THE RELATIONSHIP BETWEEN HERODOTUS' *HISTORY* AND PRIMARY HISTORY

SOUTH FLORIDA STUDIES IN THE HISTORY OF JUDAISM

Edited by
Jacob Neusner
William Scott Green, James Strange
Darrell J. Fasching, Sara Mandell

Number 60
THE RELATIONSHIP BETWEEN HERODOTUS'
HISTORY AND PRIMARY HISTORY

by
Sara Mandell
and
David Noel Freedman

THE RELATIONSHIP BETWEEN HERODOTUS' *HISTORY* AND PRIMARY HISTORY

by

Sara Mandell
and
David Noel Freedman

Scholars Press
Atlanta, Georgia

THE RELATIONSHIP BETWEEN HERODOTUS' *HISTORY* AND PRIMARY HISTORY

© 1993
University of South Florida

Publication of this book was made possible by a grant from the Tisch Family Foundation, New York City. The University of South Florida acknowledges with thanks this important support for its scholarly projects.

Library of Congress Cataloging in Publication Data
Mandell, Sara, 1938-
    The relationship between Herodotus' history and primary history
        p. cm. — (South Florida studies in the history of Judaism;
no. 60)
    Includes bibliographical references.
    ISBN 1-55540-838-9
    1. Herodotus. History. 2. Bible. O.T. Pentateuch—Comparative
studies. 3. Bible. O.T. Former Prophets—Comparative studies.
4. Ezra (Biblical figure)—Authorship. 5. Jews—History—To 586
B.C.—Historiography.   I. Freedman, David Noel, 1922-
II. Title. III. Series: South Florida studies in the history of
Judaism; 60.
D58.M36   1993
930—dc20   93-16100
                                                    CIP

Printed in the United States of America
on acid-free paper

THE RELATIONSHIP BETWEEN HERODOTUS' *HISTORY* AND PRIMARY HISTORY*

---

*   All translations of Graeco-Roman texts and of Primary History are our own unless otherwise noted. The editions used will be noted in their proper place.

Preface

Our investigation into the relationship between Herodotus' *History* and Primary History emanated from our belief that the parallels between them were too numerous to be either accidental or merely characteristic of a shared genre. Rather, they seemed to indicate a commonalty of thought, which in turn suggested that the two works were more closely bound than had hitherto been assumed. When we began our inquiry, however, neither of us expected to find as close a connection as we did.

Because the correspondences existed despite differences in language, theology, and national outlook, we first theorized that there might have been a shared climate of opinion. In fact, historic developments do suggest that some type of intellectual trend of though may have developed within and spread throughout the Mediterranean world toward the end of the 6th century, and that it continued well into the 5th. We found this hypothesis particularly attractive because Ezra, who rearranged the text of Primary History so as to form a Pentateuch and a four book sequel, the Former Prophets, is a contemporary of Herodotus,[1] the author of the work we know as the *History* (or *Histories*, or more properly, *Inquiries*). Significantly, both Ezra and Herodotus were eastern, no matter what their ethnic affiliation. And both had ties, directly or indirectly, to Persia, the suzerain of Judaea and former suzerain of Halikarnassus.

But Persian suzerainty over Judaea and its quondam suzerainty over Halikarnassus just prior to the time of Herodotus' birth is not sufficient in and of itself to posit a juncture between Ezra and Herodotus or between Primary History and Herodotus' *History.* Nevertheless, Ezra's political position vis à vis Persia, and,—if we may trust the tra-

---

1   The Ezra-Nehemiah dating controversy is difficult. In any case, we accept the 5th century (458 BCE) dating for Ezra whereby the reference in Ezra 7:8 is to the seventh year of Artaxerxes I. For the "trend back to" this dating, see J. Maxwell Miller "Israelite History" *The Hebrew Bible and Its Modern Interpreters* (Philadelphia: Fortress/Chico:Scholars, 1985, Douglas A. Knight and Gene M. Tucker, ed.) 18.

dition,—Herodotus' family's aristocratic social status and position when Halikarnassus had been subject to Persia are certainly suggestive of at least a shared climate of intellectual opinion. This possibility is not obviated by the extremely disparate political outlook that might have developed after Halikarnassus became free of Persian hegemony. In any case, we have no way of knowing how Herodotus' family or even Herodotus himself reacted to the changed political orientation of Halikarnassus.

We soon concluded, however, that even if Ezra and Herodotus had worked in an environment in which the same intellectual climate of opinion had prevailed, this alone could not account for the numerous points of correspondence between the two works. There are some very specific correlations that we simply could not charge to a commonalty of thought. For example, both Herodotus' *History* and Primary History are national epics; both had been divided into nine books at some time in their history; and both are about the same length. Both works begin with a prehistory that includes myths, fables, folk-tales, and legends that are treated as factual, and they continue in this vein well into historical time. And significantly the basic format of both works changes concomitantly and rather abruptly under similar circumstances: in Primary History, it does so at the point where the Sons of Israel are about to enter the Land, and in Herodotus' *History,* at the point where Persians are about to fight on the Greek mainland. Once the "homeland" becomes the locus of action, the narrative takes on at least the semblance of an historical narrative, albeit one that includes miracles, marvels, and divinities who act in or at least guide history. Notably, then, in both Herodotus' *History* and Primary History, historic causation is intimately tied to the will of the divinity.

We think that these parallels may have been noted in antiquity although there is no extant work in which they are described. We believe that the (Alexandrian) Hellenistic Grammarians named and "numbered" Herodotus' *History* the way they did because they were aware of the presence of some form of relationship between it and Primary History. Significantly, the Hellenistic Grammarians were innovating when they named the books of Herodotus' *History* for the nine Muses. Their method of numeration, likewise, was not the ordinary formulation by which books were numbered.

Despite the mounting evidence, we were somewhat hesitant to dismiss the possibility that all we had was an impressive coincidence. We were in a quandary because Primary History was the result of four centuries of redactional activity (from the work of the late 10th century Yahwistic Redactor through that of the 6th century exilic redactor, the second Deuteronomistic Historian) before Ezra reordered it during the 5th century, whereas Herodotus' *History,* which was also the result of repeated redactional activity, was only redacted by Herodotus himself. Still, we felt that the number of structural and theological parallels hinted at something other than mere happenstance.

Although we feared that the lack of such external data as, for instance, the works of the logographers who preceded Herodotus would hamper our investigation, we soon learned that both they and their conclusions are unnecessary to an understanding of the relationship between Herodotus' *History* and Primary History. A far greater impediment to our inquiry was the accepted belief, with which we at first concurred, that even when the stories themselves were not truthful, Herodotus was truthfully reporting what he had learned during his perambulations, and concomitantly that Herodotus believed he was writing an historical work. We soon realized that this was not valid. Rather it was exactly what the author, Herodotus, who knew what he was doing, wanted his readers to believe.[2]

Perhaps we had been led astray by Aristotle, who classified Herodotus as an historian, and even by Cicero, who called Herodotus the "father of history."[3] But most likely, as we now realize, we concurred

---

2   The distinction between the author, Herodotus, and his work's implied narrator, whom he named Herodotus, will be discussed below.

3   We, like others, overlooked Cicero's clear statement, given *on his own authority,* that in History, "everything must be traced back to what has really happened" (*omnia ad veritatem...referantur* [*de Legibus* 1.5]). The translation of *veritas* as "truth" (as, for example, in Clinton Walker Keyes translation in the Loeb edition) is misleading and obfuscates the real meaning of the statement. That Cicero uses *referantur* in the subjunctive is also disregarded in Keyes translation. Because the critical edition is unavailable to us, we have used the Loeb Latin text (*Cicero: de*

with the view that Herodotus' work falls within the historic genre because the author successfully created that illusion by virtue of his superb literary craftsmanship.

As long as we deemed Herodotus an historian of any sort, albeit not in the modern sense, we could not understand fully the structure of the *History* or the real and primal role that theology plays in it. These only became comprehensible when we began to view his work as the historical type of fiction it really is. When we realized that the *History* is a theologically "charged" prose epic in which two different but related genres, the Documentary Novel and the Roman à Clef, are combined, we began to see that Herodotus was not simply a credulous collector of anecdotal data.

It was at this point that we understood that the named narrator, Herodotus, was not the author himself. He was an implied narrator, whom the real author called by his own name. Interestingly enough, there is evidence suggesting that this was understood by the author's audience.

With this in mind, we came to differentiate between the real author and the implied narrator, the literary *persona* whom the author depicts as the narrator of the work. The Herodotean implied narrator holds to the confessional perspective of the worshipper of the god at Delphi, but we do not know whether the real author shared that viewpoint. In any case, the narrative is presented from the implied narrator's position in which gods, most notably the divinity at Delphi, act in and, hence, influence history (*pace*, von Rad). So we realized that from the confessional stance of the implied narrator, the work is historical despite its basic theological premises: but from the real reader's presumably non-confessional perspective, it is not.

We faced similar problems in our analysis of Primary History, which from a confessional outlook is a chronicle of the mighty acts of the Divinity in history. From this viewpoint, Primary History is historical despite its theological foundation: but from a non-confessional position, it is not. Even those who reject its overall historicity, how-

---

Republica, de Legibus Cambridge: Harvard, 1961 reprint of 1928 edition). The translation, however, is our own.

ever, do not treat Primary History as a conscious work of fiction. Rather they deem it as a religious document from which historic data can be gleaned.

Once we realized that neither Herodotus' *History* nor Primary History should properly be classified as histories save under a confessional rubric, we began to approach the problem from the perceptual standpoint of Analytic Criticism whereby any work, even a seemingly historical one, is to be treated as iconic. In so doing, we believe that we have also shown that the common structuring and other architectonic devices demand an acknowledgment of at least the probability that there was a direct relationship between Herodotus' *History* and Primary History.

Introduction One: Aims and Methods

In the 7th century CE, Isidorus said Moses was the "First among us," Dares the Phrygian was the first gentile, and Herodotus the first Greek "to turn his attention to history" (*Etymologiae* 1.42 Lindsay).[1] In 1944, Gerhard von Rad, overlooking Dares, described the Greeks and "long before them, the Israelites" as the only people "in antiquity who really wrote history".[2]

Von Rad particularly regards Herodotus as an historian who recognized that metaphysical forces function in the domain of worldly occurrences through "a multiplicity of omens, prophecies, and dreams".[3] Because he considers real religion and theology extrinsic to Herodotus' narrative, however, he does not equate these powers with religious phenomena. Even today some scholars take this status for granted. They assume that Herodotus' *History* is historically trustworthy, but of no theological worth. And they follow von Rad in rejecting the viability of comparing Herodotus' *History* with Old Testament precisely because he deems the events of Old Testament religious and at the same time, historical.[4]

Not everybody agrees with von Rad and disallows the possibility or even the propriety of making such a comparison. Some scholars who may or may not make a normative judgment about the theology of Old Testament, consider the text un- or ahistoric, but they still believe that historic data can be gleaned from it. Others think that Old Testament theology is valid though the text is historically untrustworthy at

---

1   For a discussion of this, see Arnaldo Momigliano "*Erodoto e la Storiografia Moderna: Alcuni Problemi Presentati ad un Convegno di Umanisti*" *Aevum* 31 (1957) 75, *et passim*.

2   Gerhard von Rad "The Beginnings of Historical Writing in Ancient Israel" *The Problem of the Hexateuch and Other Essays* (London: SCM, 1984) 167.

3   G. von Rad ("The Beginnings of Historical Writing in Ancient Israel" 171) cites Regenbogen's *Thukydides als politischer Denker* ([*Das humanistische Gynmasium:* Heidelberg, 1933] 17) which is unavailable to us.

4   For von Rad's perspective, see G. von Rad "The Beginnings of Historical Writing in Ancient Israel" 171.

best. Yet others treat sections of Genesis as primarily mythic, but they consider the remainder of Primary History historic even where the divinity acts in history or the people act in sacred time and space.

Analogously, there are those who distinguish the major portions of Herodotus' *History* that they deem factual and basically historic from those that they deem primarily mythic, legendary, pre-historic, or "fanciful." And like those who think the final redactor placed most of the mythic, legendary, pre-historic and fanciful sections of Primary History in the beginning of his work, scholars generally think Herodotus placed most of the mythic, legendary and fanciful sections in the first four books of his.

Most scholars treat the divinities differently in the respective works. In particular, they accord an historic role to the deity in Primary History, but not to the gods in Herodotus' *History*. In fact, scholars who frequently treat the myths and legends of Old Testament as historical take the equivalent myths and legends in Herodotus' *History*, particularly those that contain representations of the gods acting in history, as charming literary enhancements that should not be construed seriously.[5] Some even ignore or completely dismiss those segments of the *History* in which gods play an active role.

It is not surprising, therefore, that in spite of recent studies illustrating the religious motif that pervades and even acts as a foundation for Herodotus' narrative,[6] nobody has suggested that this is correlative with the religious motif that acts as an infrastructure for Primary History. On the contrary, many agree with von Rad, who contends that the

---

[5]   Perhaps this is why Herodotus' text, which is viewed as falling within the historical genre and is deemed worthy of respect as a Greek "Classic," is not treated as equivalent in theological probity to Old Testament.

[6]   The religious basis of the *History* is noted and summarized by David Grene in the (necessarily) generalized introduction to his translation of the text. See David Grene "Introduction" *The History: Herodotus* (Chicago: University of Chicago, 1987) 18, 20, 25-31. See also Ludwig Huber *Religiöse und politische Beweggründe des Handelns in der Geschichtsschreibung der Herod.* PhD diss.; Tübingen: Eberhard-Karls-Universität, 1965; Ivan M. Linforth "Greek Gods and Foreign Gods in Herodotus" *University of California Publications in Classical Philology* 9 (1926-1929) 1-25; *idem* "Named and Unnamed Gods in Herodotus" *University of California Publications in Classical Philology* 9 (1926-1929) 201-243.

"religious basis of the historical thought of the Old Testament",
namely, "God's management" of history even when that very regula-
tion is hidden,[7] differentiates Israelite/Judaean from Greek historiography.[8]

For such scholars, Greek historiography, of which Herodotus' *History* is a part, concerns itself solely with human history.[9] They deem
the Greek gods and/or their roles irrelevant whether or not they are involved in any event.[10]

Because we consider Herodotus' *History* to be pretty much un- or
ahistoric, we disagree with von Rad and those who follow his perspective regarding Herodotus' work. But we do believe that historic evidence can sometimes be culled from the *History*, although far less frequently than is generally presumed. Without external data to support it,
however, such material cannot be trusted. On the other hand, we always view Herodotus' *History* as being of theological merit, albeit
within its own cultural system. Granting this outlook, a comparison of
Herodotus' *History* with Primary History becomes viable.

Until now, there have not been any extensive and notably unpreju-
diced inquiries into the relationship between Herodotus' *History* and
Old Testament as a whole, and there have not been any inquiries at all
into the relationship between Herodotus' *History* and Primary History
as a whole. But there have been some important, objective studies in
which Herodotus' work has have been compared with those of his near
contemporary, the Chronicler.

Those who examine the texts come from two different disciplines
and, therefore, they often begin their work from different vantage
points. Frequently, scholars reach outside their own discipline to find

---

[7]   G. von Rad "The Beginnings of Historical Writing in Ancient Israel"
170-171, 201.

[8]   G. von Rad "The Beginnings of Historical Writing in Ancient Israel"
170-171.

[9]   See, for example, Oswyn Murray "Greek Historians" *The Oxford History
of the Classical World* (Oxford: Oxford University, 1986, John Boardman, Jasper
Griffin, Oswyn Murray, ed.) 186.

[10]   This may well reflect the Judaeo-Christian religious bias whereby foreign
gods are deemed non-gods.

external validation for or simply information about some precept. Hence, some may bring to their investigation a bias about the temporal and contextual priority of either Herodotus' *History* or Old Testament that becomes notable when one of the two works is used more to validate than to explicate the other. But when explication rather than validation is sought, and when prejudice is based on fact rather than on wish fulfillment or ideology, judgment about priority becomes useful and even basic to the analysis.

Since those who undertake these comparisons today are frequently Biblical Scholars rather than Classicists, their focus is on supporting or invalidating Old Testament while treating Herodotus' *History* as a "given." Indeed, the current trend is mostly to seek to validate the historical accuracy of Old Testament as an entirety, and in particular the chronological accuracy of Genesis on the (partial) basis of evidence in Herodotus' *History*.[11] It does not matter whether Herodotus' information is in accord with the ancient Near Eastern data, more and more of which are becoming available to us. The investigators may well use Herodotus' narrative as an historical "yardstick" by which "to measure" Old Testament and not the reverse.

On the other hand, there have been attempts to show the temporal and historical priority of Herodotus' opus to and its influence on Old Testament literature.[12] This conjectured influence is then used to support an hypothesis that even the early books in Old Testament were or at least may have been completed at a far later date than is generally believed by most academicians.

From this perspective, Old Testament seems even the more untrustworthy as a source of historical information than it really is or

---

[11]   For the use of Herodotus in the "confrontation" between the non-Judaeo-Christian histories and the scriptures, see Chantal Grell "*Hérodote et la Bible. Tradition chrétienne et histoire ancienne dans la France moderne (XVI-XVIIIe siècles)*" *Histoire de l'historiographie* 7 (1985) 60-91. See especially 60-61, 64, 66, 88, 91.

[12]   See, for example, John Van Seters *In Search of History: Historiography in the Ancient World and the Origins of Biblical History* New Haven: Yale University, 1983.

than many would like it to be.[13] Certainly, the postulated lateness demands that some considerable portion of Old Testament's allegedly primary data be treated as coming from what is at best a secondary source. And the possibility that some information may have been transmuted by the world view of Greek or Persian culture through which it was filtered makes it that much the less reliable.

This book examines the relationship between Herodotus' *History* and Primary History hopefully *"sine ira et studio."* We deem the comparison viable because we believe that both Herodotus' *History* and Primary History are essentially un- or ahistoric even though historic data may be gleaned from each of them. We also think that for the ancient Greeks, some if not all the things related in Herodotus' text may have been as theologically valid and subject to normative interpretation as Primary History is to those of the Judaeo-Christian traditions.

While we pay especial attention to the presence of analogous theological and ideological precepts, we focus primarily on the parallels between the literary and structural features of the two works.[14] Consequently, in accordance with the rules of various types of 20th century literary analyses, we hold the precept that in both there are implied narrators who are fictional *personae*, and moreover there are implied auditors/readers of the "work" of each implied narrator.

Each implied auditor/reader is the addressee of his respective implied narrator. But transcending all the latter is an overriding addressee of an overriding implied narrator, who himself encompasses all the individual implied narrators. Both the implied narrators and the implied auditors/readers have correlative roles in both works.[15]

The distinction between implied and real auditors/readers is generally ignored in the analysis of both works because of the ideological stance that demands the respective narratives be treated as primary his-

---

13   This must not be taken to mean that we treat the text as historical.

14   See below, Introduction Two. The applicability of modern forms of Literary Criticism to the analysis of New Testament literature has been demonstrated definitively by Mark Allan Powell (*What is Narrative Criticism?* Minneapolis: Fortress, 1990). Although Powell's work is primarily addressed to New Testament criticism, it is equally germane to an analysis of Old Testament.

15   For a discussion of this, see below, Introduction Two.

torical information about real people who lived in real, secular, historical time. Actually, it is the prevalence of ideologically oriented probes,
even by those who honestly try to put their own beliefs aside when ex-
amining the text, that leads to the dogma that the implied narrator and
the implied auditors/readers of Herodotus' *History* and likewise the
implied narrators/redactors and the implied auditors/readers of the diverse redactions of Primary History—including the final redaction—
are the real narrators/redactors and the real auditors/readers respectively. Thus we must stress the importance of Northrop Frye's observation that:

> When mythology modulates into ideology and helps to form a social con-
> tract, it presents data asserted to be historical, actual events in the past, but
> presents them so selectively that we can hardly take them to be really his-
> torical.[16]

Clearly then, a reading of Primary History informs us of the world
the respective authors/redactors, and particularly the final redactor, depicted as a literary construct. This invention, however, may have nothing to do with the real world in which any one of them lived. The same
is true in the case of Herodotus' *History*.

It is our hope that by showing commonalty extending beyond the
merely accidental, we may discover whether there is any actual relationship between Herodotus' *History* and Primary History. We are interested in finding out whether Herodotus could have had knowledge of
Primary History as a textual unit; or, alternatively, whether Herodotus
and his contemporary Ezra,[17] the editor who is responsible for dividing

---

16   Northrop Frye *Words with Power: Being a Second Study of The Bible
and Literature* (San Diego/New York: Harcourt Brace Jovanovich, 1990) 26. Suffice it to say that the attempt to make the "nation" conform with the ideology represented in the text is still an ongoing process today.

17   For the priority of Ezra, see J. Maxwell Miller "Israelite History" *The Hebrew Bible and Its Modern Interpreters* (Philadelphia: Fortress/Chico:Scholars,
1985, Douglas A. Knight and Gene M. Tucker, ed.) 18. If the contact was not with
Ezra himself, perhaps it was with the scribes of Ezra's era (2 Esdras 14:44). But
even if Nehemiah was actually earlier than Ezra, which we doubt, then the contact
was with the scribes of Nehemiah's era (2 Maccabees 2:13). See above, Preface,
note 1.

Old Testament so its parts became the Pentateuch and the Prophetic corpus,[18] could have had any form of knowledge of one another's work; or, finally, whether the similarities should be attributed to nothing more than a climate of opinion.

Because it is possible that some mechanical, non-literary parallels may have entered the text at a Hellenistic date, we will investigate how the Hellenistic Grammarians' editorial changes or redactions of the respective works have affected the way we now encounter Herodotus' *History* and Primary History. The presence of mutually corresponding modifications will tell us whether analogies between the two were recognized in antiquity.[19]

We do not have to prove each hypothesized correlation to support our theory that there is a well-defined relationship between Herodotus' *History* and Primary History. We need only determine that this link is possible, that it may have occurred. But the greater the congruences, the greater the probability and likelihood that there was some form of contact between the respective authors and/or that they merely had knowledge of each other's work. Barring further data, that is all we can hope for.

---

[18] For the division, see David Noel Freedman "The Formation of the Canon of the Old Testament: The Selection and Identification of the Torah as the Supreme Authority of the Post-exilic Community" *Religion and Law: Biblical-Judaic and Islamic Perspectives* (Winona Lake: Eisenbrauns: 1990, Edwin B. Firmage, Bernard G. Weiss, John W. Welch, ed.) 317-318, 324-236. See also Brevard S. Childs *Introduction to the Old Testament as Scripture* (Philadelphia: Fortress, 1979) 51, 63.

[19] On the other hand, should these be absent, we could make neither positive nor negative assertions regarding the Grammarians' belief about this matter.

Introduction Two: Literary-Critical Precepts, Techniques, and Methodology Applied to the Analysis

We take it for granted that some subjective as well as all objective literary theories beginning with Analytic or New Criticism and extending to even more contemporary approaches are viable means of interpreting literature from all times and all places.[1] Herein we disagree with John Barton, who in his extremely important and basic work accepts the perspective of those who think that Analytic Criticism is "decidedly out of fashion in the literary world — so much so that books can be written taking its demise for granted...."[2] It is our belief that Analytic Criticism, which is now deemed passé by those who see many later types of criticism as supplanting it, has neither been overshadowed nor obviated by many of the more recently defined methodologies. Rather, it serves as a foundation for and complement to them and, consequently, cannot be considered obsolete. We are not alone in holding this perspective regarding Analytic Criticism, which is still deemed viable by those who see many of the newer forms of criticism as extensions of or developments emanating from this school of thought. Unfortunately the same validity cannot be predicated for the types of analysis practiced by members of those literary-critical schools that Analytic Criticism supersedes.

It is not the purpose of this work to evaluate the various forms of Literary Criticism. However, it is noteworthy that with the exception of the older Historical Criticism, which is not to be confused with Old Testament Historical-Critical Criticism to which it bears some similarity, the role and status of each of the various types of evaluative and critical discourse are still controversial. The only real point of agreement between literary theorists is that the obsolete Historical Criticism,

---

[1]   Hereinafter New Criticism will be referred to as Analytic Criticism save when textual or external exigencies demand otherwise.

[2]   John Barton *Reading the Old Testament: Method in Biblical Study* (Philadelphia: Westminster, 1984) 142.

popular during the nineteenth and early twentieth centuries, should be, but has not yet been laid to rest.[3]

Although some wish one type of critical thought to be used exclusively, we do not reject the possibility that different literary theories may be used in combination with or in tandem to one another. Hence, we accept some premises of (the subjective) Reader Response Criticism such as, for example, that which predicates a text's existence on the basis of its being read,[4] and that which assumes the reader could influence the text by bringing to its interpretation his own insights, predilections, world view, etc. But we refuse to accede to the viability of any eisegetic interpretation.

We hold as valid and basic to our analysis the fundamental tenet of Analytic Criticism that a literary text does and, indeed, must stand alone as a self-contained artifactual or iconic entity: that is, once created, a work is an "objectified" organic whole, which is independent of its real author or his intentions.[5] Correlatively, we believe that when a reader draws exegetical conclusions about the text, he is extracting what was inherent in the artifact itself. Consequently, we deem those Reader Response postulates we view as sound to be in accord with the "iconic text" premise of Analytic Criticism.[6]

We reject the Biographical (or Historical) approach to the analysis of literature[7] precisely because it *permits* allegedly credible knowledge about an author to be extracted from his own writings and then em-

---

3   Significantly J. Barton (*Reading the Old Testament: Method in Biblical Study* 146) finds the shifting of concern away from "psychology and life-history of poets and authors and onto the finished texts that lie before the reader" somewhat more interesting than the Analytic Critics' implicit attempt to change literary taste toward "classicism."

4   This is analogous to the problem addressed in elementary physics of whether a tree falling in the forest makes a sound if there is nobody present to hear it falling.

5   We cannot agree with Mark Allan Powell (*What is Narrative Criticism?* [Minneapolis: Fortress, 1990] 4-5) that this position is pretty much thought of as extreme today.

6   We acknowledge the validity of many theories subsequent to, but not superseding Analytic Criticism and will refer to them if and when necessary.

7   We iterate that this is not to be confused with the "Historical-Critical" analysis used in biblical studies.

ployed to interpret the very works from which it had been extracted.[8] It does not matter whether data about an author or his intentions are sometimes obtained from external sources:[9] from the perspective of Analytic Criticism, even collateral material cannot justify or explain the specific format of a narrative. Correlatively, we deem it imperative that a text, which by definition can only give intrinsic information about its own creation, not be used as if it were a source of extrinsic knowledge about its author or his intention. This does not mean, however, that we deny the "given" precept that a text discloses facts about itself. Rather we refuse to treat it as divulging information about its genesis and/or its author's reasons for writing it.[10] In any case, we hold to the basic axiom of Analytic Criticism, whereby a narrative cannot be used as a source of exact knowledge about its real author or his society, but only about the characters and the society he created. Yet we also believe that the reader, who is prohibited from extracting a "faithful account" about the author or his society, may cull generalized truths from a narrative.[11]

It is imperative that these strictures, particularly that against extracting biographic material from a text to interpret that same text, be heeded in the analysis of all works. And Primary History, a work in which there are multiple authors/redactors, who are for the most part mutually distinguishable on the basis of the literary, theological, ideological, and historical viewpoints their implied narrator(s) seem to

---

[8]   This is sometimes called "expressive realism." See Catherine Belsey *Critical Practice* (London: Routledge, 1988 reprint of the 1980 Methuen edition) Chapter 1.2, page 7-14 *passim*.

[9]   Although we can learn about an author from external sources, his own use of external sources does not give us biographic information about him. Furthermore even when an author makes statements in places other than the narrative regarding his intentions in writing a particular work, Analytic Criticism frequently rejects them in interpreting that very work. It does so on the presupposition that each work, once created, has a "life "of its own.

[10]   Hence, Analytic Criticism does not militate against analysis via Form,- Tradition,- or Redaction Criticism. Rather, the various methods are complementary to one another (below, Chapter Three).

[11]   See, for example, Cleanth Brooks "American Literature: Mirror, Lens or Prism?" *A Shaping Joy: Studies In The Writer's Craft* (New York: Harcourt Brace Jovanovich, 1971) 166.

hold[12] is no exception. In fact, an analogous treatment must be applied when doing a literary analysis of the Gospels. Although as M. A. Powell points out, the authors/redactors of the Gospels "did not intend them to be viewed as fiction"; and although because of their personal religious beliefs, many scholars do not place them in a category that Analytic Criticism deems literary, from a literary perspective they are more closely related to the Roman à Clef than to biography.[13]

According to Analytic Criticism, an author's intent is extrinsic to a literary narrative. Tzvetan Toldorov even thinks this true in the case of an historical narrative.[14] Therefore, if the respective author(s)/ redactor(s) of the work(s) subject to analysis were creating a fictional, a meta-historical, or even an historical work, we may categorize and interpret the text itself as literature.

Consequently, even those tales that have been passed down from generation to generation, and changed normatively, can be subjected to Narrative Criticism. And they may even be viewed as having a single identifiable and describable implied author no matter how the narrative had come into existence.[15]

We believe Powell's stricture relegating such accounts to the literary domain is applicable to the study of both Primary History and Herodotus' *History*, each of which incorporates stories that may have been traditional or that are the product of literary artifice that the real author(s)/redactor(s) wish the reader to think have emanated from traditional sources. But the interpreter of Herodotus' *History* must be even more cautious than that of Primary History because the multiple redactions of Herodotus' work were made by only one author, whose principal character, the implied narrator acts as if he were an historian working with oral data.[16]

---

[12]   M. A. Powell *What is Narrative Criticism?* 3-4.

[13]   M. A. Powell *What is Narrative Criticism?* 3.

[14]   Tzvetan Toldorov "The Notion of Literature" *Genres in Discourse* (Cambridge: Cambridge University, 1990) 3.

[15]   M. A. Powell *What is Narrative Criticism?* 6.

[16]   Whereas most critics simply refer to the narrator, we use the term "implied narrator" so as to stress the difference between him and the real narrator, who is the real author of the work. Herodotus' implied narrator as historian imputes that many of the data he allegedly gathered from other, generally oral sources are themselves

Analytic Criticism predicates a distinction between a real author/redactor and an implied narrator.[17] The former is the corporeal person who created or redacted the work, and the latter is a fictive character who is allegedly telling the story.[18] The implied narrator is sometimes a named and sometimes an unnamed ("self-effacing") first person reporting events he (the fictive character) had "experienced" or learned about. He may be a participant ("intrusive") in the events he reports in some portions, but not in the entire narrative. Sometimes the implied narrator is omniscient and omnipresent: that is, he is all-seeing and all-knowing; he is present at events that occurred long before or those that will occur long after his time; he looks into the hearts, minds, and innermost feelings of those he depicts. He often treats and reports the products of the real author's imagination and/or speculation as if they were facts.[19]

---

primary even though they depict events in remote antiquity (below, Chapter One). He accomplishes this by intimating that the chain of oral tradition is forged so as to treat its data as inviolable. Therefore, the implied narrator wants the implied reader to believe that the oral data were unchanged in transmission and, hence, are primary evidence. We know from oral theory that this is an invalid premise even when it pertains to the work of a real, non-fictionally oriented historian.

[17]   For the role of the implied author, see Wayne Booth *The Rhetoric of Fiction* (Chicago: University of Chicago, 1961) 70-71. Some literary critics even distinguish between a real author and an implied author, both of whom are different from the implied narrator of a text. We are mainly concerned with the distinction between the real author and the implied narrator, that is, the "I" who is telling the story. We are not, however, interested in the difference between the implied author and the implied narrator. Hence, in this work, we will treat the implied narrator as if he were the implied author, keeping in mind that both really differ from the real author.

[18]   Tzvetan Toldorov makes it clear that there really is a narrative "I," who is that *persona* of which we are aware throughout the text ("Language and Literature" *The Structuralist Controversy* [Baltimore: Johns Hopkins University, 1979, Richard Macksey and Eugenio Donato, ed.] 125-133). M. A. Powell (*What is Narrative Criticism?* 25) believes that it is the *implied author* who "guides the reader" by using the device of a narrator, whom he defines as "the voice that the implied author uses to tell the story." Unfortunately, we cannot accept Powell's hypothesis that both the narrator and the narratee are "rhetorical devices" that the implied author created (Powell, *ibid.* 27). Rather, their creation must be attributed to the real author.

[19]   Journeys to places the real author has only read, heard, or simply dreamed about can, therefore, be real ports of call for the fictive implied narrator. See, for ex-

No matter what the reader believes, the implied narrator is a character created by the author. What he says, he says because the author depicts him doing so. His world is circumscribed by the author's narrative vision. It is of no consequence whether or not he is identified as fictive in the narrative itself. If the work is in a definable literary genre or in a melding of defined or even definable literary genres, the implied narrator is a literary *persona*.

The implied narrator we have just described need not be the only literary *persona* narrating the events depicted in the text. Literary works may even have secondary implied narrators who are also fictive *personae*. These secondary implied narrators may, but need not be omniscient. Belsey observes the trend in contemporary French criticism to differentiate

> between this implied narrator of the discourse as a whole, the 'subject of the enunciation', and the 'subjects of the énoncé', who are characters (including fictional narrators) with their own subordinate discourses:....[20]

In Objective Analysis and particularly in Analytic Criticism, there is a convention predicating a distinction between a real auditor/reader and an implied auditor/reader.[21] Clearly the real auditor/reader like his correlative, the real author/redactor, is a palpable, corporeal person to whom the latter directs his entire work. On the other hand, the implied auditor/reader like his correlative, the implied narrator, is a fictive character. His sole role in the narrative is that of the addressee to whom the implied narrator directs his entire discourse.[22] The implied auditor/reader is sometimes named and sometimes he is not.

---

ample, René Wellek and Austin Warren *Theory of Literature* (New York: Harcourt Brace Jovanovich, 1975, 3rd edition) 78.

[20]   C. Belsey *Critical Practice* 30.

[21]   Our implied narrator may be different than that predicated by Wolfgang Iser *The Act of Reading: A Theory of Aesthetic Response* Baltimore: Johns Hopkins University, 1978. But he need not always differ from Iser's paradigmatic implied narrator.

[22]   Because the implied auditor is fictive, "Reader Response Criticism," in which the reader actually affects the text he reads, could change the real reader's precepts about this literary character precisely because the implied narrator himself may be defined so as to view him differently than the real reader does. Conse-

There may also be specifically named auditors/addressees who are literary and acting characters within the narrative and serve as immediate addressees of direct speech or of didactic material. These individual auditors/addressees must not be confused with the real auditor/reader or with the implied auditor/reader of the entire narrative.[23] Rather, they are correlative to the specifically named implied narrators, who as we have already stated are also literary and acting characters within the narrative.

We presume, therefore, that Herodotus, the real author of the *History*, employs an intrusive implied narrator, whom he calls by his own name, to narrate the events depicted in the work. The real author depicts this first person literary *persona* by using direct exposition, but he does so by building a composite picture that develops and is enhanced upon throughout the narrative. And the depiction of action is used as a technique to define this *persona* by example.[24]

Insofar as the real author Herodotus uses the "Explicit Method" in which a "story is presented" from the perspective of a first-person narrator and/or by an omniscient author,[25] whom we call the implied narrator, he makes himself extraneous to the work he has created. Thus, the work is neither a set of memoirs nor is it autobiographical. We, therefore, must not infer that the real author did what he depicts his implied narrator, who is merely a literary character whom the author called Herodotus, either as saying he had done or actually doing.

---

quently, although Reader Response Criticism could theoretically be employed in studying the interaction between the implied auditor and the implied narrator's text, this problem would only be addressable if we could get into the mind of the implied auditor to the extent that we know how he and his expectations affect the very material he is hearing. This, however, is beyond the scope of our investigation. Moreover, it is impossible to resolve the problem without comparing far more external historic data than we possess with the evidence the implied narrator presents.

[23]   Because a discussion of specific auditors/addressees is only pertinent to a literary analysis of individual λόγοι/pericopes, we will not deal with them in this study. Any reference to the implied auditor/reader, therefore, is to the implied addressee of the entire narrative.

[24]   C. Hugh Holman and William Harmon *A Handbook to Literature* (New York: Macmillan, 1986) 81, *s.v.* "Characterization".

[25]   C. H. Holman and W. Harmon *A Handbook to Literature* 82, *s.v.* "Characterization".

The implied narrator addresses his entire work to an unnamed, implied auditor/reader. Since this implied auditor/reader is himself a fictional addressee and does not represent any real contemporary auditor/reader, textually based assumptions about the people before whom the work was read relate only to the fictive audience of the implied narrator and not to that of the real author.[26]

Although the *History* appears to be an historical work, it is not.[27] Rather, it is comprised of a combination of genres, none of which can be classified as historical. The real author composed his work in such a way that he produced a new literary genre. He superimposed the paradigm characteristic of 5th century Attic drama on that of the genres we now call the "Documentary Novel" (or "Historical Fiction") and "Roman à Clef" respectively, and he bonded this into a prose epic.

Those parts of the work in which the characters are totally fictional are cognate to the Documentary Novel. This is particularly true of the portions of the narrative that emanate from mythological stories. It is also true of those legendary stories that are told about fictional characters, but we must remember that some legends do have a real personage as their referent.

Those parts in which stories about real characters had been created by some author or bard and then handed down as part of a larger oral or written tradition just as those that were expressly composed by the real author himself for his work are cognate to the Roman à Clef.

---

[26] Despite the prevailing *consensio opinionis* that Herodotus' work was known in Athens and in many other Greek speaking regions, we must stress the validity of Stewart Flory's observation that there is a lack of "convincing evidence to show that the work was even widely known in the late fifth century" ("Who Read Herodotus' *Histories*? *AJPh* 101 [1980] 13). Flory notes that even the allusions to Herodotus' work in drama do not mean, prove, or even support the hypothesis that the *History* was well known during the 5th century BCE (*ibid.* 23).

[27] T. Toldorov's suggestion ("The Notion of Literature" 3) that even History can be treated as a literary genre and analyzed according to literary precepts is at least tangentially relevant to our argument. It would be explicitly relevant were the works in question really to fall within the historical genre, an hypothesis with which we disagree.

In both, the paradigm holds good whether or not the format is dramatic. The *History*, therefore, is not historical either by our modern definition[28] or by those held in antiquity.[29]

This does not mean that the real author necessarily conceived of his work as fictional or even as meta-historical. He may have fancied it as representative of history even though some of his data were not factual *per se* and he had actually made up other data himself. The phenomenon first noted by Geertz, whereby the organization of cultural patterns may be categorized under the rubric of "models of" and "models for,"[30] may describe the organization of literary patterns as well as cultural ones. Accordingly, Herodotus could have conceived of his *History* as a model of rather than a model for history. If so, he did not equate the representation with the actuality.[31]

It is our contention that Herodotus, whose *History* is the work of an articulate, literate, and particularly intelligent author, knew full well what he was doing when he adopted, adapted, and created evidence that he then presented as historical data in the context of a prose narrative. Since the authors/redactors who worked in the epic genre—both those authors/redactors we call Homer and the various authors/redactors known as the Homeridae—did the same thing, we believe that the frequently noted analogies between Homeric epic and Herodotus' *History* are more than coincidental. By using a format that his contempo-

---

28   Although Hayden White distinguishes between the "historical" and the "fictional" on the basis of content ("The Question of Narrative in Contemporary Historical Theory" *History and Theory* 23 [1984] 2, 21), he points out that a "dissertation was an *interpretation* of what" the author "took to be a true story, while his narration was a *representation* of what he took to be the real story" (*ibid.* 3). White's distinction between interpretation and representation is basic to our distinction between the reporting of history and the creation of some form of historical fiction—be it a Documentary Novel or a Roman à Clef—that serves as meta-history. See also C. Brooks *A Shaping Joy* 166.

29   It is a fallacy to assume that "Pathetic History" was really deemed as offering incontestable data, even in its own era.

30   For the double aspect of cultural patterns, see Clifford Geertz "Religion as a Cultural System" *Reader in Comparative Religion: An Anthropological Approach* (New York Philadelphia, San Francisco: Harper & Row, 1979, 4th edition, William A. Lessa & Evon Z. Vogt, ed.) 81.

31   C. Geertz "Religion as a Cultural System" 81.

raries would recognize as cognate with epic, the real author Herodotus may have been suggesting to his readers that he was writing some new form of epic that they were not to treat as genuinely historical. Similarly, by subtending his narrative with elements from the tragic genre, he may have been suggesting that he was writing some new form of tragedy, but one that was not to be acted out in the theater of Dionysus.[32]

Herodotus' real readers/audience(s) may have realized what he was doing as well as why he was doing it if, as the evidence suggests, most 5th century Greeks treated Homeric epic and tragic drama as representative of history while comprehending that it was not truly historical.[33] We will not speculate about the basis of this dichotomy other than to propose that the events portrayed in Homeric epic, which by the 5th century had both a religious and an educational *Sitz im Leben*, and those portrayed in tragic drama, which also had both a religious and an educational *Sitz im Leben*, were in accord with what Greeks in the 5th century BCE wished their theologically based history to be. This does not mean, however, that they were deluded. It is likely that they understood the nature of Homeric and Herodotean epic respectively exactly as we today understand that of such religious drama as the Passion Play. They and we both realize that both types of epic include ideologically and even theologically oriented non- or meta-historic data.

We also believe that the representative redactors of Primary History had used many of the same types of literary devices as did Herodotus. Because the narrative in its final form is a text in which various redactions were combined, it may have been far different from the

---

[32]   Costanzo Di Girolamo's observation (*A Critical Theory of Literature* [Madison: University of Wisconsin, 1981] 30) that "Genres that seem predominantly prosaic to us, like the novel and the novella, originated in medieval poetic genres ...." may, by analogy, be relevant to our argument that the prose narrative *History* is intimately related to both the poetic epic and tragedy.

[33]   C. Di Girolamo (*A Critical Theory of Literature* 33) notes the importance of, and difficulty inherent in "restoring a work's referentiality". See also Di Girolamo (*ibid.* 58) for a definition of epic, historical drama, novels etc. as "hybrids" composed of both fiction and non fiction; and for the referentiality whereby "a single content is proposed and accepted as fictional or nonfictional according to the author's and audience's attitude...."

format of any of the earlier redactions saving, possibly, that of the Deuteronomistic History; and, hence, we cannot say anything about the primary implied narrators of the earlier redactions beyond what the overriding redactor and his text suggest.

We must not presuppose that the ability to identify the various redactions means that we have them just as their individual redactors presented them. The inviolability of the text of Primary History may well be a late precept that was superimposed on the believing community to force it to adhere to theologically "correct" dogma. If so, we must assume that each redactor had and used the ability and freedom to edit and alter the work(s) of his predecessors so as to properly incorporate them into his own narrative framework.

The overriding redactor may have altered the *personae* and format(s) he inherited so as to bring about the architectonic unity of the work as a whole. If so, he did it in such a way as to stress his own outlook, be it literary, theological, ideological, or meta-historical. But he may well have had no such motives, and we the readers are falling into the trap of assigning an implied narrator's motivation to the author/redactor who created him.

Significantly, therefore, we have no way of knowing whether the real author/final redactor of Primary History was simply telling a good story in a form that is cognate with epic, or whether he was creating a theo-political tract in tandem with the telling of a good story in a form that is cognate with epic, or whether he was giving expression to normatively interpreted traditions held by a believing community to which he may have belonged. In any case, we are dealing with a theologically and ideologically based work of literature that is meant to seem to be a work of history. We, however, are not at liberty to impute motivation to its author/redactor.

Chapter One: Herodotus

Herodotus[1] composed his *History* without punctuation.[2] Rather than dividing the work into books, he divided it into λόγοι, which are inclusive and exclusive, major and minor self-contained segments of varying sizes. Every major λόγος contains smaller, minor λόγοι, each of which is complete. Both the major and the minor λόγοι appertain to and advance the development of the narrative, which itself is a λόγος embracing all the other λόγοι.[3]

The λόγοι configuration neither defines nor even requires the use of a particular genre nor an exclusive literary format. Accordingly, Herodotus' narrative is primarily prose. However, there are two types of poetry embedded in this prose narrative: poetry attributed to poets and poetry attributed to the oracle of a god, for the most part that of Apollo.

Sometimes Herodotus refers to the poets by name only. But when he incorporates verse attributed to various Greek poets into his narrative, he both names the poet and cites or adapts a few lines or even a stanza of his poetry (*e.g., History* 1.12, 23-24; 2.116-117, 135, 156; 3.38, 121; 4.13, 29, 32; 5.67, 95, 102, 113; 6.21; 7.161, 228; *et alii*).

---

[1]   All citations of Herodotus' *History* are from *Herodoti Historiae* Oxford: Oxford University/Clarendon, 1927, 3rd edition, Carolus Hude, ed., 2 volumes. When Herodotus is referred to solely by name, the reference is to both the real author and implied narrator of the *History* without any distinction. When the real author is to be differentiated from the (primary) implied narrator, whom he calls by his own name, we will refer to the real author or the implied narrator as such. Similar conventions hold for the implied auditor, who is the addressee of the narrative, and for the real auditor/reader, who is anyone who has read or now reads the *History*. A discussion of the difference between the implied author and the implied narrator, or between the implied reader and real reader, topics of interest to Analytic or New Critics, is beyond the scope of this investigation.

[2]   R. A. McNeal "On Editing Herodotus" *L'Antiquité Classique* 52 (1983) 125.

[3]   This is suggested by *History* 1.5, 95. For the entire work as one λόγος, and for numerous λόγοι within that λόγος see, in particular, Henry R. Immerwahr "The Samian Stories of Herodotus" *Classical Journal* 52 (1957) 312-313, 315; also see Oswyn Murray "Herodotus and Oral History" *Achaemenid History II: The Greek Sources* (Nederlands Instituut voor het Nabije Oosten: Leiden, 1987, Heleen Sancisi-Weerdenburg and Amélie Kuhrt, ed.) 99-100; *et al*.

His inclusion of verse oracles in his narrative, particularly those from Delphi (*e.g., History* 1.47, 55, 65, 66, 67, 85, 174; 3.57; 4.155, 5.92; 6.19; *et alii*) is of the greatest importance to the structure and unfolding of the entire narrative and often to that of an individual λόγος within it, and must be considered part of the architectonics. Consequently, these oracles are cited as needed to develop the plot of any of the λόγοι.

The subtending λόγος of the *History* is itself either a prose epic,[4] a novel (Historical or Roman à Clef), or a novella;[5] and its leitmotif is theological. The work as a whole, however, is a tragic type of epic novel that is synthetically formed by the fusion of several genres: Epic, Tragedy, Documentary Novel, and Roman à Clef. This, however, is a "stratified" work, whose internal literary and architectonic divisions utilize elements of these as well as of other genres.[6] For example, many of the major λόγοι are themselves epyllions that are based on or incorporate tragic themes. Furthermore, diverse genres, singly or in combination, either form minor λόγοι or are found in them: some are saga cycles; others, such as the Persian "court stories," are novellas;[7] others are prose epyllions; and yet others are prose tragedies.

There are various types of ψευδῆ in the *History*. Although the real author, Herodotus, created many of them for their "own sake," he did not fabricate all of them.[8] In fact, some ψευδῆ are variants of the same

---

[4]   This was first suggested in a rather generalized way by Malachi J. Donnelly, S. J. "The 'Epic' of Herodotus" *Classical Bulletin* 11 (1934) 11-12. But see O. Murray ("Herodotus and Oral History" 97) who rejects this classification because the Greek heroic epic lacks historicity.

[5]   See Joseph Wells "Herodotus as a Traveller" *Proceedings of the Hellenic Travellers' Club* (1926) 29.

[6]   For a work of literature as "a highly complex organization of a stratified character with multiple meaning and relationships", see René Wellek and Austin Warren *Theory of Literature* (New York: Harcourt Brace Jovanovich, 1975, 3rd edition) 27.

[7]   O. Murray "Herodotus and Oral History" 97-98.

[8]   J. A. K. Thompson *The Art of the Logos* (London: George Allen & Unwin, 1935) 62-64.

mythic[9] or legendary traditions[10] on which epic and tragedy are based; others were handed down and perhaps even received by the real author as λόγοι after having been consciously and intentionally invented by someone else.[11]

In addition to the ψευδῆ, the real author integrates into his work culturally admissible myths, legends/sagas,[12] folk tales, etc. He may have distinguished between the different genres, but his implied narrator does not do so. Cicero, for whom Herodotus was the "father of history," may have been aware of this when he classified both legends and *Märchen* as fables or stories (*quamquam et apud Herodotum, patrem historiae...sunt innumerabiles fabulae* "although even in the work of Herodotus, the father of history...there is an uncountable number of fables" [*de Legibus* 1.1.5]).[13] From our perspective, it is significant that the *fabulae* of which Herodotus was particularly fond were those legends and *Märchen* that are part of the *corpora* of Greek epic and tragedy.[14]

The real author also includes variant myths, etc., only some of which are theologically acceptable within his culture.[15] He particularly

---

[9]   Wherever the term mythic is used in this work, it denotes a story about divinities or one whose locale is depicted as being *"in illo tempore."* It is not used in the Greek sense of μῦθος, that is, any type of "story."

[10]   J. A. K. Thompson's observation (*The Art of the Logos* 62-64) that Herodotus does not give and perhaps did not know Io's "true" story, which was a sacred narrative and therefore only known "to privileged persons at the Argive shrine", may be valid. On the other hand, Herodotus may have known, but not included it because of his end-view regarding this λόγος.

[11]   J. A. K. Thompson *The Art of the Logos* 73.

[12]   Some scholars distinguish between sagas and legends, others do not. Although this can be an important distinction, it is frequently artificial. But because it is not pertinent to our analysis, we will not differentiate between the two.

[13]   The critical edition is not available to us. The Latin text is that of the Loeb edition: Cicero: *de Legibus* London: William Heinemann, 1928. The translation is our own.

[14]   For legends, see for example *History* 1.8-12; 3.154-155 *et al.* For *Märchen*, see *History* 1.108-121; 8.137; *et al.*

[15]   Some instances of myths, be they admissible or variant, are found in *History* 1.34-45; 2.73; 4.95 *et al.* J. A. K. Thompson (*The Art of the Logos* 74 ff.) wrongly defines Herodotean myths as "unconscious fiction". Rather, we suggest that Herodotus, in light of a "scientific" appraisal of myth, consciously incorporates

esteems αἶνοι, or fables (proper), and he includes them in the narrative.[16] Occasionally he disguises fables as historical anecdotes (*e.g.*, *History* 3.38, where Darius seeks to find out the response to a violation of custom regarding the treatment of the dead; *et alii*). Sometimes the real author presents the story in such a fashion that it could be used as a moral *exemplum* (*e.g.*, *History* 6.86, where the implied narrator is telling the fable about Glaucus; *et alii*). In any case, the implied narrator treats fables as variant reports of real events. Hence, for him they are historical data.

All the information the real author includes, no matter what its genre, is presented as part of a calculated response to his own literary or pseudo-historical demands.[17] Because the report of that evidence is itself a model the real author wishes the implied auditor to note, he presents it as a λόγος. Thus, for example, the real author treats the αἶνοι he incorporates as coherent stories that serve as factual data. He even has the implied narrator speak of the oldest form of αἶνος, the beast fable,[18] as a λόγος[19] that he says Cyrus related to the Ionian and Aeolian envoys (ἔλεξέ σφι λόγον "Cyrus...told them [(sic) the Ionian and Aeolian envoys] a λόγος" [*History* 1.141.1]).

The real author is consistent in his propensity not to allow his implied narrator to distinguish among the types of conventions that are joined together to form his narrative. Instead, the implied narrator presents them as if they were all of good historical value.[20] Even when a

---

myth into his fictional narrative. It is his implied narrator for whom this is unconscious fiction.

16 For the broad sense of the fable and its lack of specific confinement until a comparatively late date to animal stories although these may have been the fable's oldest form, see Werner Jaeger *Paideia: The Ideals of Greek Culture* Volume I: *Archaic Greece; The Mind of Athens* (New York: Oxford University, 1965, 2nd. edition) 68.

17 For conscious art, reflection, and choice in the *History*, see Ph. -E. Legrand "Introduction" *Hérodote* (Paris: Société d' Édition <<Les Belles Lettres,>> 1955) 160.

18 J. A. K. Thompson *The Art of the Logos* 65.

19 J. A. K. Thompson *The Art of the Logos* 66-67.

20 Ph. -E. Legrand ("Introduction" *Hérodote* 140) points out that Herodotus was following a precedent when he analyzed myth rationally. We, however, think that the real author was or may have been conscious of such a precedent when he

protocol seems to be grounded in fiction, the implied narrator treats it as an historical narrative *because for him* it is paradigmatic truth and *ipso facto* history.

At the same time, the treatment of the data as historical is part of Herodotus' "conscious art."[21] In accordance with good literary precepts, each minor λόγος has a well defined beginning, middle, and end; but its logical components are not always narrated in chronological sequence. Sometimes it begins *in mediis rebus* as is characteristic of the best Greek literature, and particularly of Homeric Epic. Sometimes it even concludes *in mediis rebus*. The denouement, no matter where it is located in the narrative of a λόγος, frequently serves as a trajectory to, if not the beginning of an entirely different and not always contiguous λόγος.

The real author, who does not have the same constraints as his implied narrator, develops any motif that permits him to introduce his new minor λόγος and to advance his narrative as he sees fit. When a minor λόγος funnels or forms a trajectory into another minor λόγος, it connects the two while preserving the individuality of each. The minor λόγοι are usually joined by some textual element, be it a theme, motif,[22] or leitmotif, emanating from an earlier minor λόγος. Notably, then, each of the minor λόγοι has its own leitmotif, which does not have to be the same as the trajectory by which it is bonded to another minor λόγος.

Each minor λόγος with its respective leitmotif is subordinated to its major λόγος with its respective leitmotif. The minor λόγοι unite to form a structural sequence of major λόγοι that are not always channeled into one another. Mainly, these sequences are semi-independent

---

depicted his implied narrator treating myth as historical data; but he himself did not *necessarily* accept the validity of this usage. Again, we iterate that we have no basis for assessing what the real author believed.

21   J. A. K. Thompson *The Art of the Logos* 116.

22   Some literary critics distinguish both themes from motifs and motifs from leitmotifs, others do not. Since the distinction seems artificial to us, we will not differentiate between them.

or independent entities that are characterized by their protagonist's or protagonists' subordination to fate, usually under Delphic ideology.[23]

Whenever the leitmotif of the major λόγος is obfuscated by the principal motif(s) of a minor λόγος, it soon comes to the fore again. But this only happens in the context of the major λόγος in which the hero follows that which Aristotle later defined as the ideal pattern of action for the protagonist in Greek tragedy. Consequently, when the real reader finally sees that the subtending leitmotif of the narrative presents the heroic figure or nation rising to the fore, committing hubris, and falling from power or dying, he understands that the *History* is some type of religious, moralizing story.[24]

As the real author intended, this very understanding leads to correct conclusions from the perspective of the implied narrator and the implied auditor/reader, but ones that are out of accord with historical reality. In addition, it wrongly suggests religiously oriented *Sitzen im Leben* for many of the minor λόγοι, while fostering the misconception that the major λόγοι share a single *Sitz im Leben*. And this, in conjunction with the implied narrator's reiterated statement that he has "heard" data (1.20.1 [ἀκούσας]; 2.29.1 [ἀκοῆ]; 2.52.1 [ἀκούσας]; 2.148.5 [λόγοισι ἐπυνθανόμεθα = ἀκούσας]; 3.117.6 [ἀκούσας]; *et alii*), has led readers to the erroneous belief that many or even most of the author's sources are oral.[25] That is, the real author has wrought his literary illusions and he has been so successful as to fool his modern readers.

So when the real author depicts many of the implied narrator's sources as being part of the folk or national heritage that has been handed down orally by priests or others whose task it is to keep the tradition, he intentionally promotes the illusion that the implied narrator is recording theological or cultic narrative as well as paradigmatic

---

23   The role of fate in the *History* has been studied by many. For Delphi as the most cited oracle, see Roland Crahay *La littérature oraculaire chez Hérodote* (Paris: Société d' Édition <<Les Belles Lettres,>> 1956) 10.

24   Hence, Hans-Friedrich Bornitz (*Herodot-Studien: Beiträge zum Verstandnis der Einheit des Geschichtswerks* [Berlin: Walter de Gruyter, 1968] 140) notes that αἰτίη denotes "a human failing in the social or religious realm".

25   For the assumption that this statement proves the oral receipt of the data, see John Gould *Herodotus* (New York: St. Martin's, 1989) 27.

truth of the sort that is usually transmitted by priests.[26] Consequently, the implicit "priestly" role of the implied narrator, who really does obtain a goodly amount of data from priests in the countries he visits, leads the real reader to accept the precept on which the entire structure of the *History* rests: the gods do act in history.

Therefore, by predicating the enactment of history on the basis of divine oracular pronouncements, the real author ties all of history to the gods themselves[27] and in particular, to the cult of Apollo and his oracle.[28] Hence even such *Sitzen im Leben* as those having their bases in the temple traditions in Egypt may have been fabricated. In any case, they are either subordinated to or based on implied and fictive *Sitzen im Leben* that, by implication, emanate from various cultic practices of Apollo's worship.

As there is an accurate paradigm for the invented *Sitz im Leben* of many λόγοι, there is an indisputably real geographic locale in which the counterfeit story is presented as being enacted. And we must iterate, as there is an original author of the *History*, there is also a

---

[26]   For the role of priests who were "effectively the ideological apparatus of society" and whose task it was to discover, articulate, and transmit "the most sacred and profound of all truths, in which were revealed nothing less than the fundamental structures of reality—cosmic as well as social", see Bruce Lincoln *Myth, Cosmos, and Society: Indo-European Themes of Creation and Destruction* (Cambridge: Harvard University, 1986) 164-165.

[27]   The use of *res divinae* by Herodotus has been studied extensively. For the relationship of the gods to human life in Herodotus, see Friedrich Focke *Herodot als Historiker* (Stuttgart: W. Kohlhammer, 1927) 56. For the divine will and intercession as a foundation of the *History*, see Ludwig Huber *Religiöse und politische Beweggründe des Handelns in der Geschichtsschreibung der Hcrod.* (PhD Diss.; Tübingen: Eberhard-Karls-Universität, 1965) 1. For Herodotus' treatment of *res divinae* as historical rather than theological, see Ph. -E. Legrand "Introduction" *Hérodote* 131; Ivan M. Linforth "Greek Gods and Foreign Gods in Herodotus" *University of California Publications in Classical Philology* 9 (1926-1929) 1, *et passim*; *idem* "Named and Unnamed Gods in Herodotus *University of California Publications in Classical Philology* 9 (1926-1929) 218, *et passim*; *et al.*

[28]   For the importance of the Delphic oracle, see H. W. Parke and D. E. W. Wormell *The Delphic Oracle* Oxford: Oxford University, 1956, *passim*; *et al.* For the oracle's particular significance to the Greek colonies (and, hence, to Herodotus presuming he really is from Halikarnassus), see W. G. Forrest "Colonization and the Rise of Delphi" *Historia* 6 (1957) 160-175; Irad Malkin *Religion and Colonization in Ancient Greece* (Leiden: Brill, 1987) 17-92; *et al.*

made-up narrator for the entire narrative. The imputation that the implied narrator and the real author are the same is the basis of the assumption that the *Sitzen im Leben* and the implied narrator's "ports of call" as depicted in the *History* are themselves authentic.[29] Confusion arises because each individual *Sitz im Leben* could be genuine; the various places the implied narrator visits are authentic; and the real author calls the implied narrator by his own name, Herodotus.

Even today the distinction between an author and his creation is and has often been unacknowledged, ignored, or simply unrecognized by those who practice Historical Criticism.[30] Nevertheless, just as in antiquity the more literate 5th and 4th century BCE Greeks understood the difference between an author and an implied narrator (Aristotle *Poetics* 1448a),[31] most modern literary critics also understand it.

But even before the 5th century BCE, an implied narrator or fictive *persona loquens*, whom the real author may have intended to be taken for an actual individual, was used as a rhetorical, sophistic, serio-comic, or even a generalized poetic type of device.[32] The 5th century evidence for this concept and usage is particularly strong. For example, Aristophanes' *dramatis personae* ridiculed Herodotus' work (*Acharnians* 68-92; *Birds* 551, 961-962, 1124-1138).[33] But this does not mean that Aristophanes spoke in his own person or that he himself

---

[29] J. A. S. Evans (*Herodotus* [Boston: Twayne, 1982] 8-10, *et passim*) points out that we don't really know where he traveled since all of our evidence comes from the *History*. Evans does not justify his conclusion on the genre of the *History*, but rather on the methodology Herodotus uses to record his experiences.

[30] Seth Benardete (*Herodotean Inquiries* [The Hague: Martinus Nijhoff, 1969] 3) may have had this dichotomy between the real author and implied narrator in mind when he noted the subjective nature of the assumption that Herodotus really believed whatever "we find it convenient for him to believe." Most commentators take the statements in the *History* at face value and judge the implied narrator to be the real author reporting his own experiences.

[31] All citations from Aristotle's *Poetics* are from *Aristotle Poétique* Paris: Société d'Édition <<Les Belles Lettres>>, 1932, J. Hardy, ed.

[32] See Bruno Gentili *Poetry and its Public in Ancient Greece: From Homer to the Fifth Century* (Baltimore: Johns Hopkins, 1988) 109-110.

[33] *Aristophanis Comoediae* Oxford: Oxford University/Clarendon, 1906, 2nd edition, F. W. Hall and W. M. Geldart, ed., volume 1. In the above citations, Herodotus' Persians, defined as Barbarians, Babylonians, and Egyptians, serve as a stock types, whom Aristophanes' characters mock.

mocked either Herodotus' work or had any specific feelings about the real author Herodotus.

Although we do not know what Aristophanes felt about Herodotus or his *History,* we do know that he recognized the existence of a distinction between an author and his literary creation.[34] And Herodotus is not the only person whose literary *persona* Aristophanes understood to be different from the man himself. If we can trust Plato (*Apology* 19c [Burnet]) and perhaps even Socrates—provided Plato's Socrates is not himself a *persona loquens,*—Aristophanes created a fictive character as a *persona* in the *Clouds* and he called him Socrates. But we must not forget that Aristophanes' Socrates was an invention of the playwright no matter what anyone in the audience may possibly have thought. He was a literary character called Socrates, not the philosopher Socrates himself.[35]

Although the real author could not expect his literary technique or his theo-political ideological stance to be understood by those who did not view the world from a perspective common with his own, the implied auditors of the *History* as a whole are contemporary with the real author, and the narrative's message is for "insiders." It is no accident, therefore, that Thucydides, whose very first sentence[36] has been inter-

---

34 See Joseph Wells "Aristophanes and Herodotus" *Studies in Herodotus* (Freeport: Books for Libraries, 1970 reprint of 1923 edition) 171. But Wells believes Aristophanes himself was making fun of the author, Herodotus, himself. In fact, as we have just noted, this was done by his literary creations, the characters in Aristophanes' plays and their targets were literary characters depicted by Herodotus. So although we can attribute the characterization to the real dramatist Aristophanes, we do not know what he himself really felt about Herodotus or about his *History.*

35 On the basis of this very distinction, Plato's Socrates decries the unjustness of assuming Aristophanes was lampooning him.

36 Θουκυδίδης ᾿Αθηναῖος ξυνέγραψε τὸν πόλεμον τῶν Πελοποννησίων καὶ ᾿Αθηναίων, ὡς ἐπολέμησαν πρὸς ἀλλήλους, ἀρξάμενος αὐθὺς καθισταμένου καὶ ἐλπίσας μέγαν τε ἔσεσθαι καὶ ἀξιολογώτατον τῶν προγεγενημένων, τεκμαιρόμενος ὅτι ἀκμάζοντές τε ἦσαν ἐς αὐτὸν ἀμφότεροι παρασκευῇ τῇ πάσῃ καὶ τὸ ἄλλο ῾Ελληνικὸν ὁρῶν ξυνιστάμενον πρὸς ἑκατέρους, τὸ μὲν εὐθύς, τὸ δὲ καὶ διανοούμενον. (*Thucydidis Historiae* [Oxford: Oxford University/Clarendon, 1942 reprint with emended and augmented critical apparatus, Henricus Stuart Jones, ed., 2 volume edition, *Tomus Prior*] ᾿ΙΣΤΟΡΙΩΝ 1.1.

preted as suggesting that he sees "himself a conscious rival of Herodotus",[37] is an insider and a near contemporary who merely pretends to
view the world in a different way than Herodotus does.[38] Actually, it is
only Thucydides' implied narrator's historical focus on "politics and
war" rather than on religion as a causal entity (or just *per se*) that
makes the two works seem different.[39]

In contrast to the real author, who never actually allows the course
of the narrative to focus on anything save religious matters, Herodotus'
implied narrator seems to concentrate on politics and war as well.
This, however, is an illusion. Actually, the doctrinal thrust of Herodotus' *History* represents the expected outlook of an implied narrator and
implied auditor, each of whom holds to a theo-historical *Weltanschauung* in which politics of any sort, much less geo-politics, play a
role that is totally subordinated to that of religious matters. The implication is that the implied auditor and the implied narrator as well consider the moral, ethical, or religious causes, precedents, and consequences of the war between the Greeks and the Persians to be particularly and even solely pertinent and historical. Political and geo-political
data are either excluded from the λόγοι or included in such a way that
their historical relevance is obfuscated or simply subordinated to their
theological consequence.

Although not everyone (then or now) understands the distinction,
the real author seems to expect the implied auditor to see the reasons
for the exclusion of politics *per se* as a topic of discussion. He also
seems to expect him to comprehend the *Sitzen im Leben* behind his
λόγοι, the fanciful nature of his peregrinations, and even the distinc-

---

37   Oswyn Murray "Greek Historians" *The Oxford History of the Classical
World* (Oxford: Oxford University, 1986, John Boardman, Jasper Griffin, Oswyn
Murray, ed.) 193. From an historical perspective, this is absolutely true. But if
Thucydides was writing a literary rather than an historical study, then on the basis
of the independence of the text from its author, we must suggest that it is Thucydides' implied narrator who is being depicted as believing that he was Herodotus'
competitor. In any case, this is only tangential to our argument.

38   It is interesting that when Thucydides or his implied narrator
(*Peloponnesian War* 1.1) by implication condemns Herodotus as a (poor) historian,
he either does not recognize or he pretends not to understand the dichotomy between
the *persona loquens* and the living man.

39   For this focus, see O. Murray "Greek Historians" 197.

tion between the *persona loquens* and the author himself. Moreover, he especially seems to expect the auditor to discern the true basis of his religious thought.[40]

Sometimes the real reader does not realize what is demanded of him until he has read a large portion of the narrative.[41] The implied narrator defines as the goal of his inquiry the preservation of the memory of the past. This is to be accomplished by recording the astonishing achievements of both the Greeks and the non-Greeks (*History* 1, superscription [below]). The implied narrator's other stated objective, a demonstration of how the Greeks and Barbarians came to make war against one another (*History* 1, superscription [below]), is secondary to and yet inseparable from the first.

Herodotus clearly specifies his intentions in his implied narrator's superscription.

Ἡροδότου Ἁλικαρνησσέος ἱστορίης ἀπόδεξις ἥδε, ὡς μήτε τὰ γενόμενα ἐξ ἀνθρώπων τῷ χρόνῳ ἐξίτηλα γένηται, μήτε ἔργα μεγάλα τε καὶ θωμαστά, τὰ μὲν Ἕλλησι, τὰ δὲ βαρβάροισι ἀποδεχθέντα, ἀκλεᾶ γένηται, τά τε ἄλλα καὶ δι ' ἣν αἰτίην ἐπολέμησαν ἀλλήλοισι (*History* 1, superscription 1-5).

This exposition of the narrative of Herodotus of Halikarnassus (is given) lest mankind's accomplishments be forgotten with the passing of time, and lest the great and wondrous deeds accomplished, on the one hand, by the Greeks and, on the other, by the barbarians, be unsung; and additionally, (this exposition of the narrative shows) for what cause they made war against one another.[42]

Despite the desire of translators, including ourselves, to break this superscription into two or more sentences, Herodotus has the implied narrator state each of his implied themes in one periodic sentence,

---

[40]   For the religious dimension of the work, see David Grene "Introduction" *The History: Herodotus* (Chicago: University of Chicago, 1987) 18, 20, 25-31, *et passim; et al.*

[41]   See, for example, Aubrey de Selincourt *The World of Herodotus* (San Francisco: North Point, 1982) 54.

[42]   We prefer to translate δι ' ἣν αἰτίην literally since the notion of cause is so important to the narrative development. The English "why," also a linguistically proper translation, obfuscates the thematic significance of αἰτίη.

which the implied auditor is expected to follow. Although this may simply be good Greek, it has literary-critical undertones. Specifically, it indicates that everything that follows is to be deemed an organically melded entity and, hence, that the ostensible division of the narrative by motifs and λόγοι is really secondary to the substantive unity of the work as a whole.

The superscription is stated by the implied narrator. But the real author, like his implied narrator, chooses what he wishes to record "lest mankind's accomplishments be forgotten with the passing of time". He creates an historically and ideologically oriented work of literature,[43] one of whose objectives is to foster the illusion that the real author *himself* was a critical historian who exercised his analytical ability on the interpretation and evaluation of various types of records.[44] Knowing this, we must distinguish between the real author's thought and that which he imputes to his implied narrator.[45]

The real author, who develops his implied narrator's account to support his pretense of historicity, shows his intent by presenting paradigmatic aspects of life instead of giving a chronological, annalistic listing of all events. Sometimes, therefore, the real author does not mention historical occurrences that are germane to the history of the war and its antecedents—particularly when they are not pertinent to the implied narrator's ideological stance or *Weltanschauung*. Sometimes, however, he alludes to, but does not record them. Whenever the implied narrator does directly refer to these events, he informs the implied auditor/reader that he will not discuss them.

---

43   See S. Benardete *Herodotean Inquiries* 3, 200, *et passim*.

44   For temple records see W. W. How and J. Wells *A Commentary on Herodotus* (New York: Oxford University, 1989 reprint of corrected 1928 edition; 2 volumes) "Introduction to Book One" volume 1, *ad* 1.1, page 53.

45   This leads to the realization that such literary devices as the abrupt anacolouthon in *History* 1.51 reflect the "thought" of the implied narrator. Various artifices are included to depict the implied narrator as a critical historian (below). Ironically, some think that these literary contrivances are the epitome of historical thought. W. W. How and J. Wells' belief that in *History* 1.51.3 Herodotus is "exercising his critical faculty on the Temple records" (*A Commentary on Herodotus ad* 1.51.3, volume 1, page 75) is particularly illustrative of this.

The implied narrator does report some data fully, however; and then he rejects them as allegedly being of lesser historical value than those depicting other versions of the same events. By this very "act," he evaluates the evidence in a manner that is congruent with his ideological stance and *Weltanschauung*. Clearly, then, when the implied narrator rejects data, he does so because he is an historian.

The real author has other motives. He is not an historian, but a writer of historical, theologically oriented fiction. He uses the notification of an implied narrator's resolve to reject evidence as a theme in the narrative. His intent in doing so is to shore up the literary rendering of the implied narrator as an historian. Consequently, he attributes any decision to expunge or include information to the implied narrator, from whom the implied auditor/reader as well as the real reader learns about it.

Obviously the implied narrator only does what the real author has him do. All excisions are made by the real author. Thus, any time the implied narrator says he has omitted material (*e.g., History* 1.51.4, 177.1; 2.3.2, 171.1-2; 4.43.7; 7.96.1 *et alii*), the decision to have him do so is that of the real author. It tells us nothing about the real author's self-image. Rather, it reflects the way in which the real author perceived and depicted his implied narrator's *persona*.[46] Because the real author understands that an historian must justify his choice of evidence, he pictures the implied narrator selecting information, making critical choices, and at times indicating what he has rejected.

To iterate, the real author depicts the implied narrator as an historian whereas he himself may simply be a literary artist. The real author and his creation, therefore, may view causality somewhat differently from one another. The implied narrator as historian suggests that each event is a cause of what follows.[47] The real author develops his narra-

---

[46]   Hence, for example, when the reference is to a mystery religion as in *History* 2.171.1-2, it also shows that the implied narrator respects the demand for religious secrecy. Again, we do not know what the real author himself felt about this.

[47]   For both Herodotus and Thucydides as "imitating the tradition of historiography as the history of events", see J. Cobet "Herodotus and Thucydides on war (sic)" *Past Perspectives in Greek and Roman Historical Writing* (Cambridge: Cambridge University, 1986, I. S. Moxon, J. D. Smart, A. J. Woodman, ed.) 1. Cobet's

tive in such a way that this concept of causality, which serves as a leit-motif,[48] is itself subtended by the leitmotif whereby fate and its ful-fillment by an act or acts performed under the volition of those des-tined to do so is the only real cause of any action.[49] This represents what the real author wishes to be the perspective of the implied narra-tor, who treats the various outrageous, criminal, and sacrilegious acts as incidents that lead to or even cause subsequent events, each of which is fated.[50] We have no basis for assuming that the real author held the same point of view.

The implied narrator's thought is characterized by two intertwined underlying leitmotifs: (1) each man, family, or nation rising to the pin-nacle of success must die, come to an end, or precipitously fall at or just after that very point in time that he reaches that pinnacle;[51] (2) at the same time and as part of the same process, the sufferer must bring about his own inescapably fated collapse. The implied narrator views the real cause of the fall of individuals or nations as predestined and, thus, antecedent to both its precipitating and its consequent cause.

The implied narrator embraces a theory of free will within the con-fines of predestination[52] or of "double motivation" that may well pre-

---

hypothesis is based on the belief that Herodotus is both real author and narrator of his *History*, however.

[48]   For the use of causation as a unifying factor, see Henry R. Immerwahr "Herodotus" *The Cambridge History of Classical Literature* I *Greek Literature* (Cambridge: Cambridge University, 1985, P. E. Easterling and B. M. W. Knox, ed.) 438; *et al.* Thus we define it as a leitmotif.

[49]   R. Crahay (*La littérature oraculaire chez Hérodote* 3) suggests that some oracles, such as that in *History* 1.13, are unveilings *"of the supernatural in time."* All of the responses given are religious in nature (*ibid.* 10). For the literary basis of the oracles, see *ibid.* 58-59, *et passim.* We believe that for Herodotus' implied nar-rator fate is intimately tied into the oracular responses.

[50]   But for the belief that there was a prevailing Greek *Weltanschauung* under which divine and human causation could be accepted concomitantly, see J. Gould *Herodotus* 70. However, Gould does not distinguish between the real author and the implied narrator.

[51]   S. Benardete *Herodotean Inquiries* 31.

[52]   But see Henry R. Immerwahr "Historical Action in Herodotus" *TAPA* 85 (1954) 32.

vail in the religious thought of the era.[53] He perceives Greek customs, not subordination to fate or lack of freewill, as distinguishing Greeks from non-Greeks.[54] Had he been referring to the implied narrator rather than the real author, we would agree with Seth Benardete's thesis that both the νοῦς of Herodotus' νόμος and the explication of the νόοι of the λόγοι are themselves the structural bond and the true overall Herodotean λόγος.[55] The real author, on the other hand, textually differentiates between the genuine and the expediting cause by depicting the latter as an action or even reaction of the victim. For him, this expediting cause is tethered to both its precipitating and consequent warrant.

Despite the difference, the real author's world view may be the same as that of his implied narrator, but we cannot prove it. For the real author, the bonds between the self-fulfilled but fated and inevitable fall of men and nations who have risen to greatness could have provided a clear paradigm for the future of the Greeks themselves. He may have wanted his real reader to comprehend what he presents the implied narrator as wanting the implied auditor to understand: even Greeks and their πόλεις, like foreigners and their states, are subject to the very vicissitudes of fate, death, and destruction that they themselves will voluntarily bring to fruition. And this scheme whereby the Greeks as an aggregate are deemed the personified hero is itself presented as a true epic "aristeia" that "tells of the hero's victory, not of his fall."[56]

---

[53] For free will with divine constraints as a 5th century belief, see Jean-Pierre Vernant "Imitations of the Will in Greek Tragedy" *Tragedy and Myth in Ancient Greece* (Atlantic Highlands: Humanities, 1981, Jean-Pierre Vernant and Pierre Vidal-Naquet, ed.) 28-62. Although Vernant directs his attention to Athenian thought, his arguments can easily be extended to embrace the thought of other Greek societies. See also A. de Selincourt *The World of Herodotus* 57-58. De Selincourt acknowledges the subordination of man to fate as pervading the *History*, but he does not recognize that this is a leitmotif. Rather he views it as merely a characteristically Greek religious outlook, which of course it is.

[54] S. Benardete *Herodotean Inquiries* 9.

[55] S. Benardete *Herodotean Inquiries* 31.

[56] For this definition of an *aristeia* within an epic context, see W. Jaeger *Paideia* 1.47.

This may account for the arrangement of the final form of the text. But despite the strongly developed religious leitmotif and the tragic format of the narrative, we cannot presume that the work was written in the sequence in which we now find it.[57] The relationship of the work's design to its order of composition is not readily obvious.

The real author may have drafted the *History* as a continuous narrative although this is not likely. According to the "unitarians," who believe Herodotus had an unified and well thought out plan from the beginning, the *History* is only apparently a work of contrasts. Granting that the consistent thematic development of the subtending λόγος with its implied religious *Sitz im Leben* and that of the moralizing *Sitzen im Leben* of most of the λόγοι suggest that Herodotus had a grand plan for his *History*, they do not show at what point in the creative process he conceived of it. Moreover, although the real author put together the first ordered compilation of the contents of his *History*, he may never have published "an authorized version" of the text. Consequently, we cannot know if what we have is in accord with the author's intent.

The unitarians' belief that the order in which Herodotus drafted the *History* is congruent with the received format is complemented by their predication of the writing of the work in tandem with the peregrinations of the author, who for them is both real author and narrator. But since all the information about these travels is based on the narrative itself,[58] there is no reason to believe that the real author went to each or even any of the places the implied narrator says he visited. Significantly, the albeit very late biography by Suidas does not discus Herodotus' voyages and his visit to Athens although these are "givens" for

---

57   But for the belief that the work was written in the received order, see Richmond Lattimore "The Composition of the *History* of Herodotus" *CP* 53 (1958) 9-21.

58   For example, see J. A. S. Evans (*Herodotus* 6-8) for Herodotus' travels as accepted as historical despite the fact that they cannot be traced because the evidence emanates from the *History* which "was written from notes, or memories that may never have been jotted down, after the travels were over: in some instances, long after."

most modern scholars.[59] Possibly he did not even go to Athens: but if
he did, he may not have stayed there for any length of time.[60]

Once we differentiate between the real author and the implied narrator, the commonly accepted belief that the real author composed the
first and last parts of the *History* in Athens and the middle part in Italy,[61] not only cannot be proven, but it must be discarded. It is based
on the conviction that Athens was the Mecca of the intelligentsia during the 5th century BCE and, therefore, it is presumed that Herodotus'
allegedly positive attitude about Athens suggests he had resided or at
least spent some time there.[62] Significantly, this is not substantiated by
the text itself and there are no external data underlying the assumption.
But without additional data, there is no warrant for the belief that
Herodotus had a pro-Athenian bias, that he had resided at Athens, or
even that he had visited it.

Were we to follow the wrong line of reasoning that allows for any
bias regarding a residence in or even a visit to a particular place, we
may also assume that if, as Valerie French suggests,[63] Herodotus did
have a pro-Spartan bias, he may have written parts of the *History*
while in Sparta. But even if French's theory that Herodotus was had
some preference for Sparta could be substantiated, it does not prove
that he visited that city-state. Because the logic on which the theories
are based is fallacious, the conclusion that he visited either Athens or

---

[59] See also Ph. -E. Legrand *Hérodote: Introduction* 23-24.

[60] But see Joseph Wells ("Herodotus as Traveller" 22), who takes it for
granted that Herodotus was well known at Athens. Nevertheless, even Wells points
out that Herodotus does not refer to the Parthenon at all, and yet he pays attention to
architecture in Ephesus and Samos (*ibid.* 25).

[61] See W. W. How & J. Wells "Introduction" *A Commentary on Herodotus*
10, volume 1, page 10-12. Even Ph. -E. Legrand (*Hérodote: Introduction* 29),
while pointing out that Herodotus does not say he went to Athens, states categorically that the richness of his information proves he went there. Legrand goes so far
as to stress Herodotus' intimacy with important Athenians (*ibid.* 29). See also Legrand, *ibid.* 30-34, *et passim.*

[62] There is no real textual support for any Athenian residency on the part of
the implied narrator either.

[63] Valerie French "Herodotus: Revisionist Historian" *Panhellenica: Essays
in Ancient History and Historiography in Honor of Truesdell S. Brown* (Lawrence:
Coronado, 1980, Stanley M. Burstein and Louis A. Okin, ed.) 31-42.

Sparta or that he had a leaning toward the one or the other must be deemed invalid without substantive data to support it.

The alleged pro-Athenian or pro-Spartan prejudice simply reflects the tragic paradigm of the work. In any case, since the implied narrator rather than the real author is predicating the inevitability of the rise, hubris, and fall of nations, even if the latter did have a pro-Spartan or a pro-Athenian leaning, this does not affect the narrative. As others have noted, in the *History* any πόλις Herodotus depicts coming to the fore must fall. And the implication is that like Persia, all of Greece is destined to become hubristic and fall. Perhaps for the real author, the war between the city-states, the Peloponnesian war, represented just that fall.

The implied narrator's allusions to specific locales that the reader may expect to see in the narrative are inserted for literary ends. Such intimations are part of a literary "topos" signaling the inevitability of those places' predetermined but self-induced ruin. Consequently, they do not inform the real reader that the real author spent time in any particular place, did his writing there, or favored it.[64]

The leitmotif, then, in which men and nations enact of their own free will the destruction that is fated for them is basic to the subtending λόγος. So even the existence of a corresponding underlying motif does not suffice to prove continuity in composition *ab initio*. Many scholars believe that Herodotus wrote different major λόγοι at different times and in different places. Although they do not agree about where, they also do not agree about when, in what order, or in what relationship to any other λόγος he composed any one of them.

The λόγος that is architectonic to all the λόγοι could, but does not have to be an afterthought. The real author may not even have had his primary motif in mind when he began writing. He may have added it while making one of his redactions, intending it to serve as a unifying theme or to be part of a previously included harmonizing argument. He

---

[64]   Likewise, the implied narrator's ignorance of certain locales tells us nothing about the real author's relationship to or knowledge of them. Thus, there is no corroboration for Kirchoff's well-accepted thesis that Herodotus composed his work in the present order but in three discrete segments (*History* 1.1-3.118; 3.119-[*circa*] 5.77; [*circa*] 5.77-9.122) *while in three different places.*

may even have done so during his last redaction to bring together divergent segments of the narrative. In any case, the motif's existence is basic to the received version of the text.

The use of trajectories is fundamental to the unification of individual λόγοι and, ultimately, to their consolidation by a subtending λόγος. The trajectories help to bind the λόγοι in a "pedimental structure" that is both "deep-seated and all-embracing".[65] Thus, it does not matter whether the real author wrote the major and minor λόγοι or even individual passages within the various λόγοι at different times and in a different order from what they are in the received text. All that counts is his putting them together to fit the overall *schema* that has long been acknowledged to be the underlying λόγος. By subsuming the narrative under an all-embracing λόγος, the real author defined the order of the narrative even though he probably did not divide it into the books we have received.[66]

Appropriately, therefore, the *History* is a lengthy, intricate account in which the various parts blend into one another to make one, unified entity.[67] The need to distinguish the individual sections is irrelevant because the *History* is a complete book.

Thematic homogeneity does not predicate a sequential narrative progression or well-balanced architectonics or even composition in the received order. There is disagreement among those who believe that Herodotus composed the *History* in the received order. Even some of the scholars who think it was so designed when Herodotus first began to write do not necessarily believe that the work has a basic unity or a balanced structure.[68] On the other hand, some who hold that the *History* has an elemental homogeneity or an ordered design do not agree

---

65   John L. Myres *Herodotus: Father of History* (Oxford: Oxford University/Clarendon, 1953) 86-87, *et passim*.

66   K. H. Waters (*Herodotos the Historian: His Problems, Methods and Originality* [Norman: University of Oklahoma, 1985] 55) suggests that the order of composition is "immaterial to the unity of the whole."

67   W. W. How and J. Wells "Introduction" *A Commentary on Herodotus* # 33, volume 1, page 46.

68   See for example F. Jacoby "Herodotos" *PW* 8 Supp. 2 (1913) *passim*; Fritz Hellmann *Herodotos' Kroisos-Logos* (Berlin: Weidmannsche, 1934) 2. See also the discussion in J. L. Myres *Herodotus: Father of History* 26-27.

that the real author wrote the λόγοι in the received order. This is possible because structural arrangement and textual unity are not inextricably intertwined in the *History*.

During the 19th century, scholars tried to compare the extant fragments of the works of Herodotus' predecessors with Herodotus' *History*. On the basis of their correct belief that Herodotus was a redactor of material collated in an additive manner, many came to the erroneous conclusion that he was not the or even an original author, but rather only a compiler or redactor of materials that had come down to him.[69] Others, while assuming the redactive postulate, still take it for granted that Herodotus was an author, and he was the author of each redaction of his *History*.

We find the arguments of those who believe that the *History* is the work of one author who made multiple redactions to be more persuasive than the arguments of those who think the *History* is the product of multiple authors. And we see them as far more convincing than those of the unitarians who believe that a single author conceptualized and wrote the *History* as a well-ordered entity having a grand design.[70]

---

[69]   The bibliography is extensive. See the discussions in J. L. Myres *Herodotus: Father of History* 17-31; Charles W. Fornara *Herodotus: An Interpretative Essay*(Oxford: Oxford University/Clarendon, 1971) 1-23. But see John Van Seters (*In Search of History: Historiography in the Ancient World and the Origins of Biblical History* [New Haven: Yale University, 1983] 9), who rejects their methodology *because* of his belief that "Herodotus did investigate directly and gather firsthand the largest part of his work". This belief does represent the *communis opinio,* although not the *consensio opinionis* today.

[70]   The progression in which Herodotus wrote the major λόγοι that form the narrative is controversial. The unitarians believe that the books were composed in the order we now have and that they show an "essential unity". For a discussion of the theories of A. Kirchoff, M. Pohlenz, and others see J. L. Myres *Herodotus: Father of History* 1, 29, *et passim.* Myres himself believes that "we have Herodotus' book essentially as he left it" (*ibid.* 89). For modern unitarians, see Seth Benardete *Herodotean Inquiries* 4, *et passim*; Amy Barbour "Introduction" *Selections From Herodotus* (Norman: University of Oklahoma, n.d. Reprint of 1929 D. C. Heath edition) *passim.*

We are not using the term "analyst" (= separatist) in the same way as P. MacKendrick ("Herodotus: The Making of a World Historian" *The Classical Weekly* 47 [1954] 148). MacKendrick believes that the analysts themselves are divided into two camps: those who believe that Herodotus desired to gather together his λόγοι "and link them on the slender thread of the war between Greek and bar-

In fact, many of the unitarians, for whose argument the organic wholeness of the work is the basic premise, have attributed this essential textual unity to Herodotus' use of the subtending leitmotif that the course of events throughout the world is determined by "a relentless fate" under which men and nations rise, commit hubris, and fall.[71] But their argument is flawed since there is no reason to believe that this leitmotif was not added at a later date in order to facilitate the real author's attempt to unite the various segments of his narrative into some form of unified entity.

Herodotus was a creative literary artist and at the same time a redactor who put his own thematic stamp on the narrative he designed.[72] He was particularly interested in religious matters, and these are well represented from the implied narrator's perspective in the thematics of the narrative. Jacoby, who divides the work into three sections that in part resemble those of Bury, shows that he understands this concern with religious matters. He suggests an apportionment that transcends book divisions. Rather it reveals a λόγοι-focused context reflecting the religious orientation of Herodotus' major theme.[73]

The multiplicity of sound and verifiable sections with dividing points determined by seams in the narrative as defined by λόγοι testifies strongly to multiple redactions. These redactions need not represent a conscious or intentional change of design. The logic of the arrangement may have been the conception of an overriding redactor, who may, but need not have been the real author himself.[74]

There is no evidence to support the hypothesis of multiple authorship, however. It is more likely that all the divisions are authentic but

---

barian" and those who believe that Herodotus was composing an ethnographic work. There are some analysts, ourselves included, who believe that both outlooks and intentions are present in Herodotus' architectonics.

[71]   See above. See also A. L. Barbour "Introduction" *Selections From Herodotus* 4-5.

[72]   As we have shown he may not have collected his data aurally during peregrinations to various places.

[73]   F. Jacoby "Herodotos" 351.

[74]   This would obviate the belief of the unitarians who affirm that Herodotus had conceptualized "one Grand Design" *when he started his composition* (above). For this unitarian dogma, see in particular P. MacKendrick "Herodotus: The Making of a World Historian" 148.

temporally and referentially different from one ancther. They are not the product of *eisegetic* activity, but rather of the real author's own working and reworking of his narrative. Consequently, a knowledge of the bases of these divisions and of their relative priority to one another would help us to understand the real author's own intellectual development and changing interests. And since the real author made more than one edition of his work, this itself may account for many of the differences attributed to the use of more than one source or type of source.

We do not know when the real author placed the λόγοι in their present order. He may have done so when he made his final redaction or at least after he had composed all of the various λόγοι of the narrative. Contemporary scholars differ amongst themselves regarding this. For example, How and Wells believe that the story of Xerxes' invasion was written before the remainder of the *History*.[75] Others think it was written after the narrative of the earlier books had been completed.

Many scholars hold that the narrative of book 2, the Egyptian λόγος, was written last,[76] and it was inserted into its present position by Herodotus more for architectonic than for historic ends. Fornara, however, has argued that book 2 shows a different, "more primitive technique" than book 1, and that Herodotus has a different *persona* and different interests in book 2 than he does in book 1.[77] He assumes that book 2 is the effort of a man who is younger than the author of book 1, and who has not yet fully developed his skills or intellectual outlook.

Fornara compares book 1 with books 7 through 9, which he believes to be far more intricate than the remainder of the *History*.[78] If Fornara's hypothesis is correct, the narrative of book 2 may have been written or perhaps conceived of as a short monograph about Egypt long before Herodotus thought about writing an history or, as we belie-

---

[75]   W. W. How and J. Wells "Introduction" *A Commentary on Herodotus* # 12, volume 1; *Commentary ad* 7.1-4, volume 2, page 124.

[76]   See W. W. How and J. Wells "Introduction" *A Commentary on Herodotus* # 13, volume 1, page 15.

[77]   C. W. Fornara *Herodotus* 8-19.

[78]   C. W. Fornara *Herodotus* 21.

ve, a literary work that is ostensibly about the Persian Wars.[79] But these theories themselves argue against the possibility that Herodotus configured the *History* under some transcending plan.

We do not and cannot know whether the real author had a preconceived plan to which the received order corresponds. Significantly, Fornara is not the only scholar who presents hypotheses that militate against the composition of the parts as segments of an unified work, but not against the integrating and/or joining of formerly independent portions into a self-contained work of literature possessing an overriding unity. This is predicated on reality.[80]

Inconsistencies in the literary sense, feeling, attitude, or tone of the narrative do not definitively indicate that Herodotus composed book 2 either before or after he had composed books 1 and 3.[81] He may have had an unspecified basis for the ethnographic coloring of book 2 that he expected the implied reader to understand. Consequently, the allegedly primitive feeling does not have to suggest anything about the time in which the real author wrote. It may simply represent either the real author's or the implied narrator's attitude to his data or to his implied reader.

Fornara's argument about book 2 is basic to our belief in a Herodotean redaction process that is somewhat comparable to the process

---

[79] For the priority of book 2, see C. W. Fornara *Herodotus* 1-2.

[80] The real author did not make the received division into books and chapters. These were Hellenistic (or Roman) and modern respectively (below). Hence, the assumption that Herodotus gave the books their current order is only partially correct even granting the constraints he may have imposed on himself when he arranged the λόγοι.

[81] There are many explanations for such anomalies as the difference between the literary "sense," "tone," "feeling," and "attitude" respectively in book 2 and those in books 1 and 3. But consistency of sense, feeling, tone, or attitude is not always a sign of an ordered development of a work. Although it is unlikely, the desire for such coherence may after all may represent a modern literary prejudice that leads to the type of dullness or flat presentation that has come to characterize pseudo-scientifically presented data. What R. B. Rutherford (Homer: Odyssey Books XIX and XX [Cambridge: Cambridge University, 1992, R. B. Rutherford, ed.] 46 note 55) said of Homer's work, "inconcinnity and disturbing elements may occasionally be used deliberately, to surprise, misdirect or otherwise intrigue the reader", is also as true of Herodotus' work as it is of any and all fine literary creations.

by which Primary History developed.[82] Whether or not we accept
MacKendrick's and Immerwahr's *schema*,[83] we must admit that the
received text of Herodotus' *History,* in which there is a clear break at
the end of books 1, 3, and 6, may well be the product of one or more
redactions. However each of the redactions was made by the real
author himself and not by different "hands" as in the case of Primary
History.[84]

The obfuscation of pertinent data regarding Herodotus' own book
divisions not only thwarts any attempt to analyze their priority through
Redaction Criticism, but it points the critic in a different direction. Because the separation of books in the manuscript tradition of Herodotus' *History* is not as clear-cut as we may wish and "readings in both
the Florentine and Roman texts cut across the book divisions",[85] we
conclude that the text was divided into books as a mechanical matter
and it has little architectonic significance. Even if Herodotus had composed different parts of the work in a different order than what we now
have, and even if he had designed them as books rather than as λόγοι,
there are no data to suggest that each of those books corresponds to the
received books.

McNeal very properly attributes the trans-book readings to an editor who had use of "papyrus rolls from different earlier editions" that
he combined, thus creating a "composite text."[86] Hence, we must look
to something other than book order if we are to study the basic structure of this work. And we agree with those who hold to the *communis
opinio* that λόγοι form the basic building blocks of the narrative. Consequently, we conclude that λόγοι are of greater structural significance
than are books.

---

82   See below, Chapter Two.
83   P. MacKendrick "Herodotus: The Making of a World Historian" 147-146;
Henry R. Immerwahr *Form and Thought in Herodotus* (Cleveland: Western Reserve University, 1966) 93, 106, 126, *et passim.* For book 6 see also W. W. How
and J. Wells *A Commentary on Herodotus ad* 7.1-4, volume 2, page 124.
84   For the suggestion that the same may be true of the poet of *Odyssey,* see R.
B. Rutherford "Introduction" *Homer: Odyssey* 43-44
85   R. A. McNeal "On Editing Herodotus" 127.
86   R. A. McNeal "On Editing Herodotus" 127.

Whether or not there is an essential unity to the *History* as it was first conceived by the real author, such a unity is present in the received version of the text. Moreover, in the extant text there are various basic architectonics, represented more by λόγοι and possibly by the order of composition than by book divisions, and these underlie the *History*'s narrative. Since the final form of the text is an unified entity and the work is λόγοι oriented, *there must be a λόγος which subtends all the λόγοι.*[87]

From the analyst's perspective, the author had to adapt and rearrange his λόγοι to fit the schema of this fundamental λόγος, whose very existence implies that it embraces them. Hence, by definition, there are one or more logically divided complexes of various sizes that had been adapted and rearranged as needed. Frequently, however, exegetes look first to books, and only secondarily to λόγοι. This difference in focus leads to the presentation of different paradigms. Therefore it is not surprising that there is little scholarly agreement about the major structural ordering.

The traditional and most obvious division of the work into two parts is the basis of many structural paradigms. Some think books 1 through 5 form a pentateuch, and books 6 through 9 a tetrateuch. For others, the work clearly falls into a tetrateuch formed by books 1 through 4 and a pentateuch made up of books 5 through 9. Some have even suggested an arrangement in which there is an hexateuch formed by books 1 through 6, followed by a tristeuch consisting of books 7 through 9. In any case, the various structures are sometimes based on books, sometimes on topics and sometimes times on λόγοι.

Herodotus' implied narrator's obvious interest in the topic of ethnography in the first part of the *History* has led people to view anthropology as basic to the work's architectonics.[88] So, to explain the appar-

---

[87]	For the book divisions and/or λόγοι, see Seth Benardete *Herodotean Inquiries* 4, 31, 153-155. We follow Benardete regarding the division and even its nature, but not regarding the justification for the division. We also accept his concept of the subtending λόγος (*ibid.* 31; also see above), but we interpret it as religious.

[88]	Herodotus interpreted anthropology *through* ethnography. See J. L. Myres "Herodotus and Anthropology" *Anthropology and the Classics* (Oxford: Oxford University, 1980, R. R. Marrett, ed.) 121-168; see also Alexander Dombrowsky

ent historicity of the latter part of the narrative, some scholars assume that Herodotus' evolving and changing interests caused him to alter his perspective as he was actually in the process of composing his *History*. And they also assume that in the process of developing the narrative, he reached a point where he began to focus on the historic.[89] Such researchers perceive the basic design of the *History* to be unbalanced to the extent that the first two-thirds of the narrative is merely an introduction to the last third.[90]

The thesis that the first part of the *History* is only ethnographically and anthropologically focused presumes a discontinuity in the composition of the narrative. It suggests that the real author stopped working on the *History* and then resumed, but from a different stance. Alternatively, it implies that the real author wrote the *History* in a continuous manner over a lengthy period, but he spent so many years in the process that his interests and world view developed into something different from what they had been earlier.

Therefore we reject the precept that ethnographic and/or anthropological interests are behind or even form the leitmotif of the first or any part of the *History*. Despite the extensive presence of this type of material, the subtending motif of the this segment like that of the entire narrative is theological. Moreover, there is no data to support either the conclusion that the real author's interests changed or that his world view was simply specious.

We can say, however, that ethnographic and anthropological data so pervade not only the first third, but the first two-thirds of the *History* that it is proper to call them anthropologically oriented even when this is not their primary focus. But this orientation is from the implied narrator's perspective only.

"Herodotus and Hippocrates on the Anthropology of the Scythians" *Annals of the Ukrainian Academy of Arts and Sciences* 10 (1962/63) 88-89, *et passim*.

[89]   See J. L. Myres *Herodotus: Father of History* 29.

[90]   R. Gayre of Gayre "Herodotus" *Mankind Quarterly* 14 (1973- 1974) 164. This is supported by A. Bauer's theory that Herodotus' *History* was first written in segments reflecting the particular topics in question. Thus, for example, Xerxes' campaign, the "report" of which comprises books 7 through 9 was composed *circa* 445 BCE. See W. W. How & J. Wells "Introduction" *A Commentary on Herodotus* # 10, volume 1, page 12-13.

Actually, Herodotus' implied narrator's interest in ethnography and anthropology does not stop when he begins to narrate the seemingly more "historical" part of the *History*. For him, ethnography and anthropology play a role in the last third of the narrative despite its (apparent) primary concern with the war.[91]

The anthropological-ethnographic interpretation is erroneous because it confuses the implied narrator's interests with those of the real author. Significantly, then, it precludes there being a unifying subtending λόγος grounded in anthropology and/or ethnology. Nevertheless the existence of such a λόγος is suggested by the arrangement of the narrative so that it falls into segments actually delimited by ethnographic subjects in particular. Ethnographically, the first part, a tetrateuch comprised of the initial four books, is concerned with non-Greeks. The second part, a pentateuch constituted by the last five books, is primarily devoted to the Persian Wars.[92]

Perhaps at one time the real author did envision an ethnographic format in which the narrative was divided into two tetrateuchs or into a tetrateuch and a pentateuch, but not as we have them. Then either of these paradigms may have been the basis of an earlier redaction of the *History*. If he had envisioned it as two tetrateuchs that are constituted by the first four and the last four books of the received text respectively, he added the Ionian revolt λόγος later.[93] This is supported by Jacoby's observation that the first part of the *History* (1.6-5.27) is epitomized by a set of independent works dealing with the foreign lands that formed part of Persia's domain, "Persia, Lydia, Egypt, Scythia, etc." Thus it forms a narrative that can be called a "Persica".[94] Clearly then, even in the received text the ethnographically and/or anthropologically based *components* are thematically defensible.

The architectonics of the *History* are not limited to an exposition of Herodotus' ethnographic/anthropologic interests, however. In fact, the

---

[91] R. Gayre of Gayre "Herodotus" 164

[92] François Hartog *The Mirror of Herodotus: The Representation of the Other in the Writing of History* (Berkeley: University of California, 1988) xviii, 248-249.

[93] If so the division presents a truer mirror than F. Hartog realizes.

[94] F. Jacoby "Herodotos" 348

paradigm that is essential to the narrative's prevailing tragic leitmotif that there must be a divinely and concomitantly self-induced fall of those who rise to great heights is neither ethnographic nor anthropologic, it is religious. Furthermore, a text-critical study makes an analysis on the basis of ethnography and/or anthropology less attractive than that based on religion precisely because it devalues this subtending pattern whereby the workings of fate or causality offer paradigmatic illustrations for the dangerous nature of high positions insofar as these result in the inevitable fall of those who achieve supremacy, be they men or nations (barbaric or Greek with their individual πόλεις).

Neither the ethnographic-anthropological analysis nor the religious perspective, moreover, is oriented toward scientific historicity. Rather, they both reflect the role that the *fiction of oral history* plays in Herodotus' narrative art, while denying or at best without acknowledging that this is an illusion that itself is a literary affectation.

Proponents of each arrangement deem their own grouping determinative of the subtending structure. And although they are not quite correct, they are not completely wrong either. In reality, all the proposed structures are present at one and the same time, but only the underlying λόγος itself predicates the narrative form. Thus, each architectonic aspect of that λόγος must be considered individually as well as in relation to one another and additionally to the book divisions.

Some think the *History* may be divided into three parts: books 1 through 4; book 5 as a transition bonding the first four books with what follows; and books 6 through 9, respectively.[95] Benardete accepts this particular arrangement as authentic. Consequently he defines books 1 through 4 as Herodotus' own thought; book 5 as the progression from the Greek-Barbarian deeds to Herodotus' own thought—that is, as a pivotal book;[96]—and then books 6 through 9 as a reflection on, and a supplement to Herodotus' own ideas about the amazing and remarkable deeds of the Barbarians and the Greeks.[97] Unitarian belief does not demand composition in received order.

---

[95]   For a tripartite division, see S. Benardete *Herodotean Inquiries* 4.
[96]   S. Benardete *Herodotean Inquiries* 4.
[97]   S. Benardete *Herodotean Inquiries* 4.

The λόγοι in the first four books present the antecedents of the war between the Persians and the Greeks. Those in book 5 depict the beginnings of the Ionian revolt that is antecedent to the spread of the war into Greece. Finally, those in books 6 through 9 show the development of the Ionian revolt into a full-scale war.

This can be specified nationally and spatially. Books 1 through 4 in which the antecedents of the war between the Persians and the Greeks are depicted are chiastically arranged by nationalities—Greek/Asiatic : Egyptian : Greek/Asiatic : Scythian—as Jacoby has shown;[98] and we believe they are chiastically arranged by spatial organization as well—West-East : (South)-East : West-East : (North)-West. On the other hand, books 5 through 9 are arranged so as to show the lessening of Persian and the increase of Greek power and, at the same time, the shifting of the spatial focus away from the East and toward the West.

In the first four books, the Greek and Asiatic affairs are intertwined and treated as paired entities. Events in Egypt and Scythia are presented as standing alone for the most part. Egypt and Scythia represent extremes both culturally, geophysically, and geographically, whereas Greek/Asiatic—the West/East—is the repeated mean in respect to the same categories. Scythia is both cold and primitive. Egypt is hot and has a far older civilization than either Greece or Persia, but it is not the oldest civilization.

Likewise, in the last five books, Greek and Persian affairs are intertwined and treated as paired entities. But there is a greater specificity and focus to the matching here than in the earlier part of the work. Moreover, in the end, Greece stands alone, at least by implication; and Cyrus, who is emblematic of Persia, dies.

The narrative unit formed by book 5 through book 6.17 treats the beginnings of the Ionian revolt. That formed by book 6.18 through book 9.122 narrates the antecedents and the events of the war from the fall of Miletus onward.[99] This latter segment of the account includes an interesting break in and change of narrative style. When the implied

---

98 F. Jacoby "Herodotos" 348.
99 F. Jacoby "Herodotos" 348. Even this is not fully correct since the Egyptian and the Scythian λόγοι also account for Greek affairs.

narrator reports the fall of Miletus, the narrative, hitherto structured strictly by λόγοι, becomes and remains annalistic.[100]

Number or letter symbolism may have played a role in the Hellenistic, but not the real author's division of the work. Insofar as we know, in Herodotus' own time there was no tradition that works were to be divided into nine books, and Herodotus himself did not so apportion his work. Consequently, the symmetry presented by 4:1:4 may be Herodotean because of the λόγοι arrangement if, as we believe, the multiple redactions had been made by Herodotus, the author, himself. On the other hand, if there were multiple redactors, each of whom was responsible for one or more redactions rather than multiple redactions by Herodotus himself, this format may have been superimposed on the narrative by a very late redactor. In any case, this 4: 1: 4 *schema* is the basis rather than the result of the Alexandrians' (or of the person or people, whoever they were, who created the units) division of the *History* into nine books.

There is another division under which books 1 through 4 present the history of civilization as if the Indo-European and Semitic cultures in the ancient Near East, Eurasia, and, insofar as it is pertinent, those societies more emanating from, than existing in Europe itself represent, are emblematic of, or are even deemed to constitute the entire world. Book 5 takes the narrative into the recent history of the eastern Greek civilizations, and it pays particular attention to the Ionian Revolt. Books 6 through 9 then carry the work to an unfinished study of Greece itself without suggesting that the *History* is really incomplete. Accordingly, the *History* may even be viewed as divided into two parts of unequal length.

Bury and Jacoby both divide the work into three sets of three books. Bury sees the first set as treating the reigns of Cyrus and Cambyses, and as including the accession of Darius; the second as depicting Darius' reign; and the third as dealing with that of Xerxes. Bury considers the work as a whole to be a *Persica* even though he suggests that the first part primarily deals with Asia and Egypt, the middle part,

---

[100]   F. Jacoby "Herodotos" 348.

Europe, and the last, Greece.[101] Jacoby, however views the three sets differently. He proposes that the first is a Croesus λόγος (*History* 1.6-94); the second a Persian λόγος extending topically from Cyrus to Darius (*History* 1.95-7.4); and the third is a λόγος presenting the history of Xerxes' expedition (*History* 7.5-9.122).[102]

But we do not think that these are the only possible divisions. The *History* also falls topically into an hexateuch followed by a tristeuch. The first six books describe the events leading up to Xerxes' campaign against Greece, the Ionian Revolt, and the progress of the war through the aftermath of the critical Greek victory at Marathon (*History* 6.103.1-116.1). This includes a death-count, which is recorded in a coda to the victory report (*History* 6.117.1-3), but not to the λόγος.

Although the account of this victory may well be the high point and, at the same time, the peripeteia of the narrative, Herodotus does not end his major λόγος here. Rather he extends his report by adding the lengthy digression that forms the conclusion of the λόγος while directing the implied readers' attention to religious matters (*History* 6.118-119); to the delayed arrival of the Lacaedaemonians (*History* 6.120); to a retrospective view of Athens in which it was suggested that the Alcmaeonidae were never really traitors, but were as much haters of tyrants as Callias (*History* 6.121-131);[103] and to a prospective view of Athens limited to the period immediately after Marathon (*History* 6.132-149) in which *religio* in general and hubris in particular on the part of both the Athenians and the Pelasgians play a role (*History* 6.134-140). This lengthy digression, moreover, is not merely fortuitous. Rather, it points the way to the Athenians' impending fall as well as that of the remaining states of Greece, albeit not necessarily concomitantly.

The last three books contain the narration of Darius' receipt of the news of the Persian defeat at Marathon (*History* 7.1.1), preparations

---

[101] J. B. Bury "Herodotus" *The Ancient Greek Historians* (New York: Dover 1958) 38.

[102] F. Jacoby "Herodotos" 351.

[103] It is here within the story of the marriage of Megacles to the daughter of Cleisthenes, the prince of Sicyon, that we find the well-known story about the Hippoclides' dance.

for the succession and the death of Darius (*History* 7.2.1-5.1), and
Xerxes' campaign together with the remainder of the war (*History*
7.5.2-9.122.4). In this part of the *History* the religious theme is eminently clear. As Herodotus delineates the rise of Persia, her hubris and
subsequent defeat at Marathon in part one, he iterates the implications
of what is stated in Book 6.118-140 and adduces her fall in part two.
Herodotus, however, has also described the rise, hubris, and fall of
others in part one of this narrative. And the real Greek reader, no matter what his πόλις, could not have missed the implication, which is
merely strengthened by the digression noted above, that his πόλις and
perhaps all Greece as well *must and will* also fall.

   This may well have been directed to the Athenians, who particularly when they attained to the epitome of glory at Marathon, had already committed, were persisting in committing, and, by implication,
would continue to commit hubris. And consequently their theology
should have made them aware that they would suffer a fall. Herodotus,
the real author, still writing during the Peloponnesian War between the
Greek states, was well aware of how great a fall that could and probably would be.[104] No longer was there a united effort by "all Greece"
against a common non-Greek enemy[105] as there had at been in the heroic era, at least according to epic tradition, and as there had been in
Herodotus' own historical era in the war against the Persians.[106]

   This is a "tragic" schema, whose first part is formed by those portions of the *History* that primarily concern themselves with the lands
that eventually made up the Persian empire (*History* 1.1.1-5.25.1). Accordingly, the second part is formed by those that primarily concern
themselves with Greek affairs and with the war between the Greeks

---

   104   The fall is the division of all Greece, not the eventual Athenian defeat that
would occur long after the time we assume Herodotus to have died. Interestingly
enough, therefore, as Jacoby ("Herodotos" 348) has pointed out, Herodotus distinguishes Athenian from Spartan history according to their kings in book 1, 5, and 6.
   105   Hence it is important that Herodotus indicates that the Athenians fought
jointly with the Pelasgians at Marathon. This reference to the presence of Pelasgians, who were the first Greeks, falsely insinuates that the battle of Marathon may
have been a pan-Greek enterprise.
   106   It has frequently been noted that Herodotus himself was probably born too
late to have any first-hand knowledge of this war.

and the Persians (*History* 5.30.1 [sic]-9.122.4).[107] Moreover, the nature of the data and the way in which they are presented support the likelihood that the division (*History* 1.1.1-5.25.1[?] and 5.30.1-9.122.4) was not superimposed on the narrative during the Hellenistic era, but rather emanates from the real author himself and is basic to his final redaction.

The three pivotal chapters (*History* 5.26.1-29.2) are not independent; but rather they serve as a linking device partaking of and thereby joining together both general topics and even as a transition between two clearly defined sections of the *History*. In fact, there is no explicitly delineated break within these chapters. Since the books were not divided into chapters until the 17th century, Herodotus could not have conceived of the segment formed by these pivotal chapters as an entity *qua* entity. If anything, he may have envisioned it as forming a bond that had roots in both portions of the narrative. The two parts of the *History* are held together by this trajectory from one major division to the other.

In the first division, book 1.1 through book 5 somewhere within chapters 25 to 29, the implied narrator's interest in causes or responsibilities is particularly evident. He describes the antecedents and beginning of the war of the Greeks with the Persians and Medes, whom the implied narrator treats as one entity and does not distinguish from one another. In any case, the real author does more than preserve the record of great deeds of Greeks or Persians, as is assumed by Myres and others who confuse him with the implied narrator.[108] Instead he shows the relationship between magnificent and/or amazing deeds and human events.[109]

By tracing the origins of the war to its antecedents while conjecturing a causal train that originates with the beginning of human civiliza-

---

107 M E. White "Herodotus' Starting-Point" *Phoenix* 23 (1969) 42-43.

108 John L. Myres *Herodotus: Father of History* 61. For a lengthy discussion and a brief but important overview of the scholarship, see Hannelore Barth *"Zur Bewertung und Auswahl des Stoffes durch Herodot (Die Begriffe* θῶμα, θωμάζω, θωμάσιος *und* θωμαστός") *Klio* 50 (1968) 93-110, esp. 93-95.

109 F. Jacoby "Herodotos" 334, *et passim*; see also H. Barth *"Zur Bewertung und Auswahl des Stoffes durch Herodot"* 93.

tion,[110] Herodotus' implied narrator demonstrates that he is not interested in cosmology and the origins of the universe, but rather in the origins of culture, which he traces back to Phrygia (*History* 2.2).[111] Consequently, Herodotus does not begin his narrative with a discussion of society's inception although, by a consummate act of artistry, he encapsulates this very significant moment in human history in his (major) Egyptian λόγος, which primarily describes a much later period. In so doing, he nearly obliterates the historical relevance of this minor, but very important "origins of culture" λόγος.

For the implied narrator, then, the origins of the war between Greece and Persia emanate from the origins of civilization, and this suggests that he is interested in both anthropology and ethnography. This, however, is not important to the development of the real author's thesis that the only things that count are the inexorable rise and fall of continents, nations, and Great Men, and the inevitability of the conflict between Greece and Persia. What does matter is that conflict was inescapable once mankind attained to civilization and once Greece and Persia arose as opposing forces. It does not matter who started the clash.

In the first five books, the implied narrator looks back from the vantage of his own time as well as from that of the more recent past to which he refers as needed. He is telling a long, involved story, much of which deals with events from earlier times. For the most part, the real author depicts him as using the "unadorned style." Hence, the text is expansive, and many portions of the narrative, although not simplistic, are in simple and loosely woven Greek.

The real author, Herodotus himself, is not consistent in his employment of the unadorned style, however. Rather, he presents this as the characteristic style of his overriding implied narrator. The real author uses an intricately wrought mode where it suits his needs, particularly

---

110 For the Greek interest in the origins of civilization, see Charles Segal "Greek Tragedy and Society: A Structuralist Perspective" *Greek Tragedy and political Theory* (Berkeley: University of California, 1986, J. Peter Euben, ed.) 55-57, *passim*.
111 Perhaps it is significant that a Phrygian history, to which Herodotus may have had access, had already been written.

when his literary argument would be augmented by the presence of a complex textual presentation. This is most evident in his structuring of λόγοι.

For example, the minor λόγοι depicting an interaction between East and West are subordinated to the thematics of the respective major λόγοι into which they are incorporated. When combined, these λόγοι are artistically treated as a subordinated but still major λόγος formed by the "Persian" or eastern segment even though they describe events of western interest. In any case, they help to bind the Persian segment to the Greek.

There is a stylistic change as the narrative progresses. In books 6 through 9, dealing with the Ionian revolt and then the war itself, the narrative gives the pretense of being more historical at least from the perspective of modern so-called "scientific" history. Herodotus' implied narrator's Greek is more "tightly woven" here and the narrative deceptively appears somewhat more impartial than before.

This allegedly dispassionate historicity, however, is a well-wrought literary illusion. Moreover, the war and its immediate antecedents are not treated as history, but as religiously paradigmatic.[112] It is in books 6 through 9 that we see that Greece like the nations who preceded her will also come to an inevitable fall from power.

Neither Herodotus nor his implied narrator has to depict the catastrophe, only the exemplar that demands it. Therefore, it is no accident that book 6 is filled with minor λόγοι depicting hubristic acts, reports of hubristic acts, and oracles regarding the consequences of hubristic acts committed by individual Greek leaders or entire peoples and/or city-states (*History* 6.19; 39.2; 49; 50; 61.1; 621-2; 66-67; *et alii*). It does not matter whether those who are hubristic acknowledge or even recognize their actions as beyond the pale. More often than not, however, they do so in accordance with the paradigm for tragic drama. And the narrative includes reports of incidents in which people realize they have committed hubris (*History* 6. 12) that Herodotus uses to advance his own thematics. Most significantly, each of these accounts is

---

112 For a summation of the religious bases of the *History* and, in particular, divine causation see David Grene "Introduction" *The History: Herodotus* 18, 20, 25-31, *et passim*.

inserted into the narrative in such a way that it clearly suggests the victory at Marathon will also have adverse consequences for the victors,
as the real reader would have known and the implied reader would
have presumed.

The heaping up of accounts of Greek acts of hubris, be they recognized and acknowledged by their respective perpetrators, recognized
and unacknowledged, or even unrecognized, heightens the literary tension leading up to the depiction of the battle of Marathon. But the
beauty of the narrative's vision is that the implied narrator reports acts
of hubris that Greeks had committed before Marathon although it is the
Greeks, and not the Persians, who will win the battle. It is of thematic
relevance, then, that all of these accounts are epitomized by the reports,
with which book 6 concludes, of notable hubristic actions by Athenians and Pelasgians, and that of the essentially unheroic Spartan failure
to reach Marathon on time. Moreover, the representation of Cleomenes
as working for the common good of all of Greece (*History* 6. 61.1)
suggests that the individual Greek perpetrators of the various hubristic
acts are, in summation, representative of all Greece. There are other
examples illustrating this coherence as well.

In any case, Herodotus stresses the architectonic and paradigmatic
meaning of this chain of hubristic actions when he depicts them as the
basis of the digression with which he ends the major λόγος. The
hubristic hero must achieve a momentous height before his precipitous
fall. Moreover, like Sophocles' Oedipus in the *Oedipus Tyrannus*, he
must keep on committing hubris in an ever escalating fashion until he
recognizes what he has done thereby.

The implied narrator had forewarned the implied reader of the
meaning and consequences of these "heaped up" accounts of hubristic
acts when he stated "It is customary for a sign to be given in advance
somehow, when great evils are about to come upon a city-state or a nation" (φιλέει δέ κως προσημαίνειν, εὖτ ' ἄν μέλλη μεγάλα
κακὰ ἢ πόλι ἢ ἔθνεϊ ἔσεσθαι [*History* 6.27.1]). Therefore, these
acts are reported in precisely the right place in the narrative. The
"tragic" model requires the account to proceed in exactly the order we
have received it if the implied auditor is to be led to expect the theologically proper result: Greece, like Persia, can and must fall, and that

fall must be from a vertiginous height as we suggested. This, however, is the perception of the implied narrator.

The real author develops his narrative in such a way that implied narrator is showing that the great and wondrous victory at Marathon itself was not itself hubristic whatever preceded may have it. For the implied narrator, the inception of Greece's fated ruin was not the rightfully attained glory gained by the Athenian and Pelasgian' victory at Marathon, a battle representing the first major Greek triumph, despite the Spartan absence, since that of the Trojan War as the tradition was handed down by Homer and as it was preserved in the folk memory. In fact Marathon is clearly the dramatic high point before the fall. As such it renders the situation of "All Greece" analogous to that of a culture hero or "great man" such as the victorious Agamemnon, at the height of his prowess, returning home to be murdered basely after the fall of Troy.

The implied narrator's depiction of the Greeks at the pinnacle of success was necessitated by the need to render their impending fall, be it imminent or delayed, the more precipitous. It is primarily presented for its dramatic qualities although the author would have been hard put to ignore such a recently and gloriously concluded historical event. Hence he serves both literary and historical ends by showing that ruin's inception began and then developed gradually well before that decisive victory, and that it was brought about by the hubristic acts of individual people and city-states respectively.

As in the case of the major λόγοι, we do not know when the real author composed the "included "minor λόγοι and/or placed them in this literary taut and significant sequence in this case or any other. All we can tell is that the author had them in place by the time of his final redaction. Clearly, the order of the composition of the λόγοι is important insofar as it could testify to Herodotus' original conceptions of the work, but we cannot say anything about it because we do not have pertinent data.

Just as we do not know the order in which the various λόγοι were composed, we do not know when or by whom the *History* was divided into book form, much less into nine books. Since the λόγοι format is predominant, perhaps Herodotus mechanically separated the narrative into books for no other reason than to render the book-rolls manageable.

Additionally, some apportionment into books, although perhaps not in accordance with the Herodotean division and, possibly, not into the nine books as we have them, was made at Alexandria during the 3rd-2nd century BCE.[113] Unlike the Herodotean division, this Alexandrian book ordering may have been done for literary as well as for purely mechanical reasons. If so, it may be the basis of the confusion of priorities whereby books and even their groupings are given more attention than λόγοι.

Since the book divisions do not always coincide with caesuras in the narrative,[114] the textual basis on which those in the extant work were made is uncertain. These divisions, as we have suggested, may not be representative of earlier or even the earliest configuration of the work as it was divided into books. Given current data, therefore, the division into nine books must be treated as if it were of lesser text critical importance than the division into λόγοι—and rightly so. On the other hand, the chapter divisions are of far less significance to our analysis. The demarcation by chapter was devised by Jungermann, first appearing in his edition of 1608 CE. And even these divisions have been changed by later editors.[115] The arrangement as we now

---

[113] For the Hellenistic division into nine books, see R. A. McNeal "On Editing Herodotus" 125-127. For the dating of the received book divisions in most but not all manuscript traditions, to the 2nd or 3rd century CE, see R. A. McNeal, *ibid.* 127.

[114] For the possibility of the Muses' names actually being applied to the books by the Hellenistic Grammarians, see A. L. Barbour *Selections from Herodotus* 4. For this as "some librarian's fancy", see P. MacKendrick "Herodotus: The Making of A World Historian" 147. But see R. A. McNeal "On Editing Herodotus" 126-127. For lack of coincidence with book divisions, see R. A. McNeal *ibid.* 126-127 *et loc. cit.* For lack of coincidence with caesuras in the narrative, see J. L. Myres *Herodotus: Father of History* 65.

[115] See for example R. A. McNeal, ed., *Herodotus Book I* (Lanham: University Press of America, 1986) x. The division into chapters therefore is of no significance insofar as our discussion is concerned.

know it may have little relationship to the real author's preconception.[116]

The Amherst Papyrus (II 12. 1. I 194, 215) of uncertain date but containing a fragment of the 2nd century BCE grammarian Aristarchus' commentary on Herodotus, is the first extant reference to an individual book, namely "A," in the *History*.[117] The Lindian Chronicle (*terminus antequam* 99 BCE) refers to book B.[118] The first reference to all nine books is found in Diodorus 11.37.6 (*scripsit circa* 60-30 BCE).[119]

There is no way of knowing whether the Alexandrian scholars, who divided Herodotus' *History* into nine books during the Hellenistic era, had as the basis of their work a received, standard edition of the text.[120] Insofar as we can tell, the first standardized text of the *History* was made by Aristarchus. McNeal suggests that Aristarchus did "for Herodotus what was clearly done for Homer."[121] We, however, suggest that by applying the same technique to both works, Aristarchus did for Herodotus what he had also done for Homer.

In the Hellenistic era, the beginning of a book division in only a few works was designated by the letter of the Greek alphabet that would seem to denote an appropriate sequential number. Nobody who spoke Greek, however, would treat this type of alphabetic sequencing as real numeration. The latter uses archaic letters and combinations of letters in addition to the Classical/Hellenistic alphabet as the denotation of numbers, and it suggests nothing more than ordering. On the other hand, the use of letters alone seems to be a form of naming. This alphabetic usage, then, indicates that those who "lettered" the books

---

[116] See R. A. McNeal "On Editing Herodotus" *passim*; P. MacKendrick "Herodotus: The Making of A World Historian" 147.

[117] Carolus Hude, who assigns a date to all the other papyri containing excerpts of Herodotus, does not do so in the case of the Amherst Papyrus. See Carolus Hude "*Praefatio*" *Herodoti Historiae* volume 1, x.

[118] R. A. McNeal "On Editing Herodotus" 125-126, and 126 note 34. For the Lindian Chronicle alone, see also J. L. Myres *Herodotus: Father of History* 65.

[119] R. A. McNeal "On Editing Herodotus" 126 note 34.

[120] R. A. McNeal "On Editing Herodotus" 125.

[121] R. A. McNeal "On Editing Herodotus" 125-126. For the literary critical value of this suggestion, see below.

were creating an acrostic so as to name, rather than using simple numeration so as to number them.

The division of Herodotus' *History* into nine books that are respectively named by the first nine letters of the Classical/Hellenistic Greek
alphabet has the same basis as the naming by letters of the same Clas-
sical/Hellenistic Greek alphabet in both *Iliad* and *Odyssey*. As the alphabetic book designation in Homer is *ipso facto* an acrostic, the first
nine letters as an alphabetic book designation in Herodotus is a truncated acrostic.[122] Perhaps it is important that all three of these works
had been composed in artificial literary dialects, each of which is
based on an Ionic substratum.

Maybe the alphabetic-naming of books in both Homeric epics was
made to correspond with the twenty-four letters of the Greek alphabet
so as to show that these works were both complete and inspired even
though the inspiration was attributed to only one Muse. And if so, the
first nine letters of the alphabet were chosen to coincide with the number of Muses in Herodotus' work so as to show that it was inspired literature like the Homeric epics although it contained narratives of the
deeds of recent men as well as those of the heroic age.[123] But unlike
Homeric epic, this work was inspired by the nine Muses and it was not
really complete.[124]

If the Grammarians deemed the work historical, they would have
attributed its inspiration to Clio, the Muse whose charge was history.
We assume, therefore, that those who named it for the nine Muses
were suggesting that this work was more than historical. Perhaps they
recognized that it was composed of an hybridized blend of genres, and
they defined it accordingly.

---

[122] *Iliad* and *Odyssey* are each divided into twenty-four books. The "naming"
of the books in the two epics differs only insofar as capitol letters are used to this
end in *Iliad* and lower case letters in *Odyssey*.

[123] For possession by the muses leading to a recounting of the deeds of heroes,
and hence the education of posterity, see Plato *Phaedrus* 245a.

[124] Philosophically, this may be related to Pythagorean Mathematics in which
the number 9 needs the addition of the 1 to complete the decade, which in the form
of the "tetractys of the decade" is the drawing or visual presentation of the sacred
number according to which the entire universe is arranged (see: Sextus Empiricus
adv. Math. 7.94-95).

There is no known convention by which prose is titled by any of the Muses' names. Notably, the Homeric epics were divided into twenty-four books that were not *named* for the Muses despite the bardic invocation of a muse either at the beginning of or within the respective narratives. Hence, the lack of extant references designating the books in Herodotus' *History* by the Muses' names prior to the 2nd century CE, when Lucian (*Quomodo Historia Conscribenda sit* 42) notes their use,[125] may not be accidental.

The employment of the Muses' names for Herodotus' books may be nothing more than a rather late tradition. If so, its attribution to the Alexandrians is anachronistic. In any case, we can only state with certainty that the names of the Muses began to be applied to the individual books in the *History* sometime between the 3rd-2nd century BCE and the 2nd CE.[126]

Even granting that Herodotus' work is something other than historical in the modern sense, the use of the Muses' names to designate books is not only late, it is non-traditional. Moreover, neither numbering nor acrostic lettering is absolutely analogous to naming unless, perhaps, there is some form of allegorical representation or even mysticism involved. Simple numbering, which as we have stated is not employed in denoting either Herodotean or Homeric books, merely shows ordering. The use of acrostic lettering, on the other hand, specifies the existence of a bond that holds as implicit a commonalty of thought regarding the value of those letters. Those who first used the Muses' names to designate the individual books in Herodotus' *History* were innovating.

The truncated acrostic suggests that there is something special and noteworthy about Herodotus' work, and this may be why the Muses' names were appended to the books. As we have suggested, those who designated the books by the Muses' names may have believed the inspiration of the nine Muses, who expanded the poet's and the histo-

---

[125] See R. A. McNeal "On Editing Herodotus" 127 and 127 note 36; J. L. Myres *Herodotus: Father of History* 65; *et al.*

[126] See R. A. McNeal "On Editing Herodotus" 127.

rian's recollection alike,[127] is the bond that links the individual parts of Herodotus' *History* together just as a single Muse's inspiration links the individual parts of the respective Homeric epics. Consequently we must iterate that whoever first employed the nine Muses' names to denote the (corresponding) nine books was treating the *History* as literature that was inspired[128] and of hybrid genre.

As we have said, it has long been recognized that the *History*, like Attic tragedy, has close ties to Homeric epic. In each of these genres, the presumed past is treated as historical even when it represents what might have happened or when it includes myths or legends.[129] Thus when Herodotus' friend, Choerilus of Samos, insinuated that the missing "new chariot" of those who wanted to participate in the Muses' "race" (fr. 1) was a tradition of prose epic,[130] he may have been suggesting that Herodotus' work was to be categorized as ἔπος,[131] which is a far broader category than epic. But in particular, he was suggesting it was really a form of epic and should be treated accordingly.

---

[127] Bruno Snell *The Discovery of the Mind: The Greek Origins of European Thought* (New York/Evanston: Harper & Row, 1960) 137.

[128] Although the real author may not have adhered to the same precepts we do about the recording of history, he may have been familiar with those principles that were (subsequently) articulated during the 4th century by Aristotle. We cannot say this with any degree of certitude, however. In any case, the acquisition of historical knowledge by divine stimulus is categorically opposed to the scientific as well as to the Aristotelian concept of the recording of history, both of which were admittedly formulated later than Herodotus' time. For Herodotus' *History* as inspired literature in Hellenistic-Roman thought, see Arnaldo Momigliano "*Erodoto E La Storiografia Moderna: Alcuni Problemi Presentati ad un Convegno di Umanisti*" *Aevum* 31 (1957) 78.

[129] For the historicity of the *presumed past* in Homer, see Kurt Latte "*Die Anfänge der griechischen Geschichtschreibunt*" *Histoire et Historiens dans L'Antiquite* (Genève: Vandoeuvres, 1956) 3.

[130] It may be more than coincidental that Choerilus composed a *Persica* in epic form.

[131] For this classification, see Northrop Frye "Fourth Essay: Rhetorical Criticism: Theory of Genres" *Anatomy of Criticism: Four Essays* (Princeton: Princeton University, 1971) 248-250, *et passim; et al.* But Aristotle, who sees ἐποποιία as correlative to tragedy (*Poetics* 1449 b), would deny this.

Technically therefore, it is significant that there is a "speaking presence" in both Herodotus' *History* and Homeric epic.[132] That Herodotus uses some literary contrivances which are foreign to Homeric epic is of little matter.[133]

Herodotus clearly emphasizes the bonds between his work and Homeric epic by his repeated usage of Homeric vocabulary, his "respect for Homeric authority," and his use of pedimental structure.[134] Although the *History* is composed in a "mixed" post-Homeric and primarily Ionic literary dialect,[135] which had probably not been used for any other purpose,[136] it includes some Homeric vocabulary.

Homer had become the "schoolbook" of all Greece and was known to all educated (Greek) men. Herodotus chose the somewhat later but still mixed literary and primarily Ionic dialect to evoke the memory of the earlier Homeric usage that he followed when he collected and incorporated the traditional λόγοι into his work. Virginia Hunter even suggests that Herodotus "pictures Homer as working rather like himself, gaining knowledge through enquiry...and at times choosing among

---

[132] We do not believe that Frye's distinction between the "speaking presence" in rhetoric and the "absence" of the poet is applicable here. For this distinction, see Northrop Frye *Words with Power: Being a Second Study of The Bible and Literature* (San Diego/New York: Harcourt Brace Jovanovich, 1990) 67.

[133] J. Gould *Herodotus* 50. For the relationship to Homer, see also *ibid.* 119-120.

[134] J. L. Myres *Herodotus: Father of History* 69, 81-82. For his reliance on Homer, particularly in book 2.116-120, see Virginia Hunter *Past and Process in Herodotus and Thucydides* (Princeton: Princeton University, 1982) 52; A. L. Barbour "Introduction" *Selections from Herodotus* 1.

[135] W. W. How & J. Wells "Introduction" *A Commentary on Herodotus* # 2, volume 1, page 2 note 2. But for Herodotus' language simply as the new Ionic dialect, see A. Barbour "Introduction" *Selections from Herodotus* 8

[136] The presence of non-Ionic words and forms makes unacceptable the hypothesis that Herodotus used the mutually intelligible Ionic dialects of the Aegean Islands that may have developed because there were Ionians living in Halikarnassus, which itself had been "assimilated in speech, manners, and interests to its Ionian neighbors". For this as the basis of Herodotus' language, see J. L. Myres *Herodotus: Father of History* 2. But see Terrot Reaveley Glover *Herodotus* (Freeport: Books for Libraries, 1969 reprint of 1924 edition) 21.

variant versions" though with a different focus to his selectivity.[137] We will emend that to say that his implied narrator may well be assumed to have done so.

The Hellenistic Grammarians or even later scholars, being well versed in Homer, understood the parallel between Herodotus' *History* and Homeric epic as we have inferred in discussing the "naming" of the books. Nevertheless, they were well aware of the differences. Nobody could overlook the most notable incongruity, length: Herodotus' *History* is approximately as long as the *Iliad* and *Odyssey* combined.[138] In particular, however, the Grammarians clearly realized that Herodotus' *History* is a national epic and Homer's and the Homeridae's accounts are not. Their normative use as such is not relevant.

Because the Grammarians (or later scholars) thought the motivation for the writing of Herodotus' *History* was related to, although different from the creation of Homer's epics, they used the Muses' names for Herodotean books as we have suggested. And the use of the Muses' names indicated far more than inspiration: it stressed that this prose narrative was particularly analogous to epic and to other forms of writings that were to be read aloud. Hence, by this usage, they verified the *History*'s classification as ἔπος.

But perhaps they had an additional and even more important reason for their designation of the books by the Muses' names. They may have done so in conjunction with Apollonian worship as reflected by the role assigned to the Delphic Oracle in the *History*. They may also have assigned these names to the books because of the work's tragic structure. But the Delphic Oracle and the tragic format are each part of the same religious entity, uniting to form an organic whole in the *History*.

Although Dionysus is the god generally associated with Greek tragedy, by the 5th century the Dionysiac and Apollonian were joined closely, but not necessarily univocally. Burkert's observation that "the tragedians love to make the Dionysian tones heard at Apollo's Del-

---

[137] V. Hunter *Past and Process in Herodotus and Thucydides* 54. We do not believe, however, that the text of the *History* gives full justification for this hypothesis.

[138] S. Flory "Who Read Herodotus' *Histories*?" 13.

phi"[139] is of great moment for our argument. In particular, our belief that the Hellenistic Grammarians tied the various genres together in their interpretation of the *History* is supported by the juncture of the Dionysiac and Apollonian with the Muses by the 4th century when Apollo was associated with them (note the plural). In fact Apollo is depicted with them on the east pediment of a temple, whose west pediment portrays Dionysus with the Thyiades (Pausanias *Graeciae Descriptio* 10.19.4).[140]

The application of the Muses' names to the books by the Alexandrians or their successors, therefore, is not merely an artistic flourish or even a trope. The Grammarians or whoever first appended the Muses' names to the books did so realizing Herodotus had intentionally imitated both Homeric epic[141] and tragic drama, both of whose elements he had united in a prose epic format. Hence, when Longinus (213-273 CE) asks if only Herodotus was completely Homeric (*de Sublimitate* 13.3), he insinuates that for him, the *History* is epic. This in and of itself shows that Herodotus' relationship to Homer was recognized in late antiquity. This does not mean that everybody understood it, however. Likewise not everybody acknowledged the *History*'s connection with drama even during Herodotus' own time.

The Muses are intimately tied to the epic and/or tragic genres. Therefore, even without the witness of the 4th century temple's eastern pediment, we can assert that the use of their names in and of itself suggests the *History* was taken for some form of epic and/or tragedy during the late Hellenistic era at least by the Grammarians. Additionally, the real author's use of λόγοι to portray events in the *History* as they might have happened rather than as they really happened places the *History* within the parameters for epic poetry as well as drama.

---

139 Walter Burkert *Greek Religion*, (Cambridge: Harvard University, 1985, John Raffan, trans.), 224. See also *Pausaniae Graeciae Descriptio* Stuttgart: B. G. Teubner, 1959, 3 volume edition; Fridericus Spiro, ed., volume 3.

140 See also W. Burkert *Greek Religion* 224.

141 For the analogy between the logographer and the Homeric bard as "a restatement of Herodotus' own perceptions", see O. Murray "Herodotus and Oral History" 107. We, however, must qualify that by stating that it was Herodotus' implied narrator who was a logographer. Herodotus, the author, may or may not have been one.

If we do accept Aristotle's definition of history (*Poetics* 1451b), Herodotus' use of λόγοι to describe what might have happened actually excludes the *History* from the historic genre. Aristotle specifically distinguishes the poet who depicts events that might have happened from the historian who depicts those that have happened (*Poetics* 1451b).[142] Aristotle classifies Herodotus as a poet or a dramatist *without realizing that he has included him in this group.*[143] Overlooking his own precept, Aristotle states that Herodotus could not be a poet (*Poetics* 1451b).[144] Clearly even Aristotle has confused the real author, who created or redacted the λόγοι, with the implied narrator, whom the real author portrayed as an historian.

The commentators or editors who named the books did not understand how the real author had been influenced by the Egyptian literary tradition in which, seven hundred years earlier, people were writing novels.[145] On the other hand, they understood the prose tragic epic nature of the genre better than we, better than Aristotle, and perhaps better than Herodotus himself.

And there is not even a hint that Herodotus denoted segments of his narrative by the Muses' names. Even though others might have classified the *History* as inspired, insofar as we can tell Herodotus the real author did not. This does not mean, however, that Herodotus classified his own work as historical.

Although we have fragments of "historical," logographic works, we still know rather little about Greek historiography or prose before Herodotus. But by contemporary, later ancient standards—including those of Aristotle who says that composition in prose or verse does not

---

142 For a Homeric analogy, see B. Snell *The Discovery of the Mind* 90.

143 For Herodotus as poet or dramatist, see G. J. D. Aalders H. Wzn (sic) "*der vader der geschiedenis*" (sic) *Hermeneus* 40 (1969) 106.

144 But see T. G. Rosenmeyer ("History or Poetry?" The Example of Herodotus" *Clio* 11 [1982] 239-259) for a different appraisal of Aristotle's concept of history.

145 See, for example, J. A. Cuddon *A Dictionary of Literary Terms* (London: Penguin, 1979) *s.v.* "Novel," page 432.

determine or exclude any literary genre,—or even by modern criteria, Herodotus' *History* is incorrectly deemed historical.[146]

Actually the *History* as an entity cannot be fully classified. It falls within the provenance of different genres that appear to merge with or overlie one another. This is not unique in 5th century BCE literature, as the overlapping of the genres used by Homer and Aeschylus as depicted in Aristophanes' *Frogs* attests.[147] In reality, there are numerous examples of "blended" or hybrid genres in antiquity. But we must still distinguish between those in which there is merely overlapping. Clearly, then, as Aeschylean drama is not the same as Homeric epic despite the overlapping of genres,[148] Herodotean *History* is not the same as a tragic drama, a verse epic, or pathetic history even when it uses or falls within the parameters of those genres.

Herodotus' *History* forms some new, hitherto unnamed type of genre. This does not mean that Herodotus or his contemporaries had not named it: only that if they gave the genre a name, they were probably the first to do so or the more ancient tradition is simply not extant.

Herodotus did not thoroughly disguise the genres he blended into his work. Some aspects of the *History* are clearly tragic; and they are narrated in such a way as to highlight their relationship to tragedy, which "more than any other genre of literature" questions rather than reflects the social reality in which it is apparently grounded.[149] The coincidences between tragedy and tragic meta-history occur precisely be-

---

[146] There are other instances of this in Antiquity. For example, for at least fifteen books of Livy's work as an extensive deliberative oration and, hence, a literary rather than an historical opus, see Sara Sindel (= Sara Mandell) "A Literary Analysis of books Thirty One through Forty Five of Livy's *Ab Urbe Condita*" PhD Diss., New York University, 1969.

[147] See Rosemary M. Harriott *Aristophanes: Poet and Dramatist* (Baltimore:: Johns Hopkins, 1986) 19.

[148] Significantly, Aristophanes depicts Aeschylus as asserting a claim to being "Homer's direct successor in the presentation of heroes and heroic virtues (*Frogs* 1034-1042)". See R. M. Harriott *Aristophanes: Poet and Dramatist* 19.

[149] Jean-Pierre Vernant "Tensions and Ambiguities in Greek Tragedy" *Tragedy and Myth in Ancient Greece* (Humanities: Atlantic Highlands, 1981, Jean-Pierre Vernant and Pierre Vidal-Naquet, ed.) 9. There is support for our thesis in Vernant's suggestion that the meter in the tragic protagonists' dialogue passages is quite close to prose (*ibid.* 10).

cause Herodotus is mixing genres so as to form a new type of work. But they also occur because major segments of the narrative, like the epic and drama that subtends the narrative as a whole, are predicated on the ancient theological λόγοι.[150]

Therefore, the *History* is more directly than tangentially related to tragedy,[151] and many exemplars of the relationship are observable in or forming the basis of individual λόγοι. Consequently we would extend the parameters of Thompson's assertion that the type of pessimism found in the Solon-Croesus λόγος (*History* 1.30-33) "is simply the philosophy of the Logos" also found in Attic tragedy,[152] to embrace our conviction that this "philosophy of the Logos" as found in Attic tragedy is an or, as is more likely, the subtending element of the entire Herodotean narrative.

The basic concern of Herodotus' tragic λόγοι is the enactment of the fated fall of princes and nations. These λόγοι depict the same type of hero in the same type of situations as does tragic drama.[153] Moreover, only a few examples are needed to prove that the actions of the Herodotean gods, and in particular Apollo and his oracle at Delphi, resemble those in Attic Tragedy. For instance, Great Men, that is, heroes, must suffer because the gods are depicted as jealous of their own prerogatives. Hence, in *History* 7.10-11, the tragic hero Xerxes is "the Exceptional Man, who suffers because he is exceptional, no matter in what."[154] In *History* 5.92, Periander acts "exactly as God is repre-

---

150 See J. A. K. Thompson (*The Art of the Logos* 121) for the use of ancient λόγοι defined as myths.

151 For Herodotus' view of the "significant shape of history in tragic terms", see David Grene "Introduction" *The History: Herodotus* 4-5. But see K. H. Waters *Herodotos the Historian: His Problems, Methods and Originality* 168-170, *et passim*.

152 J. A. K. Thompson *The Art of the Logos* 121.

153 J. A. K. Thompson *The Art of the Logos* 135. The Lydian pericope, in particular, resembles Attic tragedy. It, like other tragic λόγοι, has a historical prologue, repeated warnings, the equivalent of a tragic messenger, and the equivalent of the dramatic chorus with its prelude, strophe, and antistrophe. See also J. L. Myres *Herodotus: Father of History* 137.

154 J. A. K. Thompson *The Art of the Logos* 123.

sented by Artabanus as behaving".[155] And in *History* 7.47, 49, Artabanus specifically talks about divine jealousy.[156]

The gods appropriately punish great misdeeds (*e.g.*, *History* 2.120;
7.137; 8.129; 9.65),[157] be they defined as acts of hubris, sin, error, or
simply crime. It does not matter which god is assumed to be involved
since the godhead for the implied narrator was Apollo, whose worship,
possibly in a mystery religion context, was at its height during the 5th
century. Thus, Wilhelm Schmid's observation that Aeschylean drama
brought the new religious theme in which Apollo is both "Seher und
Sühner" into the traditional story line of the epic sagas[158] is particularly pertinent to our conviction that Herodotus was writing a prose
tragic epic.

Aeschylus, Sophocles, Herodotus, (and sometimes even Euripides)
are concerned with man's relationship to the gods and with the inexorable effect of fate on men and nations. They depict the gods acting in
history, and they make them do so both directly and indirectly by
means of their oracles.[159] Only when we acknowledge the common
theological basis of Herodotus' *History* and Greek tragedy, do we realize the role played by the gods' jealousy (*e.g.*, 2.120, 139).[160] It is no
accident that this is particularly evident in the allegedly "ancient" and
obviously theologically oriented λόγοι.[161]

Our knowledge of the history of religious belief in Greece alone
shows the simple-mindedness of the assumption that every member of
the society believed in either the divinity or the religious precept(s) al-

---

[155] J A. K. Thompson *The Art of the Logos* 125.

[156] For other examples, see D. Grene "Introduction" *The History: Herodotus*
25-28, *et passim*.

[157] J. L. Myres *Herodotus: Father of History* 46.

[158] Wilhelm Schmid and Otto Stählen *Geschichte der Griechischen Literatur*
HAW 7.1.4 (München: C. H. Beck, 1946) 548.

[159] For the role of the oracle as a temporal manifestation that may well be in a
historical context (*e.g.*, *History* 1.13, 7.178, *et al.*), see Roland Crahay *La Littérature oraculaire Chez Hérodote* 3, *et passim*.

[160] D. Grene "Introduction" *The History: Herodotus* 25.

[161] J. A. K. Thompson *The Art of the Logos* 121. Correspondences between
Herodotus and Sophocles, long since noted by many others including F. Jacoby
("*Herodotos*"), are, for example, *History* 1.32.5 and *OT* 1530; *History* 4.95.4 and
Electra 62-64; *History* 1.31.4; 7.46.34 and *OC* 1225 ff.

legedly accepted by the majority. What we can say is that practitioners of some Greek religions, including that attested by Herodotus' implied narrator, did so.[162]

In any case, Herodotus' *History* has distinct literary ties to the tragic genre. Most notable is the clarity of the narrative, a topic that has been discussed by many critics.[163] His λόγοι are presented with a vividness that makes the real reader/listener feel that he is actually present at the event and not just a recipient of a second hand report about it (Longinus *de Sublimitate* 26.2).[164] This, of course, is characteristic of tragic drama (Aristotle *Poetics* 1448a; 1449b; 1450a - b; *et alii*)[165] and, consequently, in accord with the presentation of meta-history based on tragic drama.[166]

As in drama (and in Primary History), there is hardly any description of the natural world behind the narrative. Moreover, "description for its own sake" is lacking.[167] This lack of representation is not based on audience demand,[168] but rather it emanates from the religious exigencies of Attic tragedy from whence comes the foundation of Herodotus' tragic view of history.[169]

Similarly both psychological and physiological components are missing from Herodotus' analysis.[170] Again this is characteristic of Attic drama with perhaps the exception of some Euripidean plays. Such analysis is unnecessary because the theological cornerstones of that

---

[162] Similarly the belief that all 5th century Israelites or Jews had the same belief is also simplistic, and it "buys into" Ezra's ideology, for example, regarding the "people of the Land." We can only say that some Greeks and some Israelites considered divine jealousy an actuality that may well be represented by the tragic genre, but we cannot postulate this for all.

[163] See J. A. K. Thompson *The Art of the Logos* 181.

[164] See J. A. K. Thompson *The Art of the Logos* 185-186.

[165] See J. A. K. Thompson *The Art of the Logos* 186.

[166] The relationship of Herodotus' history to tragic drama has long been acknowledged. See J. L. Myres *Herodotus: Father of History* 27.

[167] J. A. K. Thompson *The Art of the Logos* 188.

[168] As J. A. K. Thompson (*The Art of the Logos* 188-189) assumes.

[169] Thus, it is surprising that Ph. -E. Legrand (*Hérodote: Introduction* 131) states that Herodotus' opinions about *res divinae* in, for example, book 2, were historical rather than theological.

[170] J. A. K. Thompson *The Art of the Logos.* 189-191.

drama are concerned with neither the mind nor the body of its exemplars. Like most Attic drama, Herodotus' *History* presents both the
gods' will and the intercession of their superhuman power as the prevailing bases although perhaps not the determinants, which are left to
human action, of the course of history.[171]

Although Herodotus' *History* is primarily narrative in which some
poetry has been embedded, it includes direct speech and even pairs of
speeches. This usage, which may well have come from the tragic
genre,[172] increases the vividness of the narrative.[173] The speeches not
only "punctuate the narrative" but they also emphasize its pivotal
points.[174] Moreover, this composite type of narrative is not anomalous.
Direct speech is natural to the *logopoiec* genre[175] as well as to Graeco-
Roman historiography, both of which fall almost entirely within the
combined genres of Documentary Novel and Roman à Clef at their
best. Consequently, its inclusion in the narrative is to be expected.

Although our scientific concept of history makes the inclusion of
direct speech suspect, neither Herodotus' implied historian, who is portrayed as assuming that what he wrote was characteristic of history,
nor the real author, who we believe knew that his work was not historical, saw any need to exclude this vivid literary and rhetorical type
of presentation. Significantly, however, even Thucydides and Polybius,
both of whom many incorrectly deem to be far closer to our concept of
an historian, make use of allegedly direct speech that they have often
make up "from whole cloth" and put "in the mouth of" some character
so as to support their literary pretense that they are depicting events as
they really happened.

Clearly the presentation of Herodotus' narrative as a tragic Roman
à Clef and/or Documentary and even Epic Novel rather than as a work
having the format we now deem characteristic of (scientific) history

---

[171] For Herodotus see Ludwig Huber *Religiöse und politische Beweggründe
des Handelns in der Geschichtsschreibung der Herod.* 1. But see Ph. -E. Legrand
(*Hérodote: Introduction* 133) for the concept of providence as an organizing force
(as in Herodotus' *History* 3.108) either inspired or even written by Hecataeus.

[172] J. L. Myres *Herodotus: Father of History* 80.

[173] J. A. K. Thompson *The Art of the Logos* 207.

[174] J. L. Myres *Herodotus: Father of History* 80.

[175] J. A. K. Thompson *The Art of the Logos* 208.

has affected the progression of the λόγοι and possibly even that of the books. Perhaps the real author, who never explicitly defines the nature of his narrative, expected the implied auditor to realize that his work was correlative to both epic and drama.[176] Conceivably, he had not assigned his narrative any name so as to enhance that correlation.[177]

The use of the Muses' names shows that the Grammarians (or later scholars) also recognized that it was the "narrative omniscience" by which the author, whom we now know to be an implied narrator, that is a literary character, revealed "the inner states of individuals." And they clearly understood that this omniscience in and of itself precluded Herodotus' work from being properly classified as history.[178] Hence, by using the Muses' names to make the *History*'s genre obvious, they were closing the gap between what they perceived to be Herodotus' intent and his formal methodology; and they were doing so in such a way that the real reader of their own day would understand the true nature of the work.

This may well be related to the fact that, like both epic and tragedy, Herodotus' *History* was meant to be heard rather than read. Although there is some question about the place in which Herodotus recited various portions of his *History* and about the audience to whom they were addressed, there is no doubt that he did read his work aloud in public.

In a society in which aurality (sic) is equated with literacy, public readings represent publication of a text. Presenting a text for circulation either in written format or by a communal reading, however, does not mean that the text is hereinafter unalterable. When the real author read his *History* aloud, it was heard by the real author himself as well as by the other auditors who may have had a reaction to it. Most likely,

---

[176] For the dramatic nature of the leitmotif, see David Grene "Herodotus: The Historian as Dramatist" *The Journal of Philosophy* 58 (1961) 481-487, *et passim*.

[177] For the lack of name, see F. Hartog *The Mirror of Herodotus: The Representation of the Other in the Writing of History* xvii.

[178] For such narrative omniscience, see Werner H. Kelber "Narrative and Disclosure: Mechanisms of Concealing, Revealing, and Reveiling (sic)" *Semeia* 43 (1988) 1-20.

the real author later redacted his text on the basis of his own and his other auditors' responses to how it sounded as he recited it.[179]

Those who try to do Source or Redaction Criticism without considering the effect of the listeners' reaction on the real author himself, assume the real author describes how he obtained data whenever he delineates the implied narrator's methodology.[180] Many do not distinguish the real author who reads his work to real auditors, from the implied author behind the implied narrator. Hence, the real author is successful when he insinuates that the implied author is the real author. Likewise, these same people do not differentiate between the real author and the implied narrator who relates to implied auditors the course of events as *he is depicted as seeing it*.[181] These errors of perception come about because the real author is eminently successful in presenting his work of historical fiction under the guise of autobiography.

If the implied narrator is a *persona loquens*, what Booth calls the "dramatized narrator" and even more pertinently the "Narrator-Agent,"[182] as we contend, the work is fiction as we have been asserting. Therefore, the real author's presentation of material as if it had emanated from an oral tradition is not a deliberate attempt to falsify historical evidence. Rather it is a literary device to depict the *persona loquens*, the implied narrator, as a traveler and collector of diverse

---

[179] This too may add to the (false) sense of orality that modern readers seem to perceive behind the narratives in the work.

[180] V. Hunter (*Past and Process in Herodotus and Thucydides* 88), like most other scholars, believes that the author obtained most of his information from oral sources.

[181] See above, Introduction Two. These distinctions in Herodotus' *History* form a self-contained topic of study that is beyond the scope of the present investigation, however. For the implied author and dramatized narrator, see Wayne C. Booth *The Rhetoric of Fiction* (Chicago: University of Chicago, 1961) 151-152, *et passim*. For the implied narrator who is separate from the implied author see *ibid*. 156. There is a huge body of literature regarding real and implied authors, real, implied and even "dramatized" narrators, and real and implied readers.

[182] W. C. Booth (*The Rhetoric of Fiction* 151-154) makes a distinction between the dramatized narrator and the narrator-agent, but this is not of particular importance for our discussion here. The implied narrator, Herodotus, fits both of Booth's categories. He assumes one stance during some parts of the narrative and the other during others.

sorts of information, particularly oral traditions.[183] This intimates nothing about the manner in which the author himself gained his information. Although he may have done so, he does not of necessity have to have gotten it aurally.

The implied narrator, not the real author, has spoken with his informants[184] and he has done so in many places.[185] The implied narrator distinguishes between quoted and reconstructed speeches. Consequently, even the quoted speeches need not be authentic. The real author may have composed some of the allegedly quoted speeches as well as those the implied narrator suggests are reconstructed. As we have already noted, the implied narrator so often allows his readers to see the data he rejected that the process is thematic in the narrative. We do not know what the real author disregarded.[186]

There is no basis for the presumption of orality other than the implied narrator's statements that he got his information aurally. Oral report is not a permanently fixed mode of transmission. Even when a narrative has been handed down orally for a long time, it may be committed to writing. Some oral texts become fixed in form in some circles while remaining fluid in others, thus, causing divergent traditions to arise.[187] Moreover, stories frequently continue to be transmitted orally along with or even in opposition to a written text in the same circles in which they have been written.[188] This also leads to diverse traditions.

---

[183] For the implied narrator as the one who traveled and collected data, see Sara Mandell "The Language, Eastern Sources, and Literary Posture of Herodotus" *Ancient World* 21 (1990) 103-108. His travels and his dependency on oral traditions are wrongly accepted by most though not all modern scholars as those of the real author.

[184] For this as a literary convention, see J. A. S. Evans *Herodotus* 146.

[185] For the number of places, see J. L. Myres *Herodotus: Father of History* 9.

[186] S. Mandell "The Language, Eastern Sources, and Literary Posture of Herodotus" *passim.*

[187] G. W. Ahlström "Oral and Written Transmission: Some Considerations" *HTR* 59 (1966) 70.

[188] For a tripartite categorization of Herodotus' oral data and the relative work of each of the three classes of evidence, see T. Cuyler Young "The Persian Empire" *CAH* 4 (Cambridge: Cambridge University, 1988, 2nd edition) 5-6.

Modern interpreters who assume that Herodotus' data were primarily or extensively oral believe that either he received misinformation from interpreters or that the erroneous data were inherent in the rumors and reports they think he used. So those who assume that Herodotus thought his data were reliable do not agree with Cicero in thinking him the "father of lies." Rather, they conclude that Herodotus was not a very good historian or that somehow or other we have knowledge of the scientific nature of history (and its methodology) that was unknown to him.

The stated aims of the *History* suggest that the implied narrator is relating historical data. This does not mean the *History* itself is historical in the modern sense or that the real author intended his work to be considered history at all. The basic religious theme militates against the classification of the work as history even though we draw historical information from it.[189]

Thematic developments within the *History* show that the real author composed the final redaction as a tragic prose epic as we have suggested.[190] Moreover, this is closer than anything else to the genre we now classify as a novel,[191] be it a Documentary Novel and/or a Roman à Clef.[192] Without further data, there is no way of knowing the

---

[189] But see A. W. Gomme *The Greek Attitude to Poetry and History* (Berkeley and Los Angeles: University of California, 1954) 92, 93, *et passim*. See particularly chapter five.

[190] This would justify the use of the epic/epyllion genre for many of the major and minor λόγοι. F. Hartog suggests that Herodotus' work was interpreted by the public as "poetry, pleasure, fiction" (*The Mirror of Herodotus: The Representation of the Other in the Writing of History* xvii). Additionally, for ἔπη, including prose tales and orations, defined as the "genre of the spoken word and the listener", see Northrop Frye "Fourth Essay: Rhetorical Criticism: Theory of Genres" 248.

[191] But see Thomas G. Rosenmeyer ("History or Poetry? The Example of Herodotus" 239-259) for support of Herodotus' status as historian.

[192] Not quite as defined by N. Frye "Rhetorical Criticism: Theory of Genres" 248-249. Frye's distinction between ἔπος as "episodic" and fiction as "continuous" (*ibid.* 249) is important to our classification. His definition of ἔπος as specifically oral, and of fiction as written (*ibid.* 248), however, does not apply in this case. Herodotus was writing at a time when the written word was expected to be heard. But we must distinguish two facets of *audienda*: that which was to be read aloud and that which was to be performed as well.

genres under which his prior redactions of the work as a whole or even individual λόγοι within it were to be classified.

On the other hand, in the final redaction, the implied narrator is represented as working under the rubric ἔπος, which he equated with history. The real author portrays him as an historian who is writing a work of history that is to be read aloud as a performance and, hence, to be received aurally by the implied auditor, who is not really a "reader" as we understand the term. Like the real author himself, the implied narrator's classification in earlier redactions or even individual λόγοι is currently unknowable.

Nothing suggests that the real (5th century) author, writing in an Ionic dialect, intended to call his work ἱστορίη, a term which the 6th century Ionian scientists had treated as denoting "empirical investigation."[193] This title was given by commentators who classified the work as historical inquiries on the basis of their own belief that they could show the real author's intent by determining the meaning of each word in the narrative's introduction.[194] Precisely because of the long-standing convention, first suggested by Cicero (*de Legibus* 1.1.5), that Herodotus was the "father of history",[195] the English word "history" is taken from the his work's assigned non-self assigned "title." This eisegetic practice began because the real author chose the traditional format for oral narrative, using the λόγος, which originally meant "what is said," as the basis of his architectonics.[196]

The real author's treatment of the narrative in which the implied narrator reports history could have been either an affectation or a jest of some sort. But it may have been theological grounded in such a way that the god at Delphi, in particular, became the arbiter or at least the

---

193   For this usage, see W. Jaeger *Paideia* 1.155.

194   See F. Hartog *The Mirror of Herodotus: The Representation of the Other in the Writing of History* xvii. Thus, we do not really borrow the term from Herodotus but from early commentators on Herodotus.

195   *Loc. Cit.* For the assumption that the Greeks, including Herodotus, equated history and inquiry, see Mabel L. Lang "Oral History with a Difference" *PAPhS* 128 (1984) 93.

196   For this definition of λόγος, see J. A. K. Thompson *The Art of the Logos* 17.

regulator of events.[197] In fact, the *History* can be considered a narrative of *the mighty acts of the divinity at Delphi* as depicted in "relief" by mankind's effecting of the god's design.[198] Today, as in antiquity, not everyone understands that this is the most important motif of the work; and as we have seen, even Aristotle was fooled. This suggests that the implied and perhaps the real author's religious assumptions were then and are not yet now fully perceived.[199] It also demonstrates, we must iterate, that the real author's artistic pretexts were eminently success-ful.

Our growing knowledge that data gained in an ethnographic ex-change are often dependent upon the respondent's memory shows the status of information obtained by interview is, at best, uncertain. No matter what the pretense to total recall, human memory may be and often is flawed.[200]

The correctness of information is also dependent on the infor-mant's probity. This, however, is itself problematic since lying to "outsiders" is often considered justified to protect "insider" informa-tion. But even when an informant in an "oral society" thinks he is tell-ing the truth, he may not be.[201] We must never forget that that infor-

---

[197] For the interference in human events by the gods, who along with men sometimes lived and often acted in the world, see I. M. Linforth "Named and Un-named Gods in Herodotus" 211. For the oracles as consequential and as given in a historical frame of reference, see R. Crahay *La littérature oraculaire chez Hérodote* 3. For the oracle as "dramatizing the narrative" so that the reader realizes that "everything that has happened has been foreseen and announced or signified by the god", see Crahay *ibid.* 59. For the Delphic oracle as the most cited in the *History*, see Crahay *ibid.* 10. But see Crahay (*ibid.* 58-59, *et passim*) for the oracle as a "literary production", although not a "gratuitous fabrication", that is used to ad-vance the narrative and to explain obscure matters.

[198] Hence, without limiting it to Apollo, L. Huber (*Religiöse und politische Beweggründe des Handelns in der Geschichtsschreibung der Herod.* 1) suggests the prevalence of divine will and supra-human power as architectonic to the narrative.

[199] Perhaps Herodotus stressed Apollo and Delphi because of the god's rela-tionship to the Greek Colonies. For a discussion of Apollo and the colonies, see I. Malkin *Religion and Colonization in Ancient Greece.*

[200] David Henige *Oral Historiography* (New York: Longman, 1982) 76, 110.

[201] D. Henige *Oral Historiography* 110-111.

mant is a performing artist who frequently chooses to present unique interpretations of his material.[202]

Herodotus, the real author, realized that eyewitness information is often inaccurate, and that different witnesses may present very different reports of the same event, each believing his own account to be valid. Consequently he portrays the implied narrator as someone who treats the indigenous traditions he reports "as a kind of living entity".[203] Knowing that traditional information secured orally *must be tainted*, the real author may have refashioned good material to make it appear flawed so as to give it the character of oral data. If so, it was to support and authenticate his pretense that his implied narrator had really received this material aurally.

The real author also used false or perhaps merely flawed and inaccurate data to support the implied narrator's literary posture as a traveler and recorder or rememberer of orally related information. Hence, it is wrong to attribute to the implied narrator's carelessness or lack of probity errors in matters he claims to have learned by autopsy. The implied narrator is neither careless nor a liar. The real author, however, may tell untruths because he is writing fiction rather than scientific or any other form of history.

It follows that the real author may possibly have used far better[204] and by far more written sources than the implied narrator acknowledges.[205] If so, the real author altered some reports and fabricated others so as to illustrate his implied narrator's "historical" concepts.[206]

---

[202] D. Henige *Oral Historiography* 76, 109.

[203] For the oral traditions as living, see V. Hunter *Past and Process in Herodotus and Thucydides* 51.

[204] See T. C. Young "The Persian Empire" 5; see also Amélie Kuhrt "Babylonia from Cyrus to Xerxes" *CAH* 4 (Cambridge: Cambridge University, 1988, 2nd edition) 118 and 118 note 39. Kuhrt, however, has some well-founded reservations (*loc. cit.*).

[205] For the use of written sources, see T. R. Glover *Herodotus* 51-58, 76, *et passim*. See also J. A. S. Evans *Herodotus* 142-145.

[206] Interestingly enough, however, his information regarding the Scythians as well as his use of Persian sources seems to have been reliable. See Edwin M. Yamauchi *Persia and the Bible* (Grand Rapids: Baker House, 1990) 77 and 77 note 63-64.

And accordingly, he portrays his implied narrator as having obtained the data by autopsy or aurally.

Hence, these fictive accounts become part of the literary ensemble precisely because they are real to the implied narrator. And in particular they lend support to one of the most important leitmotifs of the *History*: the implied narrator obtains major portions of his data directly from living human rather than indirectly from literary sources. He claims either to have witnessed something himself or to have heard about it from those who saw it or to have learned about it from those who had heard it from yet others. This does not mean, however, that the entire work is fabricated.

Not all or even most of Herodotus' data are falsified either intentionally or otherwise. Rather, in many cases, the real author has "embroidered," amplified, and altered evidence, some of which had been factual, to fit the particular leitmotif of his subtending λόγος or even of individual major and minor λόγοι. Significantly, therefore, some of the information in the *History* has recently been authenticated.[207] The new understanding we have about the ancient Near East supports the 19th century belief that *some* of the real author's sources for that region were primary or they relied on good primary documentation. This hypothesis is now supported by our new understanding that the real author understood Aramaic and perhaps Carian as well.[208]

---

[207] For one example of this, see Valerie French "Herodotus: Revisionist Historian" 32-42, esp. 32, 39, 40.

[208] S. Mandell "The Language, Eastern Sources, and Literary Posture of Herodotus" *passim*. The total and absolute absence of Aramaic inscriptions in Halikarnassos is itself suggestive. Since Halikarnassos, a Doric colony that had subsequently become Ionic, was under Persian suzerainty, the probability that there would not be a single inscription in which Aramaic, the *Lingua Franca* used by the Persians to govern their Western Satrapies, was included is virtually nil. (For example, we even have a trilingual Stele from Xanthus in Southwest Turkey that was written in Greek, Lycian, and Aramaic [J. Teixidor "The Aramaic Text in the Trilingual Stele from Xanthus" *JNES* 37 (1978) 181-186]). We presume, therefore, that the absence of any Aramaic inscriptions in Halikarnassos reflects some destruction perpetrated after the Ionian revolt or, possibly, at the conclusion of the entire Persian War. We wish to thank Professor Eric Myers for bringing this significant absence to our attention.

Since the entire work is a literary artifice, we cannot use any part of it to confirm the orality of the real author's sources. Consequently, the theory that the errors in the *History* prove that the real author's sources were primarily oral is not verifiable. Other hypotheses based on statements within the narrative (*e.g., History* 2.147)[209] such as the commonly accepted belief that the real author relied on rumor and report must also be discarded. We may no longer attribute errors in information the implied narrator secured by interview to the real author's acquisition of misinformation or even to his lack of probity. The real author is after all a literary artist, not an historian and not simply "a pioneer in Homeric 'Higher Criticism'".[210]

---

[209] Thus, J. A. S. Evans (*Herodotus* 65) believes that both the Egyptian and the Scythian λόγοι are based on knowledge obtained in Herodotus' travels.

[210] But see T. S. Brown "The Greek Sense of Time in History as Suggested by their accounts of Egypt" *Historia* 11 (1962) 262-263.

Chapter Two: Primary History[1]

The arguments for an unitarian authorship of Primary History have long been invalidated on linguistic, literary,[2] and descriptive, although not necessarily normative theological grounds.[3] Even when an analysis of the canonical text demands an unitarian approach under normative theology, that particular tack is needed for ideological rather than textual reasons.[4] Additionally, from a descriptive perspective, normative ideology is often seen as superimposed on, rather than extracted from the narrative.

From a literary viewpoint, an investigation along "unitarian" lines must be limited to the canonical text, which is only descriptive for the period in which it was made canonical and is normative in respect to

---

1   All references to Primary History are to the revision of Kittel's *BHK* made by Elliger and Rudolph and others: *Biblia Hebraica Stuttgartensia* Stuttgart: Deutsche Bibelstiftung, 1967/77, K. Elliger and W. Rudolph, *et al.,* ed. Likewise, all citations of the text are from *BHS*. Terms referring to the constituent parts of Primary History will be capitalized in accordance with standard usage, even though the same terms are not capitalized when they refer to the segments of Herodotus' *History*, again in accordance with standard usage.

2   We do not know the literary status of any of the individual redactions prior to their inclusion into the final redaction. Consequently, we cannot agree that Meir Sternberg's hypothesis ("Whatever the nature and origin of the parts—materials, units, forms—the whole governs and interrelates them by well-defined rules of poetic communication" [*The Poetics of Biblical Narrative: Ideological Literature and the Drama of Reading* (Bloomington: Indiana University, 1985) 2]) is applicable to the individual redactions that as a composite form Primary History. It is quite possible and even probably, however, that Sternberg's assumption is applicable to the overriding redaction of the text.

3   Even Ivan Engnell, who warns the reader not to dismiss the unitarian thesis for "Genesis-Numbers and Deuteronomy-II Kings respectively" ("The Pentateuch" *A Rigid Scrutiny: Critical Essays on the Old Testament by Ivan Engnell* [Nashville, Vanderbilt University, 1969, John T. Willis and Helmer Ringgren, ed. and trans.] 51), acknowledges the basic division into a P-work and D-work (*ibid.* 51-67).

4   For Canonical Criticism as dealing with texts whose status "is based on the belief that they reflect and bear testimony to truth in a unique and unrepeatable manner", and which "are understood as embodying and reflecting...the essence of the faith and practice of the community", see John H. Hayes and Carl R. Holladay *Biblical Exegesis: A Beginner's Handbook* (Atlanta: John Knox, 1987 revised edition) 122.

its textual forebears. The belief that the work is an unified whole must not be retrojected from the canonical text to its prior, constituent redactions. Since there is an obvious distinction between the formation of the text and its final form,[5] we may be selective of our exegetic tools if we are only looking at the end product, that is the canonical text, rather than the process by which it developed or *vice versa*.[6] But from a non-unitarian point of view, things are not so simple as this. The critic must resolve the apparent conundrum whereby a literary analysis may simultaneously militate against and yet demand that the text be viewed as an entity.

In fact, precisely because Analytic Critics treat the text as an entity whereas Redaction and/or Source Critics, Tradition Critics, and Form Critics attempt to "get behind" the text, this apparent enigma can be resolved by the concomitant application of the various forms of criticism. This is particularly obvious when we acknowledge that Redaction criticism takes the "insights and perspectives of tradition criticism and form criticism" as given.[7]

Consequently, when the text is studied under Analytic Criticism, it must be treated as an icon. When it is studied under Redaction or Source Criticism it must be treated as a temporally differentiated layered compendium, each stratum of which was at one time iconic. When it is studied under Form Criticism, the different genres and their *Sitzen im Leben*, be they oral or written, must be sought and acknowledged. When it is studied under Tradition Criticism, the different stages of each individual tradition, again be they oral or written or the two concomitantly, must be sought and acknowledged.

But the fact that literary analysis ultimately looks to all of these types of exegetical techniques in and of itself shows that they are not

---

[5]   Rolf Knierim ("Criticism of Literary Features, Form, Tradition, and Redaction" *The Hebrew Bible and its Modern Interpreters* [Fortress/Scholars: Philadelphia/Chico, 1985, Douglas A. Knight and Gene M. Tucker, ed.] 151-152) observed that both authors and redactors can use identical techniques. Hence their application does not in and of itself represent a distinction between authors and redactors or even between different redactors of the same text.

[6]   This is also true in the case of Herodotus' *History*.

[7]   J. H. Hayes and C. R. Holladay *Biblical Exegesis: A Beginner's Handbook* 101.

mutually exclusive. Although they emanate from different perspectives and serve different ends, they must be used together in order to fully understand both the final or canonical form and how the received text reached it. Thus, the literary critic can pay heed to the existence of authors and redactors and their respective approaches when he practices Redaction or Source Criticism; he can pay heed to the varying genres and *Sitzen im Leben* of the essential units in the text when he practices From Criticism; he can acknowledge the development of the traditions and the correspondences between different forms of the same tradition when he practices Tradition Criticism; and he can also acknowledge that the terminative form of the text has an essential unity when he applies either Canonical or Analytic Criticism.[8] and [9] Consequently, although we are analyzing the final form of the text, we must still pay attention to the findings of Redaction and/or Source critics and also From Critics and Tradition Critics.

Hence, the well, although not universally accepted hypothesis that the component parts of Primary History, however divided, have themselves been built up either by an additive process or by an editorial process in which source strata have been combined and recombined in multiple redactions can and does affect our analysis even under Analytic Criticism. The work of the various principal redactors of Primary History (J, E, P, D, Dtr[1] and Dtr[2]) and sometimes even that of the secondary redactors of the various source strata has been fairly securely, but not totally or with absolute certainty, established despite differences of opinion about the dating.[10]

---

[8] We must remember that Canonical Criticism is not the same as Analytic. Rather, the latter demands the presence of the former.

[9] As Norman K. Gottwald (*The Hebrew Bible—A Socio-Literary Introduction* [Philadelphia: Fortress, 1985] 23) points out, "New literary criticism...looks at the rhetorical texture of the work as a finished whole". His choice of terms, however, is unfortunate since "New Criticism" is the *terminus technicus* for a particular branch of Literary Criticism that holds a text's self-sufficiency to be a literary postulate. In New (that is, Analytic) Criticism, the very fact that each text not only can, but must stand alone as if it were an artifact demands that it be analyzed without reference to any external factors. See above, Introduction Two.

[10] There is an enormous bibliography for this topic. For a summation of the scholarship and the varying opinions, see R. Knierim "Criticism of Literary Features, Form, Tradition, and Redaction" *The Hebrew Bible and its Modern Interpret-*

According to the *communis opinio* to which we also adhere, in its broadest format, there was a 10th century Yahwistic redaction (J) followed by a 9th century Elohistic redaction (E), both of which included earlier data such as 13th-10th (according to Albright) or 12th-10th (according to Freedman) century poetry as well as interpretations of allegedly earlier data that may but need not have been in verse. In the late 8th century, these earlier redactions were combined to form a JE Epic (R^JE). This was followed by the 7th century Deuteronomist (D), who wrote a separate work—now part of Deuteronomy—and who also included earlier material in his text. Then there was the 6th century Priestly Redactor (P),[11] who, as is commonly, but again not universally accepted, gave *some form of* overriding redaction to the text[12]—at least of the combined JE epic (R^JE). Although both the relative and the absolute dating of D and P are disputed, P may have given a, or possibly the determining cast to at least the Tetrateuchal narrative.[13]

At some time during the late 7th or possibly, but in our opinion not likely, even in the early 6th century, the Deuteronomistic School or the Deuteronomistic Historian ([Dtr], either Noth's Dtr or possibly the re-

---

ers 130-134. But see John Van Seters (*In Search of History: Historiography in the Ancient World and the Origins of Biblical History* [New Haven: Yale University, 1983] 16) for the assumption that Form-Criticism has replaced Redaction Criticism. Van Seters, like others who hold this perspective, believes that the latter has "little support" in the case of the Deuteronomistic History, and moreover, that it is "largely viewed as obsolete" in Pentateuchal studies (*ibid.* 16). Even Van Seters, however, classifies by the traditional redactions the various aspects of Primary History that he analyzes. For the problematics of a postexilic dating of P and D, see David Noel Freedman "The Earliest Bible" *Backgrounds for the Bible* (Winona Lake: Eisenbrauns, 1987, Michael P. O'Connor and David Noel Freedman, ed.) 31-32.

11   There are some who would place P as late as the 4th century. We do not believe that the data support such a late dating; and, in fact, we place P before the exilic Dtr2 (see below).

12   Various scholars have tried to limit P's role in the formation of the text. For a discussion of this, see Brevard S. Childs *Introduction to the Old Testament as Scripture* (Philadelphia: Fortress, 1979) 123.

13   The resolution of the question of whether P preceded or followed D, and if the former, of P's influence on D's portion of Deuteronomy, if any, is beyond the scope of this book. We, however, not only hold with those who consider D 7th Century (see below) and, as we have just noted, P exilic, but we consider this dating basic to our analysis.

dactor we now call Dtr[1], authored or compiled the Deuteronomistic History (DtrH or DH) and introduced it by framing Deuteronomy after he detached portions of what is now Joshua. This work was then redacted by a subsequent, exilic (6th century) redactor (Dtr[2] [= Noth's Dtr?]),[14] giving us a second edition of DtrH.[15] Dtr[2] may well have been responsible for some combined form of Genesis through 2 Kings, be it called the "First Bible" or the "Essential Bible" or the "Fundamental Bible,"[16] or as is more likely he may have been the penultimate redactor as Cross suggests.[17] In any case, this First or Essential Bible was ultimately re-divided and rearranged by Ezra into what

---

14   But Cross equates Noth's Dtr with Dtr[1]. See Frank Moore Cross "The Themes of the Book of Kings and the Structure of the Deuteronomistic History" *Canaanite Myth and Hebrew Epic: Essays in the History of the Religion of Israel* (Cambridge: Harvard University, 1973]) 289. The existence of a 2nd Deuteronomistic Historian is fairly well although not universally accepted. We concur with the *communis opinio* albeit with some reservation (see below). In any case, since Dtr[2] edited or redacted the work of Dtr[1] we need not distinguish between Dtr[1] and— if there really were two Deuteronomistic Historians—Dtr[2] except where necessary for our argument.

15   For the validity of the thesis of two editions of the Deuteronomistic History, see F. M. Cross "The Themes of the Book of Kings and the Structure of the Deuteronomistic History" 274-289. For two redactors or authors, each writing at a different time, see Cross, who expresses, if not the *consensio opinionis*, at least a very commonly held belief that Dtr[1] worked in Josiah's time, and Dtr[2] in the Exile and he finished circa 550 BCE (*ibid.* 287-289). Both Dtr[1] and Dtr[2] may possibly, but need not necessarily have been the same person. For Dtr[1] and Dtr[2] as the same person writing at different times, see Richard Elliott Friedman *Who Wrote the Bible?* (Perennial Library; New York et al.: Harper & Row, 1989) 145-146. For two separate people, however, the Deuteronomistic Historian and a later editor, see Richard D. Nelson *The Double Redaction of the Deuteronomistic History* JSOT Sup. Ser. 18; Sheffield: JSOT, 1981. See especially Chapter 3.

16   Martin Noth (*Überlieferungsgeschichtliche Studien I: die sammelnden und bearbeitenden Geschichtswerke im Alten Testament* [Halle: Max Niemeyer, 1943] 53 [11], 55 [13]) first states there was no Deuteronomistic editing in Genesis through Numbers. However, he modifies this, saying that Genesis through Numbers in the format used by P was not part of Dtr's work (*ibid.* 55 [13]). In any case, it is not our intent to come to a conclusion about whether or not Dtr was responsible for any editing of Genesis through Numbers beyond that which is necessary for the alteration of the end of Numbers so as to begin DtrH with Deuteronomy, and possibly so as to combine the two complexes into one lengthy work.

17   F. M. Cross "The Themes of the Book of Kings and the Structure of the Deuteronomistic History" 287-289; R. E. Friedman *Who Wrote the Bible?* 110

is basically our present form of Primary History at least as received in the Masoretic text.

This set of hypotheses about the text's format is tempered by those who find earlier source strata than Dtr,—particularly strands of J and E—represented in[18] or throughout Joshua, in Judges,[19] or even throughout Primary History. It is further moderated if, as Gottwald suggests without warrant, the various sagas or legendary traditions[20] as well as the "state and temple records that were eventually to be part of Joshua-Kings were... taking written shape" around the same time as the J and E strata were being put into written form.[21]

No matter what extraneous strata are represented in the Deuteronomistic History, and no matter when the represented traditions were first taking shape, they were subsumed in the written narrative of Primary History in a literary style that suggests they had been incorporated into the account by Dtr, who *had not* received them in an already assimilated state. From a literary perspective, Dtr may have viewed such various of elements of J and E as the sagas, legends, and legal and/or religious records that he adapted to his own needs as being no different than D, which he "framed" to make it seem as if it really belonged where he had placed it when he took it into his account.

But when we consider the text an icon to be interpreted in accordance with the precepts of Analytic Criticism,[22] we exclude the possi-

---

18   N. K. Gottwald (*The Hebrew Bible—A Socio-Literary Introduction* 247) quite properly suggests the likelihood that Dtr received the sagas (that is, the legends) in Joshua 1-12 via the Elohistic narrative; or alternatively that they were part of data available to J and E, but they reached Dtr independently of them.

19   N. K. Gottwald, (*The Hebrew Bible—A Socio-Literary Introduction* 248-249), for example, attributes a J substratum to Judges 1.

20   As noted above (Chapter One), the distinction between sagas and legends is artificial and therefore, not pertinent to our study. Some scholars do differentiate between them and sometimes the difference is significant, but each seems to differ in his determination of what is saga and what is legend.

21   N. K. Gottwald *The Hebrew Bible—A Socio-Literary Introduction* 94. This presupposes there were separate state and temple records: a fact not in evidence.

22   For the legitimacy of analyzing the text as we would any other work of literature, see David Noel Freedman "The Primary History" *The Unity of the Hebrew Bible* (Ann Arbor: University of Michigan, 1991) 2.

bility of extracting from the data any knowledge about Dtr or about his personal beliefs regarding any of the texts he may have inherited or about the (alleged) events he depicts through the eyes of his implied narrator. Actually, we can do no more than merely speculate about the author, his alleged sources, and even his world.[23] But we can comment on and draw conclusions about the implied narrator, his alleged sources, and even his world.

Of course, we can also express a view and draw conclusions about the text itself. For example, we can rightly say that by including the D's work in DtrH, Dtr made it an integral part of his narrative. Likewise, by including the book of Deuteronomy in the Pentateuch, Ezra, whom we believe responsible for this made both D's work as represented and edited by Dtr a part of his account.[24]

Hence, it is important that there is a major and clear literary break between Numbers and Deuteronomy that must be attributed to Dtr, who after all framed D. If we simply remove the greater part of Deuteronomy, which is obviously misplaced, the break between Numbers and Joshua like that between Deuteronomy and Joshua is not particularly sharp. Consequently, we can suggest the division into the Tetrateuch and the Deuteronomistic History that includes Deuteronomy was the most, if not the only viable and likely completed format found prior to Ezra's re-division of the text.

This does not exclude the possibility that one or both of the Deuteronomistic Historians, most likely Dtr[2], viewed the entire Primary History as an unified whole despite the seam between its two constituent parts. Their/his intent was to present Genesis through 2 Kings as a

---

[23]   Mark Allan Powell (*What is Narrative Criticism?* [Minneapolis: Fortress, 1990] 4-5) notes the transcendence of meaning relative to an author's intentions. Hence, the current interest in a work's implied author acknowledges something of the iconic state of any work of literature. But he also suggests that modern literary theory treats a work's *totally* iconic status as an extreme measure. We have mixed feelings, the resolution of which is beyond the scope of our present endeavor, about this latter view.

[24]   Even though we view Ezra as a rearranger rather than a redactor of the text, the very act of rearranging it according to some vision of his own permits us to call it Ezra's account.

continuous and unbroken narrative from a literary perspective.[25] Granting this, we suggest that perhaps Dtr *compiled,* without any more mechanical editing than was necessary, what was to become the Pentateuchal (sic) narrative. However, he did not compile this narrative as *a unit unto itself* since DtrH begins with Deuteronomy. The alternative view that it was compiled by P not long after Dtr[2] did his work, but again, not as a unit unto itself is not supportable since we know that Ezekiel's, Jeremiah's and P's work had been completed prior to Dtr[2]'s redaction, and possibly before the fall of Jerusalem.[26] In any case, this compilation of the Pentateuchal narrative was not quite, but almost in the form in which we now have it.

Since P preceded Dtr[2], and the Essential Bible was in place by 560,[27] subsequent changes did not alter the text substantively. Rather they primarily involved book groupings (*e.g.,* as in the 518 rearrangement in which Primary History remained a unit, and Ezra's 430 re-ordering of the text into the Pentateuch and Former Prophets)[28] and only the minimal textual editing that was needed to facilitate the presence of a sense of continuity in the narrative. But precisely because the editorial modifications based on books rather than redactions were superficial, the basic format of the book orderings is extremely problematic. In any case, it is generally although not universally assumed that

---

[25]   As a compiler and textual rearranger, there is no more need to seek Dtr's hand in the narrative of the Tetrateuch than there is to seek Ezra's in the narrative of the Pentateuch that he compiled and rearranged. Significantly, however, some do see Dtr's hand in a few places in the Tetrateuch. If so, he is more than a compiler and rearranger of the Tetrateuch, he is a redactor of the Tetrateuch. This, however, is beyond the scope of our argument.

[26]   For the priority of Ezekiel, Jeremiah, and P to Dtr[2], see Richard Elliott Friedman *Who Wrote the Bible?* (Perennial Library; New York *et al.*: Harper & Row, 1989) 167-171, 173. For the dating of P as antecedent to Jerusalem's fall, see *ibid.* 188.

[27]   D. N. Freedman "The Earliest Bible" 30-31.

[28]   See David Noel Freedman "The Formation of the Canon of the Old Testament: The Selection and Identification of the Torah as the Supreme Authority of the Post-exilic Community" *Religion and Law: Biblical-Judaic and Islamic Perspectives* (Winona Lake: Eisenbrauns: 1990, Edwin B. Firmage, Bernard G. Weiss, John W. Welch, ed.) 324-326; and below, note 31.

Primary History has two parts. There is, however, a difference of opinion about what constitutes those two parts.

The Pentateuch is now followed by the allegedly historical work, Joshua through Kings. But the Pentateuch did not become a seemingly self-contained entity until someone, we presume it was Ezra, separated it from the previously formed Primary History so as to divide the Bible into the Pentateuch and the Prophetic Corpus.[29] Hence, Ezra may be partially responsible for the manner in which the Tetrateuch and the Deuteronomistic History are joined together by Deuteronomy.

Significantly, Deuteronomy is a pivotal book in which strands of the Tetrateuch and DtrH are intertwined so as to give an illusion of originality, integrity, and primacy to the artificially created Pentateuch. Consequently, even as the text now stands, Deuteronomy is still part of both the synthetically and intentionally formed Pentateuch and the Deuteronomistic History. Accordingly, the narrative of the artificially defined Pentateuch, which most scholars wrongly think is the result of an additive process, clearly overlaps that of the Deuteronomistic History, which is rightly the result of such a process.

The combination of the Tetrateuch and the Deuteronomistic History to form Primary History (the Fundamental or Essential Bible) was effected just prior to 560 BCE. The publication of a, but not necessarily the finished form of the work can tentatively and yet with strong certainty be dated between 21 March 561 and 13 August 560 BCE.[30] This places the combined text well before Ezra's editorial work in which he did what was necessary to re-divide the Fundamental Bible into the Pentateuch and the Prophetic Corpus. By grouping Joshua through 2 Kings with the so-called "writing prophets,"[31] Ezra gave us the or at least a finished work.

---

[29]   D. N. Freedman "The Formation of the Canon of the Old Testament: The Selection and Identification of the Torah as the Supreme Authority of the Post-exilic Community" 318.

[30]   D. N. Freedman "The Earliest Bible" 30-31.

[31]   For the First Bible (ca. 560 BCE), the Second Bible (ca. 518 BCE),— which does not pertain to our argument here—and Ezra's Bible, that is the Third Bible (ca. 430 BCE), see D. N. Freedman "The Formation of the Canon of the Old Testament: The Selection and Identification of the Torah as the Supreme Authority of the Post-exilic Community" 324-326; For the compilation of Primary History

Despite any editorial work Ezra may have done in addition to or as part of the process of dividing the text into two component parts, and no matter what his intention, he did not succeed in emending the narrative in such a way that his ordering became the exclusive structural paradigm for Primary History. Not only are other formats obvious, but there are indications that they were and still are viable independent entities having architectonic integrity.

Consequently, it is not clear whether we now have a Pentateuchal narrative (Genesis through Deuteronomy, excluding the framework of the latter) and a Deuteronomistic History (the framework of Deuteronomy followed by all of Joshua through 2 Kings); an Hexateuchal narrative (Genesis through Joshua) followed by a Tristeuchal narrative (Judges through 2 Kings); two Tetrateuchal narratives (Genesis through Numbers; Joshua through 2 Kings), each of which contains the Deuteronomistic framework of Deuteronomy, with the framed portion of Deuteronomy serving as a juncture between the two Tetrateuchs; or as is most likely, a Tetrateuchal narrative (Genesis through Numbers), followed by the Deuteronomistic History (Deuteronomy through 2 Kings) into which Deuteronomy had been incorporated so as to make it part of the continuous historical presentation.

The contextual placement as well as the format of the book of Deuteronomy somewhat obfuscates those narrative divisions made on the basis of books, but not those made on the basis of pericopes. Deuteronomy, the greater part of which should be read in tandem with rather than subsequent to the Sinai pericope is canonically and traditionally grouped with the first four books of Primary History so as to form a Pentateuch in accordance with Ezra's division. But we iterate that it is also an intrinsic part of both major sections of Primary History. And it is not only basic to the literary structure of each section, it also plays an ideologically, theologically, and historically architectonic role in it.

Structurally the illusion that Deuteronomy unifies all of Primary History was effected by Dtr's framework of D so as to make it part of

---

between 560 and 540 BCE, see *idem* 317; see also D. N. Freedman "The Earliest Bible" 29. See also "The Earliest Bible" 33 for 561/560 BCE as the *terminus ad quem* for the Essential Bible.

DtrH, but of a text of DtrH that contains strands of J and E in or throughout Joshua as we have noted.[32] However, since Dtr's framing of D means, by definition, that D is being presented from the perspective of Dtr as a corporal portion of his historical work, D must go with DtrH from a literary point of view. And as we have it, D is necessarily more closely related to DtrH than it is to the Tetrateuch (Genesis through Numbers).[33]

It is actually the framework of Deuteronomy, then, that plays a bridge-like role between R[JE]'s or even P's redaction of R[JE]'s Tetrateuchal narrative and the remainder of the Deuteronomistic History.[34] The first part of Dtr's framework is meant to suggest a far closer relationship between the Tetrateuch and Deuteronomy than had hitherto existed. And this very relationship made Ezra's separation of the narrative into the Pentateuch and the Former Prophets almost inevitable.

Since Deuteronomy concludes with the death of Moses and points to Joshua's subsequent assumption of command, it both completes the Pentateuchal narrative and it introduces the leitmotifs that will then dominate the following books of Primary History: the Sons of Israel and the Land. Once the Sons of Israel enter the Land, they become a viable historical entity, thereby making the story of the conquest or settlement part of the historical books. Thus, contextually, Deuteronomy becomes the pivotal book that joins together both the Tetrateuch and the Deuteronomistic History.

The major portion of the narrative in Deuteronomy is not a continuation of that in Numbers despite the fact that it follows Numbers.

---

[32] Noth's belief that the frame of the book of Deuteronomy is part of the Deuteronomistic History has gained acceptance in most quarters. See Bernhard W. Anderson "Introduction" to Martin Noth's *A History of Pentateuchal Traditions* (Chico: Scholars, 1981) xiv. However, Brevard S. Childs' admonition (*Introduction to the Old Testament as Scripture* [Philadelphia: Fortress, 1979] 215) "that Noth's theory of chs. 1-3(4) as the introduction to the Deuteronomistic historical work is being called into question" must be heeded, but not accepted without strong and unquestionable proof.

[33] In accord with common usage, the terms Tetrateuch and Tetrateuchal narrative will apply to Genesis through Numbers rather than Joshua through 2 Kings even though the latter does form a tetrateuch.

[34] David Noel Freedman "Pentateuch" *IDB* (1962) 3. 716-717.

Rather, for the most part, Deuteronomy, particularly D, is paratactic to the Sinai pericope (Exodus 19:2b through Numbers 10:10). The juxtaposition of the two pericopes by some redactors and/or perhaps by the final redactor of Primary History[35] either represents a syncretism of the theological traditions,[36] a possible but not really probable refusal to reject any scriptural material, and the use of the one pericope to serve as a literary enhancement of the other.

Deuteronomy only picks up the story in Numbers when it joins the two different traditions so as to portray the death of Moses. Auld's treatment of the end of Numbers as a sort of appendix "which assumes the book of Joshua at all points" and his belief that both Deuteronomy and the end of Numbers were late accretions[37] suggest a literary melding of the traditions.

Therefore Auld's hypotheses also resolve the difficult problem of the lack of closure in Numbers' unresolved and uncompleted termination. Since the blending of the traditions is emphasized by the "marked Deuteronomistic stamp" in Numbers 33:50-56 as well as in other passages near the end of the book in our present redaction, it links the passages to both the Pentateuch and the Deuteronomistic History.[38]

---

[35] We use the term "final redactor" to denote the exilic (or possibly, although we do not believe postexilic) redactor who is responsible for the literary unity of Primary History. Accepting Cross' belief in the existence of Dtr[2] who wrote after the fall of Judah as different from the "final redactor" (F. M. Cross "The Themes of the Book of Kings and the Structure of the Deuteronomistic History" 287-289; R. E. Friedman *Who Wrote the Bible?* 110), we can state that the latter can not be dated before the exile.

[36] Martin Noth (*Überlieferungsgeschichtliche Studien I* 71 [29]) points out that the use of Horeb for the sacred mountain in the Tetrateuch is a later addition. Luther H. Martin's interpretation of Hellenistic syncretism on the basis of Plutarch's definition of syncretism as a joining together in the face of a common enemy (*De Frat. Amor.* 19 [cited by Martin]) as pointing "to coherent patterns of relationship that must be described in their systemic particulars" (Hellenistic Religions: An Introduction [New York: Oxford University, 1987] 11) may be as applicable to the earlier part of the millennium in which Primary History was being formed as it is to the Hellenistic era itself.

[37] A. Graeme Auld (*Joshua, Moses and the Land: Tetrateuch-Pentateuch-Hexateuch in a Generation Since 1938* [Edinburgh: T. & T. Clark, 1980] 115-117.

[38] Rolf Rendtorff *The Old Testament: An Introduction* (Philadelphia: Fortress, 1986) 149.

Deuteronomy joins the two parts of Primary History in an indissoluble bond and there is no way of knowing whether this was the express intent of such redactors[39] as Dtr[1] and/or Dtr[2], and/or the overriding redactor, or of a later arranger and modifier of the material such as Ezra. Although it is not impossible, it is improbable that the person who composed or redacted Deuteronomy obtained a well-wrought narrative by making an orderly patchwork out of readily available texts. Rather, even granting the framework, the literary unity of the narrative of Deuteronomy suggests that it was written or redacted by a creative literary artist who adapted traditional stories so that they fit into his narrative as if they had been created expressly for it.

If so and if we may additionally assume, as is most probable, that Ezra merely did patchwork, there is no validity to the stance taken by those both before and after Noth,[40] but not by Noth himself, that the Deuteronomistic Historian was a redactor of received data rather than either an original historian or a creative literary artist. Those who hold either of the latter viewpoints base their hypotheses on Dtr's use of texts that were accessible to him, beginning with Deuteronomy and ending with Josiah's story.[41] Perhaps they assume that he did not compile the material and therefore was not an original historian, or he did not create or adapt it and therefore was not a literary artist.

Consequently, although we disagree with Noth's basic premise that Dtr was an original historian, we do so more on the evidential basis suggested by Gottwald, who points out that in 1 and 2 Samuel and 1 Kings 1-11, 274 verses contain historical data whereas 1868 verses represent various types of literary traditions; and in 1 Kings 12 through 2 Kings 17, 77 verses (for Israel) and 63 verses (for Judah) contain historical data whereas 569 verses (for Israel) and 234 verses (for Judah) represent various types of literary traditions; and in 2 Kings 18-

---

[39] R. Rendtorff (*The Old Testament: An Introduction* 186) sees the Deuteronomistic writers as having shaped and connected the major *pericopes* in this work, each book of which was a separate entity having a different structure.

[40] R. E. Friedman (*Who Wrote the Bible?* 130) believes that the Deuteronomistic Historian took stories already at hand, and made additions to various sets of texts so as "to set the story in a certain light"; and this resulted in the respective books of Joshua, Judges, 1 and 2 Samuel, and 1 and 2 Kings.

[41] R. E. Friedman *Who Wrote the Bible* 130.

25, 70 verses contain historical data and 130 represent various types of literary traditions.[42] Hence, we believe that more attention must be paid to Noth's other suggestion, that the Deuteronomistic Historian was *an original author*,[43] who had a succinct plan for the depiction of the events described in the Deuteronomistic History.

The fact that Dtr drew his material from the tradition and arranged it by subjects[44] at least suggests that he wanted to present an ordered arrangement of data. Significantly, therefore, many of the sources Dtr uses are at best noted only occasionally. And without referential data that is external to DtrH, the existence of such sources as anything but a figment of Dtr's mind cannot be validated. Consequently, we cannot even suggest what sources Dtr ignored and we cannot attest to the reality of those he cited save when there is extant biblical data outside of Primary History and/or extra-biblical data pertaining to the events depicted in the narrative.

But despite this relative dearth of references, Dtr insinuates that they do really exist. And he enhances his illusion of historicity by depicting his implied narrator as referring the reader "continually to the sources for everything which lies outside the scheme of its (sic) theology of history",[45] thereby showing his real intent.

Dtr wanted his implied reader to perceive his implied narrator as an historian and, consequently, deem his work historical. His success

---

[42]   N. K. Gottwald *The Hebrew Bible: A Socio-Literary Introduction* Table 20, page 311; Table 22, page 339-340; Table 23, page 367. Additionally, Gottwald's divides the verses according to prophets and kings in the narrative up to 1 Kings 1-11. Of the literary verses, 1588 are clearly attributable to a *persona* + 280 crossover or subordinated verses.

[43]   Martin Noth *Überlieferungsgeschichtliche Studien I* 53 [11]. See also F. M. Cross "The Themes of the Book of Kings and the Structure of the Deuteronomistic History" 274. Cross treats this historian as his Dtr[1] who wrote in the time of Josiah (*ibid.* 289).

[44]   M. Noth *Überlieferungsgeschichtliche Studien I* 52 [10], 131-132 [89-90]. But see Noth (*ibid.* 82-83 [40-41]) for the belief that Dtr. used an existing account whose literary form was already fixed, which he only altered slightly for a section of his history such as the occupation of Cisjordan.

[45]   Gerhard von Rad "The Deuteronomic Theology of History in I and II Kings" *The Problem of the Hexateuch and Other Essays* (London: SCM, 1984) 205.

in this endeavor is shown by the fact that modern scholars have taken on the role of the implied reader and they perceive Dtr as giving the appearance of being an historian precisely because his implied narrator seems to use methodology that is in accordance with the historiographic procedure approved by those present-day scholars who formulate a methodology of scientific historiography. Thus, they have mistaken Dtr for the historian he wished his implied reader to perceive his implied narrator as being.

Dtr's literary illusion of historicity does not mean that he himself was not a creative writer. Rather, the contrary, that Dtr was an original author, is true as Noth demonstrated. And this permits us to draw the conclusion that the linkage between the two major parts of Primary History, however they are defined, was intentionally created.

Consequently, even if we were not fully convinced that Noth's premise is valid, but we were to admit that it is possible, we must question Mowinckel's proposition that neither the Tetrateuch nor the Hexateuch ever existed despite the fact that the Hexateuch is properly defined as a critical object.[46] Dtr may well and in fact must have edited, redacted, and significantly altered either the Tetrateuch or the Hexateuch he inherited or even both so as to portray his own conception of events and to create his own literary work. Additionally, he may have done some editing that was merely mechanical.

The same cannot be said of Ezra, who as we have noted changed the configuration of the canon so as to separate the Pentateuch from the Former Prophets that followed it.[47] Ezra clearly did no more than minor editorial work so as to support his new format.

Prior to Ezra's editorial work, the Pentateuch was still inclusively bound to Primary History, which, even as we now have it in the Masoretic text, may be seen as a work with related themes, stylistic

---

[46]   For Mowinckel's proposition that "Hexateuch" is to be treated as "a legitimate critical term", see A. G. Auld *Joshua, Moses and the Land* 31. See also David J. A. Clines *The Theme of the Pentateuch* (*JSOT Sup. Ser. 10*; Sheffield; JSOT, 1982) 83.

[47]   D. N. Freedman "The Formation of the Canon of the Old Testament: The Selection and Identification of the Torah as the Supreme Authority of the Post-exilic Community" 318.

parallels, and a connected story-line or plot beginning with the creation of everything pertaining to our universe but the divinity himself and ending with the Babylonian captivity of the Judahites in the 6th century BCE.

But this does not mean that the text had existed in that form for any length of time. We iterate that the Essential Bible much less the present form of Primary History does not predate 560 BCE[48] although it contains a great amount of material that was far older. Consequently, the proposal that there was a specific overall redaction joining the Pentateuch and the Deuteronomistic History, each of which is a "great literary" complex,[49] must be rejected precisely because the Pentateuch did not form a self-contained unit prior to 560 BCE by which time, as we have said, the Tetrateuch and the Deuteronomistic History had been joined together.

Accordingly, the process of joining the Pentateuch and the Former Prophets is neither probable nor plausible until after the Pentateuch had been created as an entity unto itself.[50] And this is not likely until Ezra had first artificially created these two divisions by re-dividing either the Essential Bible or some post-560 BCE division or rearrangement of the narrative, such as that of 518 BCE, in which Primary History was still a constituent unit.

Only after Ezra had artificially created the Pentateuch by extracting it from Primary History, could it at least be treated as an independent entity that could be found in a definitive edition.[51] In fact, it was this loose construction regarding the legality of dividing and recombining the text which permitted Ezra to separate the Pentateuch from the Former Prophets.

---

[48]   D. N. Freedman "The Formation of the Canon of the Old Testament: The Selection and Identification of the Torah as the Supreme Authority of the Post-exilic Community" 317. See also D. N. Freedman "Pentateuch" *IDB* 3. 712-713.

[49]   R. Rendtorff *The Old Testament: An Introduction* 149-150

[50]   D. N. Freedman "The Formation of the Canon of the Old Testament: The Selection and Identification of the Torah as the Supreme Authority of the Post-exilic Community" *passim.*

[51]   For this definitive edition, see D. J. A. Clines *The Theme of the Pentateuch* 11, 83.

This perspective is not accepted by everyone. The additive and redactive theories about the creation of the narrative have both been rejected by those who view Primary History from a fundamentalist or
from a confessional perspective. They have also been partially dismissed by some of those who consider themselves to be followers of
Engnell who seek the oral sources behind the narrative and then limit
their analysis of the text to this basis. Engnell himself, however,
treated the redactive hypothesis somewhat more circumspectly than did
his followers.[52]

In any case, although the additive and redactive theories are often
treated as different facets of the same process, this reflects the perspective of the individual analyst. The theories are not necessarily concomitant although we ourselves view them as such. Consequently,
some scholars have accepted the one, others have accepted the other,
and yet others have accepted both.[53]

The redaction postulate as an entity is accepted by most scholars
because it is the most viable explanation for the development of the
narrative. But the primacy of distinctive redactions, albeit not their existence, is usually questioned. Hence, if, for example, the P account really is the basis of the combined Tetrateuchal narrative and the other
hands simply represented an enrichment,[54] then with the exception of
the material in Genesis, a book that has its own problems, it may be
possible to reconstruct at least partially the *Ur*-P document that was
used in this effort.[55] Nevertheless, it is still not possible to reconstruct
a connected *Urtext* for any of the other hands.[56]

---

[52]   See I. Engnell "The Pentateuch" *A Rigid Scrutiny: Critical Essays on the
Old Testament* 50-67.

[53]   For a discussion of this regarding the Yahwist's work, see Gerhard von
Rad see "The Form-Critical Problem of the Hexateuch" *The Problem of the
Hexateuch and Other Essays* (London: SCM, 1984) 50-53; *et al.*

[54]   M. Noth *A History of Pentateuchal Traditions* 11-12. Mowinckel also
treats P as a separate source rather than "a series of insertions made by the final
Pentateuch editor" (see A. G. Auld (*Joshua, Moses and the Land* 25). For a mid-6th
century dating of P, see also F. M. Cross "The Themes of the Book of Kings and the
Structure of the Deuteronomistic History" 289.

[55]   M. Noth himself obviates the possibility of doing so for the entirety of the
Tetrateuch when he points out that in some parts of the narrative: "the arrangement
of the individual elements...was determined by the progression of the narrative con-

This is especially true of E in the Tetrateuch[57] and of Noth's *Grundlage* (G),[58] which may well have been an oral, poetic composition of the 12th to the 11th centuries BCE, relating the or at least *an* established account of the Sons of Israel and their forefathers.[59] It is not unlikely that if an early redactor did know G, he had some type of written formulation of it. On the other hand, we cannot ignore the literary significance of von Rad's hypothesis that the Yahwist himself had already given a final delineation to the form of the Hexateuch.[60]

Predetermination of form, however, is not necessarily also a predetermination of content. It is of even greater importance that the Hexateuch as we have it may be far different from the Hexateuch the Yahwist depicted. Hence we must look to more than Canonical Criticism. And whereas Canonical Criticism cannot always deal with such texts behind the text as, for example, the Yahwist's Hexateuch, Literary Criticism must do so. But Literary Criticism and Canonical Criticism have to function together even though they are not one and the same.[61] Of course the only exception to this "joint venture" can be

---

structed from the old sources" (see *A History of Pentateuchal Traditions* 13; see also 21).

[56]　This is impossible if, as is likely, Gunkel's and Gressman's hypotheses regarding the collective tradition rather than unitary documental nature of J and E are valid (see Alan W. Jenks *The Elohist and North Israelite Traditions* [SBL Monograph Ser. 22; Missoula: Scholars, 1977] 3-4).

[57]　For the lack of literary unification and homogeneity in the remainder of the Pentateuchal narrative, see M. Noth *A History of Pentateuchal Traditions* 20-21. This is not in conflict with Noth's belief that J forms the literary basis of a JE *Urtext* in which E supplies supplemental material (*ibid.* 25-32), and that we can trace the procedure of R[JE] with rather great precision (*ibid.* 33). For the difficulty in reconstruction a complete E, see *ibid.* 37. Significantly, Mowinckel believes that E never existed as an independent document. It simply represents the "long process of explanatory and corrective additions to the J epic" (see A. W. Jenks *The Elohist and North Israelite Traditions* 10, 18 note 41-42).

[58]　For which see M. Noth *A History of Pentateuchal Traditions* 38-41. For support of Noth's hypothetical *Grundlage*, see A. W. Jenks *The Elohist and North Israelite Traditions* 14.

[59]　D. N. Freedman "Pentateuch" *IDB* 3. 714.

[60]　G. von Rad "The Form-Critical Problem of the Hexateuch" 74. This hypothesis, however, presents us with problems that are beyond the scope of this discussion.

[61]　B. S. Childs *Introduction to the Old Testament as Scripture* 61.

when we analyze the canonical form—that is, the final form—of the completed text without regard to its configuration(s) prior to canonization.[62]

This being so, the mutual relationship between text and canon militates against the viability of the additive and/or redactive theory only insofar as those hypotheses account for the composition of the text as canon. The traditional belief that the texts that formed canon were originally linked in an unbroken chain is itself fallacious.[63] The redactors did more than simply add things to the text. Sometimes functioning as authors and sometimes as editors, they actually changed the narrative to reflect their own literary perspective and/or the ideological, theological or theo-political stance of their implied narrator whether or not they coincided with their own beliefs.

From a faith perspective at least and from a non-Analytic-Critical literary perspective as well, the existence of an hermeneutic process stretching throughout Israel's history whereby the community continuously reinterprets its own traditions in accordance with its own needs[64] strongly attests to the viability of the additive and/or redactive theory as the basis of the pre-canonical text, particularly when the text as an entity is seen as basic to the people's ideology and self-image. This reinterpretation postulate of textual and, albeit with decided differences, canonical composition and formation is accepted by the majority of scholars even when they believe that other theories are basically sound and are to be used supplementally.

---

[62] What James Barr (*Holy Scripture: Canon, Authority, Criticism* [Philadelphia: Westminster, 1983] 75) calls "canon 2".

[63] For its falsity in the formation of canon, see B.S. Childs *Introduction to the Old Testament as Scripture* 51. We cannot concur with J. Van Seters (*In Search of History* 4), who stresses the non-accidental and the non-accumulative nature of history writing, and thereby implies that what is true of the fiction regarding the formation of canon is also true of the formation of the pre-canonical work.

[64] James A. Sanders "Hermeneutics" *IDB* (1962) Supp. 404; For a discussion see B. H. Childs *Introduction to the Old Testament as Scripture* 56-57, 79. For reinterpretation "producing a picture more like historical fiction than sober history", see Millar Burrows "Ancient Israel" *The Idea of History in the Ancient Near East* (New Haven: AOS, 1983, Robert C. Dentan, ed.) 107.

Granting this, there are still problems. Since Noth's *Grundlage* is not an *Ursage*, but an advanced text *Traditio-Historically*,[65] we must still ask how the various sagas came to be united initially.[66] Analysis along story or saga/legend lines is most important, and Noth suggests that the saga-tradition is pretty much the foundation of the entire Pentateuchal narrative.[67] Gunkel's belief that the creation of the sagas came before any authoritative texts; that the individual stories came from different times; and that J and E were editors rather than authors of the collections which we attribute to them,[68] is partially supported, but not demanded by what we now know about oral transmission of texts.[69]

---

[65]   M. Noth *A History of Pentateuchal Traditions* 39, 39 note 145, 235, *et passim.*

[66]   Significantly, A. W. Jenks (*The Elohist and North Israelite Traditions* 14) points out the importance of sacred history as an introduction to the covenant conclusion ceremony as has been long recognized. He also indicates that a great part of the material would and could have no part in that type of recitation.

[67]   M. Noth *A History of Pentateuchal Traditions* 44.

[68]   Hermann Gunkel *The Legends of Genesis: The Biblical Saga & History* (New York: Schocken, 1964) 123-133. See also A. W. Jenks *The Elohist and North Israelite Traditions* 3-4. For the possible incorrectness of Gunkel's use of the term "Saga," see A. R. Millard "Methods of Studying the Patriarchal Narratives as Ancient Texts" *Essays on the Patriarchal Narratives* (Winona Lake: Eisenbrauns, 1983, A. R. Millard & D. J. Wiseman, ed.) 37, 48-49.

[69]   Thus, R. Rendtorff's (*The Old Testament: An Introduction* 160) assumption that Gunkel's approach (Form Criticism) is "basically incompatible" with Redaction or Source Criticism is not valid in light of modern oral theory. In fact they should be applied concomitantly.

The real problem, however, is the attribution of authorship to a work based on a traditional theme. And it extends well beyond the issue of whether the redactors of Primary History or even of Homeric epic were original authors or not.

Since Greek Tragedy is built about traditional themes, we may if we wished to be absurd call Aeschylus, Sophocles, or Euripides mere redactors. Likewise, in the case of Senecan drama built on the themes of Greek drama, and in those of the Renaissance, Elizabethan, and even modern dramas that take the same themes and in some instances the ancient dramas themselves as their bases, we could call the authors redactors or merely adapters only if we wished to be preposterous. The line between an author and an adapter as well as between a new work and an adaptation may be thin, but it can and must be drawn.

Perhaps when Gunkel rhetorically asks for a definition or demarcation of "the constituent unit in Genesis,"[70] he is asking if the Pentateuch is one unified "book," and if so, from whence came the stories or story complexes within it? These are the same two questions we ask when we seek to find the constituent unit in the Pentateuch as a whole. Gunkel himself recognized the implication of this question when he both defined the entire Pentateuch as the "most comprehensive unit" and indicated that the individual anthologies of legends from whence this came and the particular legends of which they are comprised are also units.[71] Hence, Gunkel does not look to the division into books, but rather to the division into cycles of legends and then into individual legends—that is, into greater and minor pericopes—for his constituent units.

We must not forget that the narrative as we have it was the result of a succession of syntheses and recombinations, that is literary junctures in which the redactors added to the works of their predecessors or they incorporated the parts of those works and possibly others they thought fitting into their own.[72] Actually, when J and E respectively were authoring, redacting, emending, enhancing, or simply editing their works, neither the narrative nor the books were yet fixed as we have them and the writings of the Deuteronomist and the Priestly Redactors were yet to come.

There is no justification for the assumption that P's redaction is that of the final or even penultimate redactor unless we assume that is P exilic or postexilic and post-dates Dtr[2]. Likewise, there is no basis for believing that "his" Pentateuch, if he even had a Pentateuch, is representative of "our" Pentateuch.[73] In fact, the strong data suggesting that it was Ezra who divided Primary History into the Pentateuch and

---

70   H. Gunkel *The Legends of Genesis* 42.

71   H. Gunkel *The Legends of Genesis* 42.

72   Scholars are not in agreement about which of these procedures the various redactors followed.

73   Thus, Frank Moore Cross ("The Priestly Work" *Canaanite Myth and Hebrew Epic: Essays in the History of the Religion of Israel* [Cambridge: Harvard University, 1973] 294-295) dates the Priestly "systematizing expansion of the normative JE tradition in the Tetrateuch" to the exilic era. See also B. S. Childs *Introduction to the Old Testament as Scripture* 123.

the Prophetic Corpus,[74] militate against the inclusion of the Pentateuch as a designated unit in P's redaction.

The hypothesis offered by others that the new data *may still have been able to be incorporated into the Pentateuch* in Ezra's day (which may possibly have been the mid-5th century BCE)[75] must be rejected albeit tentatively. If it were valid, Ezra would have been responsible for more than a canonization or a mere re-editing of the Pentateuch, and he rather than a "final" Exilic redactor who preceded him could have incorporated new data into the work of the Deuteronomistic History after its second redaction (by Dtr[2]).

Rather, we must iterate our belief that Ezra made mechanical alterations. And where necessary, he made patchwork literary, but not substantive changes in the text. He was not changing the data themselves but reordering them so as to support his textual divisions whereby he "canonized" the Pentateuch as a separate entity. The canon was not closed until much later.[76]

The hypothesis that the books were put together from the various textual strands by Ezra[77] must also be rejected although not on the ba-

---

[74] We believe that Ezra was the first to do a simple analysis, using the term in its original Greek sense, in which he broke apart the completed narrative of Primary History so as to form two separate entities: the Pentateuch and the Former Prophets. But this presumes that by definition the constituent units had been joined together so as to give at least the illusion that Genesis through 2 Kings was a coherent whole prior to Ezra's editorial activity.

[75] For Ezra as having led returnees to Jerusalem in either 458 BCE or 397 BCE, see R. H. Pfeiffer "Ezra" *IDB* (1962) 2.214. The earlier date is more likely, and consequently Ezra was a contemporary of Herodotus.

[76] But see also A. G. Auld *Joshua, Moses and the Land* 111. In fact B. S. Childs (*Introduction to the Old Testament as Scripture* 64) dates the close of canon with Ben Sira in the 2nd century BCE; and James A. Sanders (*Canon as Paradigm: From Sacred Story to Sacred Text* [Philadelphia: Fortress, 1987] 65) dates its close to the final period of the 1st century CE. H. H. Rowley ("Canon of the OT" *IDB* (1962) 1. 500) sees three stages in the development of OT: the original composition; organization and collection of the works; canonization of the works.

[77] In addition to the accepted J, E, P, D, Dtr[1], and Dtr[2] redactions, there is evidence of independent works that were used by the redactors and/or incorporated into both the Pentateuchal and the Deuteronomistic narratives. There is a great body of literature dealing with this. See, for example, F. M. Cross *Canaanite Myth and Hebrew Epic, passim;* R. E. Friedman *Who Wrote the Bible?* 218-219.

sis of the existence of an earlier, but not necessarily preexilic dating of P or Dtr, the nature of the text, or the lateness of the conflation.[78] It must be dismissed because the text does not include any reports of the Restoration or of events from that era,[79] even though this glaring lacuna can be explained and justified on non-historical bases.

Both a theo-political substratum and/or a literary superstructure can be determinative of the boundaries of an historical work. Therefore, the absence of any direct reference to the restoration in the narrative rather than the lack of redactional activity at that time could represent censorship on the basis of theological *Realpolitik*. Consequently, it is feasible that both the Tetrateuch (rather than the Pentateuch) and the Deuteronomistic History, which from a literary perspective must have included D as we have already noted, may have received their final redaction in a similar manner to one-another, possibly during the same

---

For Ezra, see R. E. Friedman, *Who Wrote the Bible?* 217-218. We cannot agree with J. A. Sanders (*Canon as Paradigm: From Sacred Story to Sacred Text* 29), who suggests that Ezra brought the "essential Torah" back from Babylon. This "essential Torah" was not yet a closed canon and, thus, not yet identical to the Torah as we know it. We also cannot agree with A. R. Millard ("Methods of Studying the Patriarchal Narratives as Ancient Texts" *Essays on the Patriarchal Narratives* 36), who dates the final joining of the traditional strands of the Patriarchal narratives to the exilic or postexilic period. But he does not suggest an Ezran re-division of the Essential Bible.

[78]   In fact this late dating is commonly accepted. See, for example, D. J. A. Clines *The Theme of the Pentateuch* 97. But for the formation of the Pentateuch not long after "P" *in the 5th century*, see Ernst Sellin *Introduction to the Old Testament* (Revised & Rewritten by Georg Fohrer; Nashville: Abingdon, 1968) 192. See Otto Eissfeldt (*The Old Testament An Introduction: The History of the Formation of the Old Testament* [New York *et al.*; Harper & Row, 1976] 563-564) for the "traditional view" which ascribes the entire canon to Ezra. This is not really in contradiction to M. Noth's (*A History of Pentateuchal Traditions* 44-45) vision of a clear historiography which began in court circles with the "formation of Israel as a state". For a postexilic "codification of the ritual" as defined by P, see Julius Wellhausen *Prolegomena to the History of Israel* (Gloucester: Peter Smith, 1973) 408-409; see also Sellin/Fohrer (above) 185.

[79]   For the suggestion that this indicates an exilic dating, see D. N. Freedman "Pentateuch" *IDB* 3.712.

Restoration era.[80] Without proof of some form of censorship, however, this hypothesis must be rejected on textual grounds alone.[81]

The formation of the text into books is another matter entirely and must be approached in a different way. We suggest that this was basically and primarily a mechanical process.

And until scholars who seek to identify something logical and coherent in the structuring of the individual books see that they cannot do so precisely because the books have been artificially defined by a mechanical division of the narrative, they will not be able to get behind the received order of many of the book divisions in Primary History or even that of some of the pericopes.[82] On the other hand, the use of the various forms of textual criticism taken as a whole[83] has led to a marked success in the determination and delineation of the sources or redactions.[84]

Consequently, we believe that each of these individual types of criticism affords a practicable, but not a complete approach to the analysis of the text. An unilateral application of a methodology does not suffice for valid exegesis. Only when the results of all of the types of analysis are conjoined can we obtain a relatively clear perception of the meaning and structure of the text. Hence, despite Engnell's belief to

---

[80]   For the various text traditions before the "stabilization of the Hebrew text" in the 1st century CE, see B. H. Childs *Introduction to the Old Testament as Scripture* 92.

[81]   See above. Since it cannot be established textually, the burden of proof rests with those who want to posit a late dating.

[82]   M. Noth (*Überlieferungsgeschichtliche Studien I* 46 [4]) notes that the book division in DtrH was secondary. We believe that the same is true of the entire Primary History.

[83]   Sharp distinctions were not always and are not to be drawn clearly between the methodology employed in analysis via such sub-disciplines as *Formgeschichte, Traditionsgeschichte, Redactionsgeschichte, et al.*, as we have already hinted. Although they must be drawn between these approaches and that of Analytic Criticism, this too must be viewed in conjunction with the others (above). Hence, although their functions are to be kept separate, the analytical techniques are not. There is a vast body of literature treating these topics. For Gunkel and his students in particular, see B. S. Childs *Introduction to the Old Testament as Scripture* 115.

[84]   Therefore J. Van Seters' rejection of Redaction Criticism as a viable entity must itself be rejected.

the contrary, their concomitant application is demanded if a thorough analysis is to be achieved.[85]

The Form-Critical school believes that the form must precede the redaction as the basic element of analysis. Clearly, however, pericopes in various genres, which themselves frequently include pericopes in multiple genres, have been fashioned, developed, or simply used by the individual redactors.[86] It does not matter whether the specific genres were part of the traditions the redactors received, and hence were ready formed before they were included in the narrative, or whether the redactors themselves formatted the particular pericopes into the genres they wanted.

The inclusion of traditions, be they oral or written, in any part of Primary History does not rule out but rather often lies behind the existence of redactions of the text.[87] Although in some instances a particular tradition may represent a later addition, this does not occur frequently enough to vitiate the belief that the narrative is more redactive than additive in nature. It suggests that various redactors admitted data that were either syncretistic *per se* or that were resultant on and representative of the syncretism of various religious practices with those religious conventions they deemed Israelitic.

Our critique, however, is made the more difficult by our lack of knowledge of the broad literary format of the individual component redactions. There are a few pericopes that may have been conceived of as individual books even before the formalized division of the narrative into books was made. Perhaps, as is likely, they sometimes, but not

---

85   G. M. Tucker *Form Criticism of the Old Testament* 25 note 4; J. Coert Rylaarsdom "Introduction" *Form Criticism of the Old Testament* by G. M. Tucker, vii. Thus, Ivan Engnell's concept of an oral tradition clearly fits into the combined type of analysis. Although this was largely rejected when it was set forth, this was a result of the climate of opinion at that time. It may well have been deemed viable had it been offered just a decade after Engnell's death, concomitant with the rise of all the new investigators into oral theory in both Classics and Anthropology.

86   For a partial listing of the genres and the frequency with which they occur in the delineation of Israel's "history "prior to the monarchy, see N. K. Gottwald *The Hebrew Bible—A Socio-Literary Introduction* 142-143.

87   See, for example, D. N. Freedman "Pentateuch" *IDB* 3. 714.

necessarily, differed from the books as we have them in the received version of Primary History.

Genesis, for example, shows definite signs of literary framing since it begins with a temporal discontinuity and it ends with "an implicit change of subject" and focus.[88] And, therefore, it may have been envisioned as a unified pericope or possibly even a book on a literary level by whichever redactor combined the various sources included in it.

We do not know whether the individual redactors of the various sources themselves had delineated a separate major pericope which was eventually incorporated into Genesis or whether the included material was part of a pericope or book which incorporated material that is now included in Exodus. In the latter case, the descent to and exodus from Egypt may have formed a separate pericope into which the Joseph Novella, hitherto also an entity unto itself, was inserted.

Because 1 and 2 Samuel, like 1 and 2 Kings, was one book in the tradition inherited by the Masoretic text,[89] Samuel and Kings may have been treated separately by either Dtr[1], Dtr[2] or both. Also we do not know which or even if both Deuteronomistic Historians[90] divided the Deuteronomistic History—including Samuel and Kings—in the received sequence or if some unnamed editor did this at a later date.[91] In

---

[88]   D. W. Baker "Diversity and Unity in the Literary Structure of Genesis" *Essays on the Patriarchal Narratives* (Winona Lake: Eisenbrauns, 1983, A. R. Millard & D. J. Wiseman, ed.) 198-199. For the value of framing in "establishing a value and a canonical text", see George Aichele, Jr., *The Limits of Story* (SBL Semeia Studies; Philadelphia/Chico: Fortress/Scholars, 1985) 22.

For the shift in tradition from the Patriarchs "as peaceful nomads" to the Israelites as "a 'people'...living in uncertain social and legal position among a foreign people" at the beginning of Exodus, see R. Rendtorff *The Old Testament: An Introduction* 6. This point of demarcation, however, does not form the division between two major *pericopes* (see below).

[89]   Although the divisions we have are very old, they may not have been treated as canonical before the Hellenistic era, at least for the Septuagint's *Vorlagen*. For the suggestion that we should be content with the "more modest results" of identifying the various strands of tradition, see O. Eissfeldt *The Old Testament An Introduction* 139-143. This, however, begs the question.

[90]   Following F. M. Cross *Canaanite Myth and Hebrew Epic passim*. See also R. E. Friedman *Who Wrote the Bible?* 107-110. Also, see above.

[91]   R. E. Friedman (*Who Wrote the Bible?* 104) suggests that if we were to ascertain "Who wrote Deuteronomy?' we would also find out "who produced six

any case, this did not occur after 540 and most likely not after 560 BCE.[92]

Likewise, since, as Cross has noted, the Priestly Redactor presented his "epic tale" in the text of Exodus/Leviticus/Numbers in such a way that the "stations" of Israel as it traveled to the Moabite Plains became framing devices that made each station a unit,[93] either he or one of his sources may have treated the material included in this unit as one book. If the latter, we cannot even hazard a guess as to whether P was originally responsible for this or, concomitantly, at what prior time in the history of the narrative's development it first was to be found.

Our lack of ability to find the origin of the book divisions and/or the constituent pericopes of Primary History is especially troublesome since one of the characteristics of the narrative is that the pericopes often overlap book divisions just as λόγοι do in Herodotus' *History*.[94] Consequently the only book sections that are well defined are those that coincide with the partitions between major pericopes.

The first such coincidence only seems to, but does not really occur between Genesis and Exodus. Although Genesis ends with an implied closure, this is not indicative of the type of essential break in the narrative that marks the completion of a major pericope. Rather, Genesis concludes with the end of a major pericope, but one subordinated to an even greater major pericope and, therefore, categorically serving the same function as a minor pericope, the Joseph Novella .

This novella is a component in the major pericope of Israel's descent to, stay in, and departure from Egypt. But it is the escape from Egypt and the "salvation" that matters most. Hence, the major Egyp-

---

other books of the Bible", namely, the Deuteronomistic History. And at the same time we would learn who divided Samuel and Kings.

[92]   See above. For the compilation of Primary History between 560 and 540 BCE, see D. N. Freedman "The Formation of the Canon of the Old Testament: The Selection and Identification of the Torah as the Supreme Authority of the Post-exilic Community" 317; see also idem "The Earliest Bible" 29. See also "The Earliest Bible" 33 for 561/560 BCE as the *terminus ad quem* for the Essential Bible.

[93]   F. M. Cross "The Priestly Work" 308.

[94]   The chapter divisions are very late. Traditionally they are dated to the 13th century CE.

tian pericope ends at Exodus 14:31 with a statement of Israel's salvation: it does not conclude with the end of Exodus 15:21 as is often assumed. The latter rather is a coda that also serves as a transition to the
very brief pre-Sinai Wandering pericope (Exodus 15:22-19:2a) that is
itself transitional from a literary perspective.

Despite the sharp demarcation between Numbers and Deuteronomy, there is no real closure at the end of Numbers. Rather, the closure
occurs at the conclusion of the Sinai pericope, which ends at Numbers
10:10. This is followed by the not so brief transitional pericope
(Numbers 10:11-36:13) in which the Sons of Israel go from Sinai to
the "plains of Moab at the Jordan at Jericho", where (: מוֹאָב עַל יַרְדֵּן יְרֵחוֹ
בְּעַרְבֹת [Numbers 36:13]) Moses gives them instruction, enjoining
Yahweh's rules and regulations upon them. And this introduces the
new, major pericope, the Conquest.

Hence, although the transition from the Sinai to the Conquest pericope begins at Numbers 10:11 and extends through the end of Numbers, the Conquest pericope does not begin at the transition's conclusion. Rightfully, the narrative should skip the greater part of the book
of Deuteronomy, which has theological, but not literary validity within
its greater context. It should begin again at Deuteronomy 27, a complex
chapter[95]in which the implied narrator presumes that the terms of the
Covenant have already been accepted (27:9-10). Moreover, since the
Conquest pericope should and does finish at the end of Joshua 12, it is
not really possible to make a case for the existence of literary closure
signaling the end of a major pericope at the conclusion of Numbers.

Deuteronomy 1-26, which presents an alternative version of parts
of the Sinai pericope, is "included" within, and framed by the ongoing
narrative that takes the Sons of Israel from the mountain of the divinity
up to and into the Land. From a literary perspective, the included text
becomes part of the same account as the Sinai pericope just as from a

---

95   Significantly, therefore, Deuteronomy 27 alludes to Shechem, the cult
center of the federation before the monarchy (Anthony Phillips *Deuteronomy The
Cambridge Bible Commentary on the New English Bible* [Cambridge: Cambridge
University, 1973] 178). And Deuteronomy 28 shows the hands of both D and Dtr.
(*ibid.* 190). For the complexities see A. Phillips *Deuteronomy* 178-182.

History of Religions perspective, the two texts suggest some form of syncretism.

It is impossible to tell whether the syncretism has brought about the literary melding or the literary melding, the syncretistic presentation. The consequences of this juncture, however, are as clearly defined as a geometric proof: the existence of the combined account has led people to assume the congruity of the two different pericopes and their respective sacred mountain; the belief in their congruity has led to the delusion that Sinai and Horeb are two names for the same sacred mountain; and, finally, the presumption that there is one sacred mountain with two names demands that the giving of the Law at Horeb be deemed a literary reiteration of the giving of the Law at Sinai.[96]

Significantly, Deuteronomy's Horeb pericope concludes with Deuteronomy 26 and is followed by Deuteronomy 27. But Deuteronomy 27, as we have just stated, really begins the Conquest pericope that should have started at the end of Numbers. Hence, Deuteronomy 27 serves as the juncture between the transition from the Sinai pericope (Exodus 19:2b-Numbers 10:10) and the Conquest, and, likewise, between the Horeb pericope (Deuteronomy 1-26) and the Conquest. Therefore, Deuteronomy 27 through Joshua 12, the Conquest pericope itself, is the logical ending of the segment of the narrative whereby the implied narrator takes Israel into the Land.

Although there seems to be a major break at the end of Judges, this is an illusion that is not supported by the narrative development.[97] Eli, Samuel, and Samuel's sons, who "judged" Israel (1 Samuel 4:18, 7:15; 8:1), are *ipso facto* Judges, but not necessarily with the modern connotations. Hence, the pericope in which Israel was led by Judges only concludes with the dishonor of Samuel's sons (1 Samuel 8:3).

---

[96] Hence, the book is now called Deuteronomy, from the Greek—the Second Law, once the congruence is accepted. We do not know whether it or its precursor had any other name than that afforded by the first Hebrew word in its first verse prior to this. Actually, we know very little about how the books of the Hebrew text were named even in the early Second Temple period.

[97] Perhaps the book of Ruth is located between Judges and 1 Samuel in the LXX for literary even more than for theological reasons. It accentuates the illusion and fosters the belief that there is a sharp break between Judges and 1 Samuel.

A new major pericope, the Kingship pericope, begins at 1 Samuel 8:4. This is divided into several pericopes, each of which must also be classified as a major pericope although it is subordinated to the extensive, overriding Kingship pericope. From a literary perspective, therefore, it is notable that these pericopes often overlap one another as is generally to be expected of minor rather than major pericopes.

The first of these major but subordinated pericopes, the kingship of Saul, does come to an end or literary closure at the conclusion of 1 Samuel with the depiction of Saul's death. But even this closure at the end of 1 Samuel is obfuscated, perhaps reflecting the ancient tradition in which Samuel was one book.[98]

Although the medieval division of Samuel was made for practical reasons, the coincidence whereby a practical break is also of literary consequence was surely an added benefit that may well have affected their treatment of the text. There is no significance to the fact that the now canonically divided text ignores the literary and theological chain, whereby the Davidic Kingship pericope begins at 1 Samuel 16 and continues into 2 Samuel forming a bridge between the now divided books, and it continues yet further into 1 Kings forming another bridge between books that are separate in the received text. The treatment of the Davidic Kingship pericope as a thematic linkage between 1 and 2 Samuel represents a reclassification, but not an alteration of the narrative. Certainly this text was continuous and without need of junction or connection when Samuel was as yet undivided. The break caused by the book division, and its concomitant topical bond, then, are both artificial even though the narrative itself is basically unaltered.

It is therefore notable that 1 Samuel, which ends with Saul's death, does conclude at a logical break point. Moreover, the coda to the description of Saul's death with which 2 Samuel begins (2 Samuel 1:1-27) may well show the best aspect of David's *persona*. When

---

98 Hence, Hans Wilhelm Hertzberg (*I & II Samuel: A Commentary* [Philadelphia: Westminster, 1964] 236) feels that it is better to take 2 Samuel 1:

"as the end of the Saul-David complex; although in its way it is a prelude to David's elevation to the throne, it still more brings the reign of Saul to a close, particularly with the eulogy."

David laments alike the death of his sometime enemy, King Saul, and that of his friend, Saul's son Jonathan (2 Samuel 1:19-27), he clearly understands that Yahweh's anointed king and his logically legitimate successor have been killed. *Ipso facto*, then, he comprehends the full baneful meaning and consequence of the death of Yahweh's anointed even though it seemingly portends something good for himself.

The type of textual bonding we have been describing itself seems to find legitimacy because of a apparently similar, although really quite different ligature that is found between the kingship of Saul and the Davidic Kingship pericopes. Here Dtr uses a thematic overlap to show the tragic nexus. From a literary perspective, then, the Davidic Kingship pericope is not only preceded and heralded by the symbolic action in which Samuel tears Saul's robe (1 Samuel 15:27-28), but it begins well before the completion of the kingship of Saul pericope.

This overlaying of pericopes is not a mechanical contravene. Rather, it is a technical literary device, whose most important function is to increase the narrative's interest while suggesting a functional unity. It accomplishes this by showing that not all matters relating to the succession occur linearly in time, but rather they sometimes overlap each other. The falling and rising heroes (or Great Men) are intended to be viewed in juncture to one another: thus, as the reader sees Saul's fall, he sees David's rise.

Clearly, then, it is in accord with sound literary precepts that the two major pericopes, the kingship of Saul (1 Samuel 7:2-31:13) depicting his rise, fall and death, and the kingship of David (1 Samuel 16-1 Kings 2:11) depicting his rise, fall and death, are and must be perceived as intentionally overlaying one another. Consequently, it is no accident that Dtr portrays the rise and fall of David as one major pericope, comprised of a number of minor pericopes positioned in literary, but not necessarily a strictly temporal sequence. He does so to enhance the literary tension of his narrative. Likewise, it is toward the same end that his description of David's rise does not follow, but rather is reported in disjunctive tandem to the delineation of the rise and fall of Saul. Significantly, each is a major pericope, comprised of a number of minor pericopes positioned in literary, but not necessarily a strictly temporal sequence.

The suite of minor pericopes depicting Yahweh's rejection of Saul's kingship, David's call, the divine and human acknowledgment of David's succession, and David's right to kingship in 1 Samuel forms a trajectory leading up to and becoming part of 2 Samuel's Davidic Kingship pericope. But the latter does not end in 2 Samuel. Rather, it bridges 2 Samuel and 1 Kings so as to end with David's death in 1 Kings 2:11. This results in a lack of closure at the end of 2 Samuel while intimately tying Solomon's regnum to David's.

Meaningfully, therefore, the material in 1 Kings 1-2:11 could have been placed at the end of 2 Samuel or at the beginning of 1 Kings. It was included in Kings, (now 1 Kings since Kings, like Samuel, was divided into two books during the medieval era), for the mechanical purpose of making the two books, Samuel and Kings, of approximately the same size. But it was also extended into and made part of Kings for literary and ideological ends.

By interrupting the originally independent Throne Succession Narrative at 2 Samuel 20:22 so as to include such data as the expiatory execution of Saul's descendants with the exception of Mephibosheth (2 Samuel 21: 1-9) and the burial of Saul and Jonathan (2 Samuel 21 12-14), Dtr basically iterates and stresses that Saul's kingship is rejected, and he shows that that rejection includes all of Saul's line. He thus emphasizes the theological perspective whereby the Davidic kingship is both viable and legal.

But when he inserts into the Throne Succession Narrative an extended report of the vicissitudes of what seems to be the remainder of David's "active" life, Dtr shows that he is interrupting the original narrative so as to depict something even more theologically and literarily meaningful than the rejection of Saul's line and the viability and legality of the Davidic kingship. What Dtr both shows and stresses is David's fallibility.

For Dtr (or at least for his implied narrator), King David's fallibility, which we may properly call hubristic rather than sinful, is the major literary, tragic, leitmotif of the Davidic Kingship pericope. Dtr depicts David as an heroic figure, who is better than most men by far. But Dtr's David has a tragic flaw: namely, that very same type of "excess," of which various sorts of intemperance and their concomitant

rash actions are often the result, that is characteristic of those
(anthropologically defined as) Great Men. It is no accident, therefore,
that the material Dtr or possibly Dtr's sources included in the narrative
as well as the diverse texts already incorporated in the Throne Succession Narrative Dtr used stress the contrasts and contradictions in
David's personality that are concomitant with the albeit later concept
of the Greek tragic hero.[99]

Dtr adheres to what we now consider the "Tragic Paradigm." He
depicts a reversal of the narrative's action and David's concomitant
fall as resulting from David's hubris, which itself was a product of his
tragic flaw(s). Moreover Dtr develops his portrait of an hubristic
David so as to set the scene for the depiction, in Kings, of a debilitated
and thereby fallen David, who has to be induced to anoint his successor, Solomon. In turn, Solomon is depicted as the rightful and in fact
righteous king from both a theological and ideological perspective; and
this in despite of Adonijah's better claim to the throne as the oldest living son.

Dtr enhances the dramatic effects and the suspense of his narrative
by delaying his discussion of Solomon's right to be heir until David is
on his deathbed. Although everything in this portion of the narrative
leads up to the Solomonic ascension, the denouement whereby he is en-
titled to be enthroned is a surprise; and the actual enthronement is
abrupt. Moreover, in terms of the drama, it is significant that Solomon's mother, Bathsheba, had once been the wife of Uriah the Hittite,
whom David had placed "in harm's way" in the hopes of causing his
death.

In fact, Dtr depicts David as trying to disguise the murder of
Uriah, for which he was ultimately responsible, as a chance death (2
Samuel 11:2-27). And this attempt to disguise his culpability for what
must be called a murder from a theological and possibly even legal

---

99   Perhaps we may even propose a possible 6th century eastern influence on
Greek tragic form. The Greeks themselves pictured Dionysus as Theban born and at
the same time *an eastern divinity, who migrated to Greece*. This is beyond the scope
of out work and we shall pursue it elsewhere.

perspective, even more than the actual causing of Uriah's death, may have been the apogee of David's hubristic actions.

Despite its tragic format and its literary unity, we do not know if the Davidic Kingship pericope was one unit that was separated when a division was made between Samuel and Kings, whenever that was done, or if Dtr composed this pericope in such a way that it overlapped traditional book divisions that were already in place when he authored and developed his narrative.

We believe, however that the book divisions were imposed on the text of Primary History as a whole at a later date and/or they were secondary, as Martin Noth suggested although he limited this to DtrH (above).[100] But in any case, we can note the literary correctness of the disposition of the Davidic Kingship pericope whereby the Throne Succession Narrative is interrupted and its conclusion becomes part of Kings rather than Samuel, where it more rightfully belongs. Additionally, the fact that it serves the ideological and even the theological ends of the Solomonic era as well as the literary ends of Dtr suggests that this is an old tradition which Dtr adapted it enhance his tragic vision.

From both the ideological and the literary perspective alike, this juncture suggests that the confusion and inherent possibilities for disaster with which David's kingship came to a close were to be resolved by the Solomonic assumption of the throne. But from a literary perspective, it also shows the innate contradictions in David's nature that make him an example of the ideal tragic figure as later defined by Aristotle.[101]

And more significantly, the supplemental material, often in the form of minor pericopes that someone, possibly Dtr added to the Throne Succession Narrative, forms part of the trajectory leading to the exceedingly important minor pericope describing David's death. In

---

[100] M. Noth *Überlieferungsgeschichtliche Studien I* 46 (4).

[101] Interestingly enough, David's *hamartiae* (ἁμαρτίαι) resemble those of Aristotle's exemplar, Sophocles' Oedipus. In both cases the "errors in judgment" or sins—two concepts that are not really as different from one another as both Biblical scholars and Classicists wish to make them—are evinced by a lack of control of temper. And in both cases the hero acts with sexual impropriety whether knowingly or not. This is beyond the scope of our work and we shall pursue it elsewhere.

any case, Dtr clearly juxtaposes the literary representation of the *persona* of this very human man of contrasting and sometimes conflicting traits with that of Solomon, a man whom he depicts as a "flat character," whose personality and actions are dull and yet ideologically perfect. David and Solomon are not presented as isomeric but as antithetical images.

From an ideological and theological perspective, then, the literary bridge between Samuel and Kings that is effected by the minor pericope with which the implied narrator depicts David's death and the firm establishment of Solomon's kingship (1 Kings 1:1-2:12) is extremely meaningful. And, from a literary critical perspective, 1 Kings 2:10-12 may be the most crucial segment of that pericope.

10 וַיִּשְׁכַּב דָּוִד עִם־אֲבֹתָיו וַיִּקָּבֵר בְּעִיר דָּוִד

11 וְהַיָּמִים אֲשֶׁר מָלַךְ דָּוִד עַל־יִשְׂרָאֵל אַרְבָּעִים שָׁנָה
בְּחֶבְרוֹן מָלַךְ שֶׁבַע שָׁנִים וּבִירוּשָׁלַ͏ִם מָלַךְ שְׁלֹשִׁים וְשָׁלֹשׁ שָׁנִים:

12 וּשְׁלֹמֹה יָשַׁב עַל־כִּסֵּא דָּוִד אָבִיו וַתִּכֹּן מַלְכֻתוֹ מְאֹד:

And David slept with his fathers and he was buried in the city of David. And the days in which King David (ruled) over Israel (amounted to) forty years. In Hebron he had been king for seven years and in Jerusalem, king for thirty three. And Solomon sat on the throne of David his father and his kingship was extremely secure (1 Kings 2:10-12 MT)

By juxtaposing the last three verses of the pericope whereby the death formula is not followed by a new ascension formula, the implied narrator symbolically ties the reigns of the two kings together so as to portray the Solomonic kingship as a and in fact the continuation and extension of the Davidic, thereby giving theological as well as legal validity to Solomon's rule.

In contrast to Solomon, David had not attained a sure kingship at first even though his reign was supported by the godhead. Meaningfully, although there is no mention of the godhead in the depiction of Solomon's ascension, the narrative stresses the stability of his kingship by immediately defining it as secure.

Thus, this juxtaposition of the death of a now enfeebled David and the ascension of a firmly "seated" Solomon is an "inverse" type of parallelism that heightens the mutually contradictory literary tones found in the two pericopes of the two kingships. Moreover, this particular juxtaposition specifically serves to unite the respective narrative presentations of David and Solomon so as to make them seem to be two facets of one entity. Since the inclusion of this passage as a minor pericope in 1 Kings serves mechanical, literary, theological, and ideological ends, we may gather that its placement is neither whimsical nor accidental.[102] Rather, it is part of a well ordered narrative.

Because Kings, like Samuel, had been one book in the Hebrew tradition and was not divided into two books until the middle ages, it is not surprising to find a lack of a clear closure at the end of 1 Kings. Moreover, the anomalous literary nature of the depiction of the rule of Ahaziah, a narrative commencing in 1 Kings 22:51 and extending into 2 Kings, does not in and of itself afford any definitive information about how Dtr viewed the text. But the three verses (1 Kings 22:51-53) with which the now divided book ends do form a sort of coda, suggesting that they were consciously included in 1 rather than 2 Kings by those medieval scholars who divided the work. And since this seems to reflect the intent of Dtr, for whom there was no major division at this point, the medieval scholars who divided the book must have had some understanding of Dtr's literary and ideological ends.

In fact, Dtr's intentions are made manifest by the manner in which the juncture of 1 and 2 Kings forms a set of back to back literary "brackets" or an inverted framework, perhaps best defined as a combined retrospective and prospective locus on either side of which the narrator depicts the leading characters doing evil. 1 Kings ends on the backward looking comment that Ahaziah follows the "way" of his parents, and his evil is particularly compared with that of his father Ahab (1 Kings 22:52-53). 2 Kings, however, is forward looking since it begins with Ahaziah's physical injury after Ahab's death (2 Kings 1:1-2). Even in an undivided text this juncture would have been notable.

---

102   By placing this text in 1 Kings rather than 2 Samuel, the redactor chose to stress that the reign of Solomon was resultant upon Davidic kingship, and also that there was no perceptible break in the chain of command despite the various attempts to seize the throne prior to Solomon's ascension.

Dtr continues to develop his ideologically based depiction of the steady deterioration of both states that had begun with the dividing of the kingdom at the death of Solomon. Although he represents both kingdoms as practicing evil, he shows partiality to Judah while simultaneously condemning the Judahites, and particularly the Judahite kings. Hence, Dtr developed the literary leitmotif whereby the evil practiced by some kings in the Southern Kingdom is sometimes mitigated but not eradicated by a tending toward the good. For example, according to Dtr, even Asa had not removed the high places (1 Kings 15:14), and the same is said of Jehoshaphat (1 Kings 43).

The narrative rendition is such that the reader is torn between pity and fear, a status not only expected of the viewer of Greek tragedy in the following century, but predicated on the theological bases that located Attic drama in the three Dionysiac festivals rather than on some form of secular stage.

In contrast to his rendition of Judah's evolving debasement and deterioration, Dtr uses a bolder brush to paint Israel's evil, which seems almost to be unmitigated. Nevertheless, even in the narrative about Israel there is an undertone of possible good, particularly in 1 Kings 17 to 2 Kings 10. Although this has properly been attributed to Dtr's use of some Northern sources, it serves a very important literary end: it "foregrounds" the evil inherent in the action of the kings and the people of this state, thereby making its presentation the more striking.[103] Consequently, even when reading about the Northern Kingdom, the reader is drawn between compassion and dread, pity and fear.

In Primary History as we now have it, therefore, there are elements of formal theologically oriented drama that is specifically in tandem with 5th century Greek tragedy. Moreover, the dramatic roots of such particulars are often enhanced by a sense of closure in the narrative; and this is part of an impressive literary technique whereby the basic elements of the narrative's structure are defined. Thus, the coincidence

---

[103] For example, Dtr depicts the Israelite victory at Aphek (1 Kings 20:26-30) in the midst of the Ahab pericope. Clearly, he altered the material so as to make Israel's victory resultant upon the Aramean's sin. But underlying this and basic to the literary depiction of the sin—which may have no relationship to historical reality— is the historical fact that Israel defeated Ben-hadad at Aphek.

between the end of a major pericope and the end of a book, if the narrative was first formed into pericopes and then divided into books, is of the greatest importance. Unfortunately, we may assume this order of composition since it is the most logical, but we cannot take it for granted.

There is a major pericope coinciding with the closing of a book only at the end of Deuteronomy where it is artificial. Other such congruences fall quite properly at the end of Joshua and Kings respectively. The literary closure at the end of Kings concludes its own major pericope and the entire work at the same time. Consequently there is an absolute sense of completion and ending at the major break between 2 Kings and the next section of Old Testament. This forms a literary separation between Primary History and what follows. Thus, given the canonical divisions, Ezra's ordering of Primary History as a Pentateuch and the four book sequel we know as the Former Prophets may have occurred before anyone separated Samuel and Kings so that each formed two books.

We do not have an *Urtext* from which the various versions of Primary History emanate and we do not know with any degree of certainty when[104] or even whence they originated.[105] But the nine book format of the canonical form of the Masoretic Text of Primary History in combination with the presence of ascertainably pre-monarchic poetry[106] embedded in an essentially and primarily prose narrative is of such great moment that it cannot be stressed strongly enough.[107]

---

[104] M. Noth (*A History of Pentateuchal Traditions* 45) believes it neither necessary nor possible to attain to "a *precise* dating " of the chronology of the textual composition. See also *ibid.* 229, *et passim.*

[105] But see Frank Moore Cross (*The Ancient Library of Qumran & Modern Biblical Studies* [revised edition Grand Rapids, Baker Book House, 1980 reprint of 1961 Doubleday edition] 168-194, and especially 188-194) for an attempt to determine the provenance of various recensions of the text.

[106] See, for example, David Noel Freedman "Early Israelite Poetry and Historical Reconstructions" *Symposia Celebrating the Seventy-Fifth Anniversary of the founding of the American Schools of Oriental Research (1900-1975)* (Cambridge: American Schools of Oriental Research, 1979, Frank Moore Cross, ed.) 87-88.

[107] The tradition in the Septuagint that combines Samuel and Kings to form one work that is divided into four books (1-4 Kingdoms) and precedes it with Ruth,

The data from Qumran and the surrounding regions suggest that there were different types of texts as well as several families and different versions of texts by the mid-2nd century BCE in Palestine itself. The Septuagint[108] by virtue of its differences from Masoretic Text, the Samaritan Pentateuch—a recension not a version,[109]—and citations in selective Apocryphal and Pseudepigraphical writings all imply that at that time there were at least two versions in the ancient Near East, and even in Alexandria and Jerusalem itself. And even the Septuagint was not a single, unified version, but rather it was "a collection of versions made by various writers who differed greatly in their methods, their knowledge of Hebrew, and in other ways".[110]

Despite the respective differences in the Masoretic Text and the Septuagint as we have received them, Genesis through 2 Kings is a meaningful albeit mutually different unit.[111] Because of the additive and redactive nature of Primary History's composition, we are unable to tell with any certainty if at all when the various units of the narrative in the proto-Masoretic Text—(MT being the version we use in this analysis)—or even when those in the pre-Christian Greek text that eventually became the canonical Septuagint were arranged in their re-

---

which is part of the "Writings" in the Hebrew Bible, may be later than that in the Masoretic Text, even if the *vorlagen* of LXX as a whole, possibly, but not necessarily represents an earlier set of traditions than MT.

Interestingly enough if J. Barr (*Holy Scripture: Canon, Authority, Criticism* 128-129) is correct, Josephus' (*contra Ap.* 1.37-42) division of the prophetic books begins with the order: Joshua, Judges with Ruth, Samuel, and Kings. With the exception of Ruth, this is the Hebrew order. Although Josephus does not indicate that these may have been part of a complete work serving as Primary History, he suggests that they are deemed part of Israelite history well into the Restoration era.

[108] See J. Weingreen (*Introduction to the Critical Study of the Text of the Hebrew Bible* [New York: Oxford University/Clarendon, 1982] 30), who gives the *communis opinio* that this was begun in the 3rd century BCE. This dating, however, is not of importance for our argument.

[109] J. Weingreen *Introduction to the Critical Study of the Text of the Hebrew Bible* 25.

[110] Ernst Würthwein *The Text of the Old Testament: An Introduction to the Biblia Hebraica* (Grand Rapids: Eerdmans, 1979) 52.

[111] For the narrative as one book, see Peter D. Miscall *The Workings of Old Testament Narrative* (SBL Semeia Studies; Fortress/Scholars: Philadelphia, Chico 1983) 1. For Primary History *per se* as a meaningful unit, see David Noel Freedman "The Deuteronomic History" *IDB* Supp. (1962) 226.

spective received order so as to join together into one overriding narrative respectively.

The book divisions themselves could be the work of either the final redactor or one of the canonical redactors.[112] Although it is generally believed that the standardization(s) of the text(s) was effected prior to the beginning of the Maccabean era,[113] that is before 164-161 BCE, or possibly even prior to the 3rd century BCE,[114] it is probable that this happened far earlier. Certainly, however, the divisions were most likely in place by the exilic era when the Fundamental or Essential Bible was edited and published or they were made not long after that. Hence, Alter's suggestion that "the editorial combination of different literary sources might usefully be conceived as the final stage in the process of artistic creation which produced biblical narrative"[115] is valid only if we exclude the division into books and their respective canonical ordering as part of that process.

On the other hand, the literary significance of the division into books is (falsely) witnessed by the "Bible as Literature" type of work we are currently seeing, some examples of which endeavor to give a literary analysis of the Bible book by book, treating each book as a separate entity.[116] Such attempts do not achieve their desired end precisely because of the presence of the overlapping pericopes. But these very failures prove *ipso facto* that these book divisions are only meaningful where there is a definite concurrence between the end of a book and a major pericope.

---

[112] The "fixing of a standard text" of the Hebrew Scriptures is believed to have been achieved by c. 135 CE. See J. Weingreen *Introduction to the Critical Study of the Text of the Hebrew Bible* 12. The official text, however, may well have been standardized long before then.

[113] See F. M. Cross *The Ancient Library of Qumran & Modern Biblical Studies* 165. But see R. Rendtorff (*The Old Testament: An Introduction* 74) for a date just prior to the Hellenistic era.

[114] For example, the possibly immediate *Vorlage* of the Septuagint is at least datable to the 3rd and perhaps even 4th century BCE, but the Samaritan Pentateuch is not nearly as old. See D. N. Freedman "Pentateuch" *IDB* 3.713.

[115] Robert Alter *The Art of Biblical Narrative* (New York: Basic Books, 1981) 133.

[116] See, for example, *The Literary Guide to the Bible* Cambridge: Harvard University, 1987, Robert Alter and Frank Kermode, ed.

We must iterate and reiterate that no matter how we classify them now, it is a logical and basic hypothesis that the book divisions throughout Primary History were later than and, hence, secondary to the chain of major pericopes; and that this chain itself is of greater literary meaning than the individual major pericopes, many of which may have had an independent history as a self contained entity. Likewise the chain of minor pericopes that as a unit form a major pericope is of greater literary meaning than the individual minor pericopes, many of which may have had an independent history as a self contained entity.

It is even possible that there was no chain or possibly a different chain of major and/or minor pericopes in earlier redactions. Each of the various redactors ordered the data with which he chose to work in accordance with his own priorities, be they literary, theological, ideological, historical or anything else.

Although we often refer to the component books of Primary History, the narrative is more properly defined as a series of major pericopes that often include one or more sets of minor or major subordinated pericopes. Although the major pericopes in particular—both subordinated and non-subordinated—funnel into one another, for the most part hypotactically via trajectories, they occasionally include paratactically reported events.

And, as we have seen, the pericopes often transcend book divisions, which in and of itself confirms the priority of the pericopes. Consequently, we again stress our belief that the book divisions themselves are artificial and the nine book format had been superimposed on an already existent narrative sometime, but not long before the redaction of 560 BCE.[117]

The minor pericopes represent a separate literary problem from the major even though the two operate as melded entities. Like the major pericopes, the minor ones also funnel hypotactically into one another. But occasionally, where it advances the narrative, they are paratactic to one another.

---

[117] The eleven book format under which Samuel and Kings are each two books, as we have noted above, is medieval.

Each minor pericope leads the story line into the next minor peri-cope until the end of a major pericope is reached. At that point there is usually a break in the narrative even though there are still trajectories leading into the next major pericope. The trajectories between minor and major pericopes permit the junction of different redactions without an apparent break in the subtending structure of the narrative. Wher-ever such interstices are internal to a pericope, be it major or minor, they reinforce the perception that the narrative is a unity.

All the major and many minor pericopes of the first four books are of composite nature, showing evidence of the hands of various redac-tors. This is also true of the Deuteronomistic History although to a lesser extent. In any case, the existence of obvious and not so obvious seams in the narrative suggests there was an overriding redactor of Primary History who cut and trimmed the text in accordance with the subtending architectonics. These cuts and splices in part become obvi-ous to the reader at the junctures and/or as the narrative unfolds.[118] On the other hand, some people also make the unwarranted assumption that there is an overriding redactor of the Pentateuchal narrative.

We iterate that if Primary History was received by Ezra in pretty much the form we have it, and since Ezra was responsible for re-divid-ing that history into the Pentateuch and the Former Prophets as we bel-ieve, then by definition the Pentateuch had not been a separate unit; and, moreover, the overriding redactor had to have preceded Ezra.

In any case, the overriding redactor, who may, but need not be re-sponsible for the division into books, worked with one of the earlier exilic divisions or orderings of Primary History. The possibility that he worked with an even earlier, possibly preexilic, text-form than is rep-resented by the divisions is obviated by the exilic dating of Dtr[2], who may then be the overriding redactor. But it is more likely that he was the penultimate redactor as we have already suggested.

---

[118] As we shall see in Chapter Three, the entirety of Primary History in its ca-nonical form parallels formal 5th century BCE Attic Greek tragedy as defined in the 4th century (sic) by Aristotle. The fact that the Aristotelian predications are not definitive for all 5th century, but rather for certain exemplars in Sophocles' drama (5th century), is not relevant to our discussion.

Whoever he really was, that same overriding redactor, be he the one who partitioned the narrative into books or not, must have combined the component parts of the text so as to form Primary History or he worked with the text after its composite parts had been combined.

Since the former is more possible, the overriding redactor might be the person who placed Deuteronomy in its present position.[119] And this prospect is reinforced by the likelihood that the overriding redactor may have been responsible for the separation or division of some earlier form of Numbers. Most likely this proto-Numbers was edited and redacted so that its proper conclusion, the death of Moses now found only in Deuteronomy and lacking in the canonical Numbers, and so that the strands of the JE Epic now found in Joshua could be transitional[120] while serving as a proper conclusion to Deuteronomy itself.[121] If this is the case, then by definition, this redactor can be dated no earlier than the era of Dtr[2].

And of necessity, therefore, P must precede Dtr if there is only one historian or Dtr[2] if there are two. Consequently, as we have already suggested, this overriding redactor of Primary History most likely did his work just before 560 BCE when the first major division of the text

---

[119] If so, there may only be one Deuteronomistic Historian as Noth presumed, and he must have been working during the Babylonian Exile.

[120] These strands form a trajectory between the respective Sinai/Horeb pericopes and the beginning of a new major pericope, the Conquest.

[121] The fact that the end of Numbers is truncated has long been recognized. See, for example, John B. Gabel and Charles B. Wheeler *The Bible as Literature: An Introduction* (New York: Oxford University, 1990, 2nd edition) 97, *et passim.*

Although there is a break between minor pericopes here, there is no break between major pericopes. Numbers 36 should have been followed by the equivalent of Deuteronomy 34 with verse 34:9 excepted. Deuteronomy 34 itself, again with verse 9 omitted, would make a very fitting conclusion to Numbers. Deuteronomy 34:9, on the other hand, is either a transitional verse or it belongs to a new pericope. Properly it should fall at the end of Deuteronomy if the former, or at the beginning of Joshua if the latter.

Maybe Deuteronomy 34:9 is misplaced because Dtr was attempting to collate data that had formerly been at the end of Numbers with his own ending of Deuteronomy, whose text either D (by definition then without the framework) or Dtr himself had inserted between Numbers and the JE traditions with which Joshua begins.

took place. And as we have shown, he was not Dtr/Dtr[2] himself but rather some unnamed redactor who edited the work just after him.

Although our analysis cannot beyond this point in the textual development, we can state with a measure of certainty that the overriding redactor was not simply a joiner of parts. Possibly the belief that overriding redactor was not an original author or that no such redactor existed, taken together with the concomitant theory that the books as individual entities existed *ab initio* though not necessarily in the form we have them, hence, allowing for the modification and changes wrought by those we now designate J, E, R[JE], P, D, and Dtr[1] & [2], comes from a postexilic and possibly post-canonical period when it was assumed that the text could not be altered substantially. This hypothesis, however, is vitiated by the existence of these same multiple redactions (J, E, R[JE], P, D, Dtr[1] & [2], *etc.*), whose viability clearly attests to an ongoing and far more than mechanical modification of the text.

Even the process of redaction demands original thought.[122] Each redactor chose what portions of the narrative to include and he chose what to omit. He made a conscious decision that certain data and certain stories belonged in the text and others did not.

Consequently, we can only say that at some point during Solomon's reign the Yahwist composed or edited his text; and, as has been noted by others, he did so within the context of the David-Zion traditions. In fact, he edited these traditions in light of some literary or even some artfully presented theological vision that caused him to stress those axioms he attributes to his implied narrator.[123]

During the next century, the Elohist, like the Yahwist, created a text in accordance with some literary or even some artfully presented theological vision that caused him to stress those axioms he attributes

---

[122]   Hence, J. B. Gabel and C. B. Wheeler (*The Bible as Literature: An Introduction* 5) suggest that each "piece of writing in the Bible expresses a *subject*...." They define this subject as something existing within the author's own awareness and as a representation of what which the author truly wants to reveal (*ibid.* 5).

[123]   Crucial to an understanding of the entire Primary History, Analytic Criticism does not demand that the convictions of an author and his implied narrator coincide.

to his implied narrator.[124] Moreover, E did one of two things. Either he composed or edited a text of his own on the basis of the earlier federation narratives that had been in existence for several centuries and whose precepts are grounded in the Exodus and Sinai traditions, or he redacted the J's David and Zion oriented text according to his own principles whereby the federation narratives were preeminent. In any case, we cannot definitively exclude either possibility.

In the Elohistic narrative we have inherited, the implied narrator's principles do seem to emanate from some form and configuration of early federation narratives with their Exodus and Sinai traditions. But at the same time, they do seem to acknowledge some aspects of the Yahwistic traditions.

Possibly the Elohist chose those parts of the Yahwist's narrative he wanted to vary, those he wanted to leave alone, and those he wanted to supplement and then he proceeded accordingly. In so doing, he clearly changed the text he had received. Therefore, he was an original author as well as an overriding redactor of the Yahwist's text.

If, on the contrary, the Elohist had edited or developed a complete narrative that was parallel to, rather than an edition of the Yahwistic narrative, then he was an original author and an overriding redactor of those federation traditions that he had inherited and adapted. In either case, he was not an overriding redactor of the text as we now have it.

By analogy, if the Elohist had used a text that paralleled the Yahwist's, the redactor of the JE Epic (R^JE) must be considered an overriding redactor who chose what parts of J and what of E he wanted to retain, to reject, to combine, etc. R^JE did more than put his stamp on the narrative. He basically combined and redesigned it so as to join together the Exodus and Sinai with the David and Zion traditions. Again we note that he did so in accordance with some literary or even artistic-theological vision that caused him to stress those beliefs he attributes to his implied narrator.

---

[124] In any case, since we are viewing this from a literary perspective, we must not attribute the attitude of the implied narrator to either J or E respectively. We do not know what either redactor really believed, only what each wanted his implied reader to believe his implied narrator believed.

The Priestly Redactor has been identified as "a single literary figure whose style one can recognize often at first glance."[125] He must also be deemed an overriding redactor of the R[JE] material, and an original author, who gave his own stamp to the work. Once again, however, we must not attribute to the Priestly Redactor the beliefs of his implied narrator, who is merely his literary creation.

Although it may be historically likely that P is iterating his own ideology, particularly in light of his exilic dating, we cannot justify this from a literary perspective. Hence, what matters is that like the other redactors, the Priestly Redactor created his narrative in accordance with some literary or even artistic-theological vision.

And in any case, P is not the overriding redactor of Primary History.[126] Nevertheless the two could be and have been confused with one another because P's implied narrator's theological perspective is so important to the overriding redactor that he tends to give preference to P's text when deleting parallel or variant strands.[127]

In respect to the creation of the narrative, the Deuteronomist does not differ from the other redactors. In the Deuteronomist's work, Israel's history is so summarized that it suggests that D once stood alone as a parallel account to that of Genesis-Numbers. Hence, it was far more than a parallel to the Sinai pericope.

Just as the extant portion of the Deuteronomist's work as redacted by the Deuteronomistic Historian offers an alternative version of the Sinai Pericope, the hypothesized *Ur* D account did not supplement, but rather offered an alternative version of Israelite and pre-Israelite history. Somebody, perhaps even an earlier redactor of those data received by the Deuteronomist, chose to include a truncated version of that his-

---

[125] See, for example, Sean E. McEvenue "A Comparison of Narrative Styles in the Hagar Stories" *Semeia* 3 (1975) 65.

[126] Hence, A. Phillips (*Deuteronomy* 229), for example, assumes that P's account of Moses' death "supplements" that of Dtr as "a result of the formation of the Pentateuch by attaching Deuteronomy to the Tetrateuch...."

[127] S. E. McEvenue "A Comparison of Narrative Styles in the Hagar Stories" 67. McEvenue's incorrect assumption that this overriding redactor is the Pentateuchal editor (*ibid.* 67) does not vitiate his primary point about the redactor's preferences.

tory in his account. This, however, is only explicable on a literary basis.

Significantly, the Deuteronomist refused to be a continuer or expander of the J and E traditions, either alone or in their combined format. He presented a new narrative in which he summarized, often in adapted form, those parts of the JE Epic his implied narrator accepted as valid, and he simply ignored any other parts. As we shall see, in some places his narrative has several secondary implied narrators. Thus, from a literary perspective D is far more complex and subtle than the work of the earlier redactors.[128]

The Deuteronomistic Historian, who placed the work of the Deuteronomist in his narrative, extended Israel's story far beyond that depicted by the earlier redactors. His implied narrator put his own moral mark on the entire narrative of Deuteronomy if only by virtue of the framing context. As in the case of the earlier redactors, we could only suggest a coincidence based on alleged ideology and theology if we presume that each redactor's faith was the same as that of his implied narrator.[129] From a literary perspective, we can say nothing about Dtr's beliefs or moral outlook, but we can only discuss that of his implied narrator. As in the case of P, they may coincide; but this is not provable.

In any case, Dtr too was an original redactor or author. But the prophetic writings, some parts of which are themselves primary evidence for the various periods Dtr reports, are ideologically oriented and only tangentially give historical data. And Chronicles, the only source that serves as a parallel to Dtr's work, was written later and comes from a totally different *Weltanschauung.* Consequently we cannot say to what extent Dtr changed or modified the material on which he relied.

The Deuteronomistic Historian chose to include some very old poems in his narrative. The "Song of Moses" (Deuteronomy 32), which

---

[128] Thus, for example, if we quite properly presuppose the core of Deuteronomy to be a literary inclusion in the Deuteronomistic History, we must ask why the Deuteronomistic Historian framed and probably adapted it, and why the final redactor of Primary History chose to retain it in tandem with Genesis-Numbers.

[129] The identicality of the two is a fact not in evidence.

bears a clear relationship to Dtr's implied narrator's theological stance,[130] is in fact from the 10th-9th century.[131] Deuteronomy 33 is even earlier, primarily emanating from the 11th century although parts of it also suggest the early monarchy.[132] On the basis of oral transmission theory, however, we can state without reservation that Dtr must have received these poems in written form.

He may have included the poems in his narrative so as to suggest that his entire narrative is also very old and emanates from the time it proposes to describe. This fictive stance is particularly important in the case of Deuteronomy because Dtr may have wished to suggest that that book or at least its core is the Torah to which 2 Kings 22:8 refers.[133]

Deuteronomy (D and Dtr combined) encapsulates the events already reported in the Tetrateuch, despite the variants in presentation. Thus, it also serves as a literary, that is, narrative juncture between the depiction of Israel before its conquest and settlement of the Land and that of Israel conquering and dwelling in the Land. But because this division is a theological as well as a literary construct, it may well reflect older traditions. It may, however, simply reflect the thought of the Deuteronomistic Historian and if Dtr is not the overriding redactor, of the overriding redactor whoever he is, or simply of the respective implied narrators of both.

As the redactors are original authors, the implied narrators are fictional characters even when named for historical people. Just when an implied narrator seems to stand out as an individual entity, either his *persona* is modified to dovetail with that of other redactors' implied narrators or the real author/redactor develops some form of anacol-

---

[130]   A. Phillips *Deuteronomy* 216.

[131]   For the early dating, see David Noel Freedman "3. Divine Names and Titles in Early Hebrew Poetry" *Pottery, Poetry, and Prophecy: Studies in Early Hebrew Poetry* (Winona Lake: Eisenbrauns, 1980) 101.

[132]   D. N. Freedman "3. Divine Names and Titles in Early Hebrew Poetry" 99.

[133]   We cannot accept the common hypothesis that the redactor(s) were not perpetrating "an act of literary deception" or that the "authors were no doubt perfectly sincere in believing that Moses either did say or should have said these things" or that "the authenticity of 'the book of the law' was not questioned in 622 B.C." (J. B. Gabel and C. B. Wheeler (*The Bible as Literature: An Introduction* 75).

outhon in the text. Both of these processes allow for the doublets in the narrative.

Once we accept the alterability of the text, we can see that the presence of doublets that can be justified, albeit on a literary basis, as part of the textual development. These doublets attest to originality of each redactor's though. They are more than formulaic entities, and they are not simply different versions of a story that the redactor had to include in his narrative because they were part of an established and primary tradition. Rather, the redactor elected to include them whether they were part of such a tradition or whether they were part of a secondary and concurrent one or whether he created them for ideological or, more likely, literary ends. It is no mere coincidence, therefore, that from a literary perspective these doublets always seem to develop the plot line and leitmotif of the pericope of which they are a part.

Primary History is in narrative form.[134] The accounts found in the pericopes are related by an omniscient implied narrator (the primary or overriding implied narrator),[135] who supersedes the respective implied narrators of the various redactions of the text. And in accordance with the conventions of Analytic Criticism, this narrator is not to be identified with any of the redactors including the overriding redactor.[136] The

---

[134] The nature of a narrative demands that a story be narrated. This, however, does not militate against the inclusion of direct statement within the course of the narrative.

[135] Named or unnamed, an implied narrator's presence is generally perceived by his intrusion into the plot development. The very fact that any narrator's presence is observed, demands that he be considered a *persona* within the text and, thus, an implied rather than an actual narrator.

[136] But see Robert Pollen *MOSES and the DEUTERONOMIST (sic): A Literary Study of the Deuteronomic History* Part One (New York: Seabury, 1980) 18, 215 note 11; *idem* "Reporting Speech in the Book of Deuteronomy: Toward a Compositional Analysis of the Deuteronomic History" *Traditions in Transformation: Turning Points in Biblical Faith* (Winona Lake: Eisenbrauns, 1981, Baruch Halpern and Jon D. Levenson, ed.) 193-194.

Polzin's basic premise, however, that the "Deuteronomist (*sic* Dtr) is the 'implied author' of this work" is in contradistinction to literary theoretical definition of an implied author as different from both the implied narrator and the real author. Hence, his rejection of Booth's basic premise (215 note 11) suggests that Polzin accepts the so-called "Historical" literary method, under which a text is as-primary implied narrator usually moderates conversation in such a way that even when he seems to allow someone (a secondary implied narrator) to speak for himself—that is, to use first person speech,—he remains the ever present, omniscient third person who is really reporting that event.

This primary or overriding implied narrator is present both *prae initium* and *ab initio*, that is, prior to and from the beginning of Elohim's creating experience in Genesis 1:1.[137] Because he is omniscient, he knows what the literary *personae* including all men and all gods such as Yahweh, Elohim, Yahweh Elohim or any other divinity or hypostasis of a divinity think, feel, believe, do in private, *etc.* This it is not surprising that, for example, in the Priestly account with which Genesis begins (1:1-2:4a), the implied narrator knows what the divinity did in the very act of creation just as he knows the same things in the Yahwistic account of creation that begins in Genesis 2:4b. And he also knows how the divinity reacted and responded to his creative acts.[138] The literary presentation rests on the precept of an implied narrator, who has gotten into and remains in the mind of the godhead and of all of the other *personae* in the narrative; but he presents his report as if he were an historian.

Although the overriding implied narrator's presence is found in texts attributed to all of the hands that redacted Primary History, it is not possible to decide which redactor first created the possibly composite literary *persona* that we now find. He may have been a creation of the final redactor or of one of the earlier redactors, who effected some combination of the various narrative or redactional traditions. In

---

sumed to give real information about its real author, whose beliefs are implied by the narrative itself.

Polzin's use of newer and acceptable literary analysis is made less acceptable by his assumption that the real author's views can actually be extracted from the narrative by an analysis of framing, a literary means of forcing the implied reader to focus inward on the text. The framing merely indicates that which the author wants his implied reader to believe.

[137] However, his presence prior to the creation is by implication only.

[138] This narrative omniscience so pervades the text that it would be impossible to list all of the examples.

any case, each redactor may have had a particular overriding implied narrator, who may but need not have been an historian.

Moreover, along with the overriding implied narrator for all of Primary History, there is more than one implied narrator in some portions of the narrative. Some of the secondary implied narrators may have been overriding implied narrators of earlier redactions of specific strata of the text.

Sometimes, but not consistently, the omniscient primary implied narrator of all of Primary History is the dominant figure in the pericope even though he is never named. It is he who tells the story as an "explicit presentation" in the third person or even, when necessary, by becoming a first person narrator and telling the story in "direct exposition" as if he were quoting.[139] At other times, but also not consistently, the omniscient primary implied narrator, who himself is a literary construct of the author(s)/redactor(s), drops into the background.

When there are also secondary implied narrators, they are—fictively at least—literary constructs of the primary implied narrator. They are most often seen as respective individual literary *personae* in the work of the Deuteronomist, whose image of the primary implied narrator is made to fade into the elapsing narrative so as to enhance the illusion that one of the secondary implied narrators, respectively called Moses, Yahweh, or Israel, is reporting events he himself experienced or even brought about. The reader only sees those aspects of Moses', Yahweh's, and the Israelites' respective *persona* that the implied narrator wishes him to see.

Significantly in Deuteronomy the primary implied narrator is himself the literary *persona* who presents Moses' and Yahweh's speeches and the Israelites' responses at the Mountain of God as if they were direct discourse; and he does so as part of his own report. Thus, Moses, Yahweh, and the Israelites all seem to be describing historic as well as current events that reach a climax, but do not culminate in the Horeb experience and the Covenant conclusion.

---

[139] C. Hugh Holman and William Harmon *A Handbook to Literature* (New York: Macmillan, 1986) 81-82, *s.v.* "Characterization".

In fact, Dtr's attribution of the adapted summary of R[JE]'s data to these literary *personae* who are secondary implied narrators gives the narrative an illusion of authenticity and theo-historical probity that the text may not have otherwise had. The implied reader may forget that the primary implied narrator is still present and, consequently, that the report is not authentic. However, the real reader cannot or at least he should not do so.

Despite the foregrounding under which the secondary implied narrators are treated as literary *personae*, they are, insofar as the narrative is concerned, placed in that position by the implied narrator himself. That it is the real author who so depicts each of them is not relevant. What matters is that whenever the *persona* Moses responds to the *persona* of the godhead or *vice versa*, or when either responds to the *persona* represented by the collective Sons of Israel, the primary implied narrator always introduces and concludes that speech. In other words, the author depicts the primary implied narrator as framing direct discourse with third person narrative.

In Deuteronomy, therefore, there is no real dialogue despite the presence of first person narrative. Additionally, the summary nature of the text of Deuteronomy together with the flat presentation that intentionally characterizes the narrative in which the events leading to Horeb are depicted, makes even the first person speeches seem like third person narrative rather than the direct address they purport to be.[140] It is this very illusion that suggests to the implied auditor/reader that the data are authentic.

It succeeds in its aim of deluding the implied auditor/reader into believing in the historicity of the speeches. And these resultant misguided beliefs held by that auditor/reader serve the purpose for which they were intended: they lead him to think that Moses himself is the real narrator of not only Deuteronomy but of the entire Pentateuch, a supposition that is not supported by the text.[141]

---

[140] This is particularly true of those speeches attributed to Moses.

[141] For a brief but significant history of the scholarship dealing with this problem, see J. B. Gabel and C. B. Wheeler *The Bible as Literature: An Introduction* 84-98.

The author(s)/redactor(s) of Deuteronomy have constructed their narrative in such a way that even some modern readers of the entire Pentateuch take on the role of the implied auditor/reader and are also deceived. Hence, those modern readers for whom the Torah is God's word given to Moses merely seek to justify how Moses can narrate the report of his own death. They do not question their basic premise that Moses was "publishing" the text as authorized by the godhead, who had given it to him on Sinai. And since the text had been given at the mountain of God, they of necessity equate Sinai with Horeb.

Despite this very successful literary illusion, we conclude that Moses is not the primary narrator or the primary implied narrator of Deuteronomy and/or the Tetrateuch; and, therefore, he is not the over-riding implied narrator of the Pentateuch. Granting the presence of a number of one or two verse statements placed in the mouth of the literary *persona* Moses, particularly in Exodus, for the most part his actions are depicted by the overriding and even by individual subordinate implied narrator(s) in reported speech.

Only in Deuteronomy do we seem to see Moses himself as a significant first person implied narrator of the text. But this is a literary device, and even when he is speaking in his own voice, he is a secondary implied narrator whose *persona* is being depicted and whose actions are being reported by a primary implied narrator.

Moreover, even though his first person narrative is allegedly being quoted by the primary implied narrator, there is no substantiation for the assumption that his statements really are quotations and, hence, that we are reading Moses' actual words.

In fact, several things militate against the historicity of the Mosaic speeches. Unless we can attest to the existence of Moses as an historical person accompanied by scribes who actually wrote his words as he said them, we are only dealing with statements about an allegedly real person that at best were handed down orally for a period of time.

All our knowledge of oral transmission indicates that significant changes in the speeches must have developed as they were reported and re-reported. Hence, even if these remarks had been written down long before the Deuteronomist's era, there is little likelihood that they had a close relationship to Moses' utterances—granting there was a Moses (*pace* Albright). Of equal significance is the literary convention by which an author can place the words in the mouth of a *persona*, be he a fictive or historical character, he would have been likely to have said on a particular occasion.[142]

Assuming Moses is historical, this is in accordance with the literary tenets for works we now define as Roman à Clef. But assuming he is a fictive character with no historic antecessor, it falls under those of the Documentary Novel.

Therefore, even when the literary *persona*, Moses, is depicted as speaking in the first person, we the readers must realize that the quotations are not what we deem quotations; and, that we are relying on the integrity of the primary implied narrator regarding both the statements and the existence of the historical person from whom they allegedly emanate. But we must not forget that that primary implied narrator is himself a literary creation of the author or redactor, who may but need not believe the data which he includes are authentic.

Consequently, we can take for granted that Deuteronomy's Moses is an implied narrator, who is himself a literary creation of the implied narrator of Deuteronomy, who himself is a literary creation of the author(s)/redactor(s) of some version of Deuteronomy that may have included the work of the Deuteronomist and of the Deuteronomistic Historian just as Dtr is the overriding redactor of D. On the other hand, the implied narrator of Deuteronomy may simply have been a literary creation of the Deuteronomist alone, and he was inherited, retained, and extended by the Deuteronomistic Historian. That is to say: Moses was depicted as the implied narrator of the implied narrator of D. Dtr then built upon and developed that fictive, bracketed literary image of Moses' narrating the events depicted in the text.

The primary implied narrator of Deuteronomy differs from the real narrator, that is the author(s) of the text,[143] but he also differs from the overriding redactor of Primary History. We iterate that the implied nar-

---

142   This literary convention, for example, is found in all the allegedly historical writings of the Greeks and Romans. Examples are to be found in Herodotus, Thucydides, Polybius, Livy, Tacitus, Josephus, *et al.*

143   But see R. Polzin *MOSES and the DEUTERONOMIST (sic): A Literary Study of the Deuteronomic History* Part One 18, 215 note 11.

rators on any level are *created* literary *personae*. The real narrator is the respective author or redactor, who formulated each of the various pericopes.

Theological premises to the contrary, the text is first and foremost a work of art. It too must be deemed a fabricated literary effort, then. This does not mean, however, that the redactors only drew from their imagination and their craft so as to create each story or even each pericope in the narrative.

Where they did not create material out of "whole cloth," the various redactors took stories that may, at one time, have been formulated and handed down as part of oral traditions. These stories may possibly have had their bases in the cult, the folk traditions, the mythology, the legends, the theological strictures, the laws, or the history of the people. But this does not indicate that they had been had been transmitted orally, or solely orally, until the time of the redaction into which they were incorporated and/or had been received aurally, or solely aurally, by the redactor.

Whether they were heard aurally as part of an oral tradition or heard when a written work was being read aloud or whether the work was simply being read by the redactor, the stories may have been and most likely were transformed. The redactors did not necessarily present the pieces in the same format or characterized by the same *Sitzen im Leben* from what they had emanated. Rather they put them forth in such a way that they seem to have issued from the past, be it remote or more recent, and in fact from the period and even the various *Sitzen im Leben* to which they are attributed in the narrative.[144]

Like the stories themselves, these *Sitzen im Leben* may have been radically different from those of their origin. The redactors alleged fictive "situations in life" as necessary. Hence, their narrative insinuated the presence of an underlying *Sitz im Leben* related to a oral tradition having cultic, folklore, mythological, legendary, legal, or historical roots. But when it suited their needs, they depicted events and hence, their implied respective *Sitz im Leben* in such a way that they seem to

---

[144] This does not mean they really emanated from the particular *Sitz im Leben* depicted. In some cases, scholars have shown the real *Sitz im Leben* behind the narrative differs decidedly from that in the narrative.

have been taken from and had their bases in a culture that expressed its most important traditions in writing.

The orality of the antecedents of the allegedly or by implication oral traditions or stories is sometimes if not often questionable. That the paradigm for the "damsel in distress" narratives in Genesis 12:10-13:1, 20, 26:1ff is not unique to these texts suggests that Robert Polzin's observation of the circular reasoning implicit in the attribution of orality to the pericopes in which they are depicted[145] is more significant than he believes it to be. In fact, this model is itself part of a larger one that is paradigmatic for many of the texts assumed to have an oral basis. Moreover, if the *Sitz im Leben* justifies the assumption of orality and if the supposition of orality itself explains the *Sitz im Leben*, then we must ignore both and deal solely with the final form of the text. In this type of situation, we cannot get behind that final form despite the attestation of Form Critics to the contrary.

In light of this, it is noteworthy that the changes in narrative style as Primary History develops are usually attributed to the oral nature of the sources in the Tetrateuch, and to the Deuteronomistic Historian's greater reliance on written texts. Any redactor or author wanting to suggest that his narrative was grounded in oral tradition could accomplish his objective by presenting pericopes that emulate oral narrative. This does not mean that he did not use written sources, but rather that he did not want to seem to have used written sources.[146] The presumption of orality may reflect the redactor's success in having created an illusion to that end.

The question of the true orality of any part of the roots of Primary History is really a non-sequitur to our problem, however. It is not even particularly relevant to it because our narrative is written and it is based on earlier redactions (J, E, P, D, Dtr), most if not all of which had been received in writing, by the sequential redactors themselves,

---

[145] Robert Polzin "'The Ancestress of Israel in Danger' in Danger" *Semeia* 3 (1975) 82.

[146] Perhaps some traditions had been handed down in oral form. As is well accepted, however, oral stories can continue to circulate orally long after they have been put into writing. In fact, it is this duality that often leads to variant traditions about the same event.

but ultimately by the overriding redactor of Primary History. Furthermore, we may presume that each of the redactors at least put his own mark on the text.

Notably, a stabilized text is a written text. As others have shown, the core or deep structure of an oral tradition may remain unchanged. But because each oral performance is a performance, be it in sacred or secular context, the outer structure varies in accordance with the various parameters of that performance (*e.g.,* the performer, the audience, the time and other external constraints).

Although the Israelites or their forebears may well have had texts that were only handed down orally, and some oral traditions were being handed down concurrently with the written redactions, a purely oral tradition, if it ever existed, had been transmitted during the distant past and, hence, was not relevant to the final form of the text. Moreover, we must seriously question the precept on which the presumption of the prior orality of the texts is based: namely that the early pre-Israelites and pre-monotheistic Israelites alone of all the ancient Near Eastern peoples either had a scribal tradition that they did not use or they were illiterate.[147]

There can be no doubt that there was a well-developed scribal tradition by the Solomonic period when the Yahwist was composing his work. Moreover, Solomon's diplomatic interaction with other monarchs of the ancient Near East, if we can trust Dtr's representation as reflecting any form of historicity, itself suggests that the Sons of Israel had knowledge of other cultural traditions, and that they were aware, although we cannot tell to what extent, of foreigners' views about them and their nation (the United Monarchy).

This predicates information received in some written format in addition or even in contradistinction to an exclusively oral exchange of

---

[147] Hence, D. J. Wiseman ("Books in the Ancient Near East and in the Old Testament" *The Cambridge History of the Bible* volume 1 *From the Beginnings to Jerome* [New York/New Rochelle: Cambridge University, 1975, P. R. Ackroyd & C. F. Evans, ed.] 37-38) thinks that the "first attributions of literacy" were ascribed to the middle of the second Millennium BCE; that Moses recorded both laws and legal determinations as well as at least one song, the covenantal curses, and "memoranda connected with the Israelite journeys" etc.

knowledge. Even when it is likely or even probable that a story had an oral prehistory, it is often impossible to determine whether a particular oral tradition incorporated in either Primary History (or for that matter in Herodotus' *History*) was received in either one or both forms; whether it had already been incorporated into a broader format when a redactor received it; and, when or even where it first created or first put into writing.

In the case of Primary History, it is sometimes hopeless to attempt to decide when such a hypothetically heretofore oral tradition, be it in oral or written form, was merged into the account inherited by a particular redactor of the narrative. We do not and frequently cannot know whether any redactor had a text before him (no matter what an implied narrator such as Herodotus, Moses, or even Yahweh, says). And if we could know, in many cases, we still would not be able to ascertain with any degree of certainty what texts he had used. Moreover, because many traditions continued orally after having been written down, there is always uncertainty regarding some form of "contamination" of any allegedly oral report. We cannot know whether any one of the redactors really did hear the allegedly oral reports the narrator or implied narrator says he had heard, or whether a redactor is supplementing his written texts with information obtained from oral reports or *vice versa*, or whether a redactor created material because it fit the course of his narrative.

This does not mean that we must reject all attempts to identify oral traditions embedded in the written text or even the possible place of origin of either a tradition or of the written text itself. In fact, in Primary History, at least a modicum of success has been achieved in this endeavor.[148] And even the status of some of the early pre-redactional material now embedded in the texts of Primary History has been determined with some relative degree of certainty.

Accordingly, when von Rad suggests that the Yahwist, for example, had collected ancient traditions, which he then assembled, amplified, and even reformatted, he does not specify their prior status as oral

---

[148] For Herodotus, see W. W. How and J. Wells *A Commentary on Herodotus* (2 volumes; New York: Oxford University, 1989) 1.20-32. But see above for a different interpretation.

or written. Rather, von Rad suggests that the Yahwist already pos-
sessed his data,[149] but they were no longer peculiar to or located in
those places where their cultic associations had once been "living traditions".[150]

We must iterate that with current data we cannot know whether the
Yahwist or for that matter any other redactor received any material in
oral, written, or both forms. This may even be true of that of the redactor whose work a subsequent redactor supplemented, overwrote,
changed, or edited. Since there was a literate caste as represented by
the scribal guilds, and since there was also a tradition of orality in the
ancient Near East, a great amount of data may have been received
orally, in written form, or both. However, the archaic—not archaizing—format and linguistic usage of some data, particularly the poetic,
suggest they had been obtained from written works and then were re-
phrased so as to seem to have come from oral traditions. But without
some type of confirmation, we are not able to identify that which any
of the redactors created and that which they emended and adapted in
order to enhance their narrative.

As our argument has suggested, there is no basis for the assumption that the redactors of Primary History are merely those who edit
and hand down traditions. Again we stress that like all authors, they
may well have created data and generated traditions to suit their literary and/or theo-political needs.

Just as we question the orality of allegedly oral sources, we must
question the implicit or even explicit claim that there is written data
behind those portions of the text that allegedly are based on them.
Written sources other than that of the sequential redactions can only be
presumed when there is some parallel and/or external documentation
supporting their existence.

These proof texts and/or external supportive data may be artifactual. They may be written works that show no influence by and are
tangential to the biblical text. They may also be other, but different
biblical texts (*e.g.,* prophetic or exilic writings) or even some written

---

[149] G. von Rad "The Form-Critical Problem of the Hexateuch" 48.
[150] G. von Rad "The Form-Critical Problem of the Hexateuch" 49.

document itself that clearly serves as a basis for the biblical text in question. And we know that there are Second Temple era texts that prove that there were different biblical textual traditions (see above), although we cannot always state when these traditions originated.

We must not assume that any text is based on written information or on those specific written sources, which may or may not exist, to which a redactor attributes it. Data allegedly extracted from real works, and even named sources themselves may be products of a redactor's imagination. Hence, statements suggesting that materials came from the "Book of the Wars of Yahweh," "Book of the Righteous," Solomon's "Annals," the "Annals of the kings of Israel," the "Annals of the kings of Judah" or any other identified work must be treated as questionable unless they are upheld by reliable supportive documentation.

On the other hand, we must not rule out the use of written data. Correspondences between the ancient Near Eastern Law codes and the Covenant Code as well as portions of other legal material included in the Pentateuchal narrative, "parallels between patriarchal customs and those of more or less contemporary societies, evidenced in the Mari and Nuzi texts,"[151] the presence of songs from the possibly 13th (Albright) but more definitely 12th (Freedman) through the 10th century in a relatively unaltered form and in archaic Hebrew in both the Hexateuch and the Deuteronomistic History, the annalistic nature of the narrative in 1 and 2 Kings all suggest that various redactors and possibly the overriding redactor as well may have had far more written data than we generally assume.[152]

---

[151] Peter R. Ackroyd "The Old Testament in the Making" *The Cambridge History of the Bible* volume 1 *From the Beginnings to Jerome* (New York/New Rochelle: Cambridge University, 1975, P. R. Ackroyd & C. F. Evans, ed.) 70. See also D. J. Wiseman "Books in the Ancient Near East and in the Old Testament" *idem.* 44.

[152] J. Van Seters' hypothesis that the redactors may have had knowledge of the inscriptional data from the ancient Near East (see, for example, John Van Seters "Oral Patterns or Literary Conventions in Biblical Narrative *Semeia* 5 (1976) 139-154) leads to the supposition that they were not particularly concerned with historical truth, which for them is a relative rather than an absolute matter. But the theory that they were aware of the inscriptional data has been contested on the basis of the differences between the inscriptions and the reports in Primary History (see, for ex-

Our knowledge of the transmission of oral literature is the primary basis for our belief that the redactors used more written texts than is generally assumed, and this is especially true regarding the archaic Hebrew poetry incorporated into the narrative. If any of the redactors of Primary History, the earliest of which, the Yahwist, wrote in the 10th century, had received the archaic poems orally, *ipso facto* he could not have had them in their original form. As we have stressed, oral transmission always reflects editing, emending, and changing, relative to the time and circumstances of individual oral performances and performers. At the same time it presumes that the performer believes in the exactitude with which he transmits the spoke word. His conviction about this is so strong that neither he nor his audience would acknowledge the fluidity of the "text" even if they could do so. That is, the performers and their audiences habitually attribute to the oral word the accuracy we attribute to the written.

Clearly, then, if the reports of the traditions had been received orally, they would have been so different from their Urtext that we could not possibly have dated any segments of these poems to the earlier period. Rather, as with the prose parts of Primary History, we could only suggest they were based on earlier traditions. Granting this, either the redactors were archaizing, which does not seem likely, or they were relying on written versions of the poetry.

The description of Israel's origins is another thing entirely. It does not matter, for our purposes, whether the traditional precepts regarding Israel's origins are valid or whether Mendenhall's and Gottwald's thesis is valid. Both Israel's origins and its history are described by the

ample, David M. Gunn "On Oral Tradition: A Response to John Van Seters" *Semeia* 5 (1976) 155-163). These differences, however, can easily be explained on a literary basis.

Only if we assume that the redactors of Primary History were recording history as we now conceive of it and that they were not creating an ideological-literary narrative, must we presume a slavish adherence to the texts and data that any redactor may have used for information. If, on the other hand, we realize that the various redactors were presenting an ideologically oriented literary narrative, we obviate the meaningfulness of the entire problem of the probity with which they adhered to their sources. Moreover, by acknowledging that our redactors treat that literary narrative as ideologically colored fictionalized history in a tragic, theo-political format, we come to the understanding that truth for them is a relative, not an absolute matter.

overriding implied narrator of Primary History in accordance with the theological precepts that he wishes to be perceived by the implied auditor/reader, who like the implied narrator is a literary construct of the real author/redactor.

But this primary implied narrator is represented as an historian who believes that he is reporting valid historical data. Although it is possible that the author(s)/redactor(s) of the narrative also thought that the data was historical, our lack of information attesting to their private convictions about the facts prevents us from coming to a conclusion in this matter.

In any case, it is we, the real readers, who wish to find and consequently seek that which is behind those strictures regarding Israel's origins. If Mendenhall and Gottwald are correct, the portion of Primary History's narrative dealing with Israel's origins has no basis in historical fact.

Chapter Three: Herodotus and *Primary History*

Each redactor of Primary History, and Ezra, the Restoration era Judaean who rearranged and modified the same Primary History, pays attention to the relationship of a man or a state to the divine. Herodotus the 5th century (real) Halikarnassian author of the *History*, and the extant 5th century Greek tragic playwrights, do likewise.[1] Moreover, there are two interrelated things that particularly concern each of them: the effect of the godhead or the not so impersonal force of divinely appointed fate on men and nations; and mans' response to that fate in particular, and to the sacred in general.

Specifically, the interest in fate causes the authors or narrators to pay especial attention to the situations of conflict in which Great Men, states, nations of consequence,[2] and/or divinities are involved. This predicates a depiction of interactions in which men are opposed to men, state to state, nation to nation, gods to gods, or some combination thereof.

The respective author's/redactor's interest in fate focuses on its inexorable course, which itself inevitably forms a leitmotif that subtends the narrative. Fate's inexorable course is only "foregrounded" when it is ideologically and/or literary necessary so as to make and stress a particular point, to serve as a proverbial type of exemplar, or otherwise to lend definition to the narrative.

From a literary perspective, the means by which a man's, state's or nation's fate is assigned or even how knowledge of it is imparted to its recipient is a different matter from his working out of that predestination. Consequently, when it suits their needs, the authors or redactors ignore this aspect of the topic. But whenever necessary, they change their literary focus and foreground the phenomena associated with the way in which humans come to learn about their destiny, thus causing

---

[1]   The same can be said of the mid-7th century author/redactor/bard of *Iliad*. It can also be said of Euripides, but there is controversy regarding the latter.

[2]   If the reception of Aeschylus' *Persians*, produced in 472 BCE, is representative, however, the Athenian audience was not particularly sympathetic to drama about contemporary events, even when their own πόλις had been the victor. This attitude need not be assumed for presentations in other genres.

that very allotment of fate or, what is more important, its revelation to its recipient to play a definitive role in the narrative.[3]

Hence, sometimes a hero's, state's, or nation's destiny is depicted as resultant upon an oracle, a vision, or a covenant; and sometimes it simply develops as an implicit facet of the narrative. Sometimes it is assigned at birth—be it human or national,—sometimes later. And sometimes its allotment is presumed on the basis of developments as they are depicted in the narrative.

Often the hero, state, or nation learn what is fated early enough to counteract that fate should he believe in it and would the possibility of obviation exist. Unfortunately the theological and dramatic cast of the each of the narratives makes impossible any attempts to prevent a literary character's lot from taking its theological and literary prescribed course even when variant fates are proposed for the same individual.[4]

Because humans are depicted as bringing to fruition a divinely imposed fate, there is a blurring of the margin between the holy and worldly. Thus, it is not surprising that both Herodotus' *History* and Primary History, often ignoring liminality completely, do not generally distinguish sacred time from secular and sacred space from secular.[5] Rather, when a god is a *dramatis persona* or when he is simply behind the events of the drama, attention is paid to the role played by the divinity himself.

And it is precisely because the narratives show the god's transitory manifestation, that is the appearance of the supernatural as if it were natural in history, that they succeed in their literary illusion of blurring and even obliterating the distinction between secular, liminal, and sacred time and space. Significantly, it is this lack of differentiation that also defines the world depicted in Greek tragedy. All times and places, be they secular, liminal, or sacred, meld into one unified macrocosm. In this state of worldly-otherworldly oneness, a god acts directly or indirectly with equal meaningfulness.

---

[3] For example, this happens in Sophocles' *Oedipus Tyrannus*.

[4] One of the best known examples of a man's apparently having the ability to choose his fate is Achilles as depicted in *Iliad*.

[5] This is also usually true of Attic drama.

In Herodotus' *History,* Primary History, and 5th century Attic drama, we find times in which all of the action is consequential upon some assumed, but not necessarily enunciated action of a god. In this instance, the god may be conjectured to have acted directly in the world of the *dramatis personae,* even though the audience or reader is not a participant in the action itself. But when an oracle is the mediator who informs the hero of the divine will,[6] the representatives of the god and man actually interact in the reader's/auditor's presence. When the god, in his own shape or that of another being or entity visits the hero, who may be awake or sleeping,[7] to whom he manifests himself and informs him of his divine will, god and man interact in the reader's/auditor's presence.

The authors or redactors of all of these works make their presentation in such a way as to show the unique function of the godhead, who for Herodotus or at least his implied narrator, is primarily but not always the god at Delphi in various manifestations. In fact, as Crahay properly observed, the basic function of the oracle in Herodotus' work is to dramatize the narrative so as to show the unique function of the god in history.[8]

Herodotus' implied narrator's belief in the existence of foreign gods, whom he does not scorn,[9] illustrates the presence of the acceptable godhead's guiding hand in the rise and fall of nations. Therefore, this presentation serves the exact same purpose as that of the implied narrators of Primary History who make multiple attempts to express a denial of foreign gods *qua* gods, whom they do scorn.

But even more significantly, both Herodotus' and Primary History's implied narrators stress the relationship between the rise or fall of each nation and the state's leader's adherence to what is willed by

---

6   For the role of the oracle as a temporal manifestation of the divine in a historical context (as, for example, in Herodotus 1.13, 7.178 *et al.*), see Roland Crahay *La Littérature oraculaire Chez Hérodote* (Paris: Société d' Édition <<Les Belles Lettres,>> 1956) 3, *et passim; et al.*

7   A dream theophany is still a materialization of the divinity.

8   R. Crahay *La Littérature oraculaire Chez Hérodote* 59.

9   Ivan M. Linforth "Greek Gods and Foreign Gods in Herodotus" *University of California Publications in Classical Philology* 9 (1926-1929) 218.

the godhead. Hence, they emphasize the defeat of a nation as a consequence of (often repeated and escalating acts of) hubris or sin.

The parallelism between the end results of these two seemingly
conflicting sets of beliefs is quite remarkable. Because the 6th century
redactors and the 5th century arranger(s) of Primary History were pos-
iting a monotheistic godhead, whereas Herodotus, despite his focus on
Apollo, was not, there seems to be a difference between the two. But
this incongruity is an illusion. And in fact, the correspondence becomes clear-cut when the reader realizes that Herodotus' implied narrator accepts a multiplicity of divinities, but still tends "to speak of the
divine element in the world *as if* (sic) it were characterized by the indivisibility of the god of the pure monotheist."[10]

The gods depicted by the Greek dramatists and Herodotus were
portrayed as literary *personae*. For the implied audience of the dramatists or the implied auditor/reader of Herodotus, however, they were far
more than that. In fact, Linforth's notion that "The Greeks of the fifth
century B. C. believed in the actual existence of their Gods"[11] is basically applicable to the implied reader or audience of Herodotus' implied narrator as well as the implied audience of the plays. Moreover,
since the omniscient and omnipresent implied narrator of the *History*
frequently treats the events of the past in accordance with the norms of
his own present day, and since the characters in the plays are partici-
pants in events that occurred in the past, the idea that the literary *personae* being depicted felt that the gods really existed may be predicated
for the implied audience of the allegedly actual events described by
Herodotus and the dramatists respectively.

This conviction, however, is not necessarily applicable to the real
reader or the listener-audience of these works either in antiquity or today. Because we sometimes confuse the implied reader or audience
with the real one, we erroneously conclude that when Herodotus and
any of the Greek dramatists, but particularly Aeschylus and Sophocles
depict the workings of the divine in history, they are presenting the re-

---

[10]   Ivan M. Linforth "Named and Unnamed Gods in Herodotus" *University
of California Publications in Classical Philology* 9 (1926-1929) 218. For the gods
as real see I. M. Linforth "Greek Gods and Foreign Gods in Herodotus" 1.

[11]   I. M. Linforth "Greek Gods and Foreign Gods in Herodotus" 1.

flections of a believing society in much the same way that the redactors of Primary History do in very similar circumstances and clearly toward the same end.[12] This error is compounded by the supposition that the redactors of Primary History or the members of the society of which they were a part all really subscribed to the theological precepts, including the presupposition that the divinity acts in history, they depicted. It is further compounded by the dogmatic rather than historical presumption that the "faithful" son of Israel of any period in question, including that of Ezra's day, of necessity differs from the "faithful" Athenian.

Although Herodotus' implied narrator's concern with the gods is basic to his narrative, superficially at least the gods are not his focal point. His major interest is the chain of causes (αἰτίαι) that brought the Greeks and Persians to war with one another.[13] For him these causes are the result of human actions. But at the same time, they are always in accordance with the divine plan that primarily but not exclusively emanates from Delphi. Hence, the implied narrator's aim and his approach are each theologically paradigmatic.

As is well known and as we have noted (above, Chapter One), there are numerous correspondences between Herodotus' work and Greek tragedy in general. Although we like to think of Greek drama as man focused, it is really predicated on and interested in the relationship between Great Men, that is heroes, and the gods. More specifically, it is in their relationship to their fellow men that many tragic and Herodotean Great Men play out their relationship to the divine. Hence, despite the frequent, but not ubiquitous multiplicity of godheads involved in the action of Greek tragedy and despite the predominantly singularity of the godhead in Herodotus' *History* in which both men and nations primarily play out Apollo's will whether or not they want to do so, there is a parallel between the exclusively tragic genre and the over-

---

12 The *communis opinio* that this is not true of Euripides has been shown to be invalid by Jon D. Mikalson *Honor Thy Gods: Popular Religion in Greek Tragedy* (Chapel Hill and London: The University of North Carolina Press, 1991) passim.

13 John L. Myres *Herodotus: Father of History* (Oxford: Oxford University/Clarendon, 1953) 47.

riding Herodotean genre. And as we have shown, this is a combination of epic, Roman à Clef, and Documentary Novel.

The same relationship exists between Great Men and the various gods in Primary History who, by the time of the Exile, had been subsumed into the monotheistically worshipped godhead. Significantly, therefore, Primary History is pervaded by the same type of dramatic elements that are found in Herodotus' *History*, which itself is pervaded by the elements of Ionic epic, to which it is subsequent insofar as we know, and Attic tragedy with which it is relatively concurrent.

In each, there are a number of pericopes in which the respective redactors depict events as they might have happened rather than as they happened, and others in which they give more than one portrayal of the same event. Despite his assurance that the transcription of Herodotus into verse would not make him the less an historian (εἴη γὰρ ἄν τὰ ʽΗροδότου εἰς μέτρα τεθῆναι, καὶ οὐδὲν ἧττον ἄν εἴη ἱστορία τις μετὰ ʽʼηετρου ἤ ἄνευ μέτρων [Poetics 1451b]), Aristotle basically contradicts himself as we have shown. Because Aristotle defines the poet as speaking of events which might have happened and the historian as speaking of those which have happened (τῷ τὸν μὲν τὰ γενόμενα λέγειν, τὸν δὲ οἷα ἄν γένοιτο [*Poetics* 1451b]),[14] by his definition, both Herodotus and the various redactors of Primary History are (like Homer—for Aristotle—or the redactors of Homeric Epic—for us)[15] poets and not historians.

---

14   Bruno Snell (*The Discovery of the Mind* T. G. Rosenmeyer, trans. [New York/Evanston: Harper & Row, 1960] 90) points out that Homer also does not fit this paradigm. The Homeric works were ideologically deemed to represent early Greek history in the same way that the mythological and legendary stories in Genesis were ideologically deemed to represent early pre- and early Israelite history.

15   Although there have been numerous attempts to prove the unity of Homeric authorship, we find none of them sufficiently convincing to vitiate the belief in multiple authorship or at least multiple redactions. Although the parallels between the "Homeric Question" and Redaction Criticism in Primary History are clear, and, in some cases, the early research into the redactions of both works was done by the same scholars or by scholars who were familiar with one another's work, the study of this particular relationship is beyond the scope of our present work.

Hence, it is not surprising that the historicity of parts of both Primary History and Herodotus' *History* has often been questioned.[16] What is interesting, however, is that only the earlier, "mythological" parts of the respective works are subject to skepticism. The last four books of both works are mostly taken for history.

But even in these so-called historical books, dramatic and narrative elements predominate. We iterate that throughout both Herodotus' *History* and Primary History the natural background of the narrative is not described. Moreover, "pure description," that is "description for its own sake" is lacking.[17]

This lack is not resultant on audience demand.[18] But rather, it reflects the fact that representation without an ultimate end was characteristic neither of epic nor of the religious exigencies of Attic tragedy which are fundamental to Herodotus' pseudo-tragic history.[19] And this type of representation is simply not necessary to enhance the literary sense, feeling, attitude, and particularly the tone of Primary History.

Similarly the explication of emotional and physiological elements is missing from Herodotus' analysis.[20] And it is also missing from Primary History in its received form. Again, this is characteristic of Attic drama, which, with perhaps the exception of some Euripidean plays, is concerned with neither the mind nor the body of its exemplars. As in Greek tragedy, Herodotus' implied narrator and those of the various redactors, or at least the overriding redactor of Primary History present the respective god's will and the intercession of his superhuman power as the prevailing bases, although perhaps not the de-

---

16   We must remember that Herodotus did not define his work as a "History" but rather an "Inquiry." Moreover, he chose the λόγος, which meant "what is said" (J. A. K. Thompson *The Art of the Logos* [London: George Allen & Unwin, 1935] 17) and which was a traditional format for oral narrative, as the basis of his architectonics.

17   J. A. K. Thompson *The Art of the Logos* 188.

18   As J. A. K. Thompson (*The Art of the Logos* 188-189) assumes.

19   Thus, it is surprising that Ph. -E. Legrand (*Hérodote: Introduction* [Paris: Société d' Édition <<Les Belles Lettres,>> 1955] 131) states that Herodotus' opinions about *res divinae* in book 2, for example, were historical rather than theological.

20   J. A. K. Thompson *The Art of the Logos*. 189-191.

terminants since these are relegated to human action, of the course of history.[21]

Moira (μοῖρα), nemesis (νέμησις), phthonos (φθόνος), ate (ἄτη) and hubris (ὕβρις), as well as other basic elements that form the underlying causes in the rise and fall of heroes, city-states, and occasionally nations in almost all of the works of Aeschylus, Sophocles, and even in many of Euripides' works are the roots of the rise and fall of each nation in Herodotus' *History*. They are the foundations of the presumed, but not depicted, eventually forthcoming fall of Athens and the subsequent fall of Sparta as well. It is perhaps quite significant that the real author, Herodotus, did not live to see the fall of either of these two city-states (πόλεις). But he could predict them as well as an ensuing disaster for all Greece.

Herodotus himself may have been and probably was responsible for the religious format of his λόγοι. There is no real basis for the assumption that Herodotus took his religious format from narratives and reports he had obtained and then applied it to his own account, as, for example, some assume he did in his the case of Cyrus and Cambyses.[22]

We do not know, however, whether this simply reflects a climate of opinion or an Herodotean intention to create a prose epic in tragic format. Our uncertainty is magnified by the fact that the same essentially religious concepts play a role in the pre-Socratic philosophies— however disguised—as well as in Attic tragedy.[23]

---

[21]   For Herodotus, see Ludwig Huber *Religiöse und politische Beweggründe des Handelns in der Geschichtsschreibung der Herod.* (PhD Diss.; Tübingen: Eberhard-Karls-Universität, 1965) 1. But see Ph. -E. Legrand (*Hérodote: Introduction* 133) for the concept of providence as an organizing force (as in Herodotus *History* 3.108) either inspired or even written by Hecataeus.

[22]   For this belief, see J. L. Myres *Herodotus: Father of History* 53.

[23]   In this chain, μοῖρα is antecedent to the ὕβρις which itself brings about ἄτη and its consequent φθόνις or νέμησις. This inevitable chain is to be found in a number of places. A representative example is the Scythian story of Artabanus' warning in the Croesus λόγος.

In any case, Herodotus' employment of theologically charged precepts in his *History,* whether for paradigmatic[24] or simply descriptive ends, is of major consequence. The various theological foundations and bases of the chain of causes (αἰτίαι) do play an architectonic role in the *History.*

In a work so concerned with the manifestation and acting out of what is fated, it is no accident that there are four major literary passages in which he presents μοῖρα as a man's fated end: that of Croesus (1.91), Cyrus (1.121), Polycrates (1.142) and Arcesilaus (4.164).[25] Since Herodotus primarily uses μοῖρα as "a share" or part of something,[26] these four passages are anomalous. He may have intentionally altered the λόγοι in which they are found so as to stress these essentially religious concepts and to reflect the prevalent belief in the theological basis of justice.

This same focus on the theological basis of justice is found in various strata of Primary History as inherited by Ezra. Alan Jenks has shown that the major theological emphasis of the 9th century Elohistic stratum of Primary History is, amongst other things, the:

> reflection on moral problems of sin, guilt, and forgiveness, with a general sensitivity to moral issues; and a thoroughly religious understanding of history.[27]

This metaphysical mode of historical thought is also characteristic of the 7th century Deuteronomist, who envisions Israel's entire historical development in terms of religiously defined categories. And this results in a "strongly didactic presentation of history."[28] Likewise the same viewpoint permeates the 6th century Priestly redaction. Moreover, in both redactions of the Deuteronomistic History, especially as it

---

[24]   In this case, it resembles the paradigmatic intent of Aeschylus' *Persians.* For Aeschylus' *Persians,* see William Chase Greene *Moira: Gate, Good, and Evil in Greek Thought* (New York: Harper & Row, 1963) 112-113.

[25]   J. L. Myres *Herodotus: Father of History* 48.

[26]   J. L. Myres *Herodotus: Father of History* 48.

[27]   Alan W. Jenks *The Elohist and North Israelite Traditions* (Missoula: Scholars, 1977) 66-67.

[28]   A. W. Jenks *The Elohist and North Israelite Traditions* 121.

is included in the final redaction of the totality of Primary History, we see a rather close,[29] but not exact parallel to the Greek tragic concept, which insofar as we know is subsequent to the redaction of the Essential Bible, but not the re-edited work of Ezra.[30] (1) Israel sins but the sins are hubristic and they are often the result of some form of divinely inflicted madness (ἄτη). (2) The Lord afflicts Israel. (3) This should lead to a recognition—implied though never really illustrated—in which Israel cries out to the Lord. (4) Then there is a reversal in which the Lord sends a savior.

This whole paradigm is repeated over and over but not *ad infinitum.* The preexilic Dtr[1] knew that the northern kingdom of Israel had fallen to the Assyrians in 722 BCE. The exilic Dtr[2] as well as other 6th century redactors and 5th century compilers or arrangers of any portion of the text each knew that the southern kingdom of Judah had fallen to the Babylonians in 586 BCE. Perhaps this knowledge itself is reflected in the overriding redactor's choice of what is clearly a tragic format for Primary History.

Significantly, therefore, W. Lee Humphreys has demonstrated that Primary History is replete with pericopes that are not only tragic in genre but are in the same format and contain the same elements as 5th century Athenian tragedy.[31] Humphreys has very properly applied R. B. Sewall's precepts[32] to individual pericopes in Old Testament. But Humphreys did not realize that the entire Primary History is itself intimately related to tragedy and is in (a somewhat modified, and possibly prior) analog of Greek tragic format.

Primary History commences with a short prologue (Genesis 1-11). This is followed by the introduction of the hero: *not Yahweh but rather the line that will eventually become the Israelites.* This hero is of noble lineage and better than most though with a tragic flaw, namely its pro-

---

[29]   *Nemesis* does not seem to be present in Primary History, however.

[30]   Despite our presumption that we can trace the development of Greek Tragedy on the basis of the scanty extant plays and in particular on the internal progression of the Aeschylean corpus, we really know very little about the entire process.

[31]   W. Lee Humphreys *The Tragic Vision and the Hebrew Tradition* Philadelphia: Fortress, 1985.

[32]   R. B. Sewall *The Vision of Tragedy* New Haven: Yale, 1952.

pensity to rebel repeatedly against the divinity whom it has chosen to worship. This tragic flaw brings about a series of events culminating in an explicit "recognition" and "reversal of the action."

The paradigm is particularly clear in the Deuteronomistic History. Israel's leaders' sins eventually lead to the division of the "united kingdom" into two nations, Israel and Judah. The leaders' continuing errors in judgment and/or sins eventually lead to the collapse of Israel in 722 and of Judah in 587/6.[33] The stress on the leaders' sins is characteristic of Dtr. And, moreover, we may assume that this is an ideological as well as a literary innovation because the writing prophets, composing their works during the latter part of the time frame depicted in DtrH— the eight, seventh, and sixth centuries—were castigating their own contemporaries; and in contrast to Dtr, they emphasized the peoples' rather than the leaders' sins.

The theological and literary parallels between Primary History, Herodotus' *History*, Aeschylean, Sophoclean, and even Euripidean Drama, then, are striking. Nevertheless the Attic dramatists were writing plays for presentation at the religious festivals, and Herodotus and the redactors of Primary History were each writing an ostensibly historical narrative.

There are also significant differences between the works in question. The narratology, including textual development, of Primary History and of Herodotus' *History* differ markedly from that of Attic tragedy, which is composed in verse. Most importantly, Attic tragedy is meant to be viewed, not read or simply heard. Hence, it is primarily in first person monologue and/or dialogue format rather than in a third person account.

Greek tragedy also contains some third person narrative, particularly, but not always in the choruses. Occasionally third person narrative is included in and, hence, is framed by the first person narrative of an individual character whose task it is to fill other characters and incidentally the audience in on background data.

---

[33] Primary History presents two characteristics of tragic drama, recognition and reversal, as occurring in Babylon.

On the other hand, the major portion, if not all of the narrative of Primary History is fictively treated and presented as if it were meant to be heard by an implied auditor rather than to be read by an implied reader. But the narratology suggests that with the possible exception of Deuteronomy,[34] which seems to be different even though this might not really be the case,[35] the opposite is true. In any case, the text of Primary History is primarily an omniscient third person prose narrative in which there is a relatively small percentage of first person narrative, and in which there is embedded an extremely small amount of narrative poetry that is from a far earlier period.

Analogously, Herodotus' *History* is to be read aloud to or by the implied reader/auditor. And it is primarily an omniscient third person prose narrative with a relatively small percentage of first person narrative and an extremely small amount of embedded poetry, much of which is also in third person narrative emanating from an earlier time—although not as early as the poetry in Primary History.

Like Primary History and Greek tragedy, Herodotus' *History* is replete with individuals who do commit hubris and suffer some form of divinely induced madness (ἄτη), which consequently leads to their own as well as their people's affliction. In fact, even when these characters themselves survive, their nation suffers. As we have seen and as

---

[34]   Robert Polzin (*MOSES and the DEUTERONOMIST (sic): A Literary Study of the Deuteronomic History* Part One [New York: Seabury: 1980] 10) notes that "the reporting speech of the narrator comprises only about fifty-six verses of the book." For a list of these verses see *ibid.* 29.

[35]   Perhaps Dtr treated the material he included in Deuteronomy as primarily first person so as to enhance his ideologically significant "you are there" illusion. Under Rabbinic normative theology today, each Israelite is considered a signatory to the Covenant whether or not he was present at Sinai or Horeb.

Although we do not know when this dogma was first accepted as valid and we cannot assume that it was normative for all or even any of the redactors of Primary History or even for the ἔθνος of the Jews during the Second Temple period, Dtr's first person presentation suggests that he may have held this tenet. We cannot make any suggestions about D's belief since we do not know whether the presentation emanating from D is representative of Dtr's overlaying perspective or of his own.

In any case, Dtr's decision to use first person must be deemed literary either in spite of, or in addition to any ideological justification for it. This usage represents a conscious choice on the part of the author/redactor even though it may be mandatory for the implied author/redactor as well as for the implied narrator.

the representation of the Persian defeat suggests, Herodotus is especially concerned with ἄτη and hubris as they relate to the implied fall of states and nations:[36] that is, he is concerned with the grand scale depiction of *History* despite his attention to the particular.

The actions of human beings are only of importance when they illustrate or actually bring about the greater thematic resolution of the *res divinae* of states and nations. It is their aggregation and not their individuation that is of significance in the divine scheme of events—as Herodotus is well aware. This attitude may be the result of Herodotus' more primitive and less ethical treatment of divine jealousy than that found in Pindar[37] or that of other Greeks of the time. Significantly, however, Herodotus' treatment of *res divinae* is no different than that of Aeschylus or Sophocles. Grene's observation that for Herodotus there is some form of divine plan within whose context Great Men act in such a way that divine jealousy must of necessity be manifest, and his observation of the divine protection of righteousness as being in accord with the world's plan[38] may well reflect a conservative 5th century religious *Weltanschauung*. The same may be said of Primary History, particularly DtrH.

The various redactors of Primary History, Ezra, and, with the exception of some of the pre-Socratic philosophers, most Greek writers both before and during the 5th century BCE, treat the gods as real and depict them as acting both directly and indirectly in history. They use various means to show the gods as effectively making their will known to man even though it is not always readily accepted by him.

In Herodotus' *History* as in the literature of the ancient Near East and in the Elohistic strata of Primary History, the gods frequently use oracles and dreams to make their will known to man (*e.g.*, Genesis 20: 3,6, 8; 21:4; 46:1-4 [possibly P]; *et alii;* Herodotus 1.209-210; *et alii)*.

---

36   William Chase Greene *Moira* 86-87.

37   W. C. Greene *Moira* 84, 87. We do not agree with Greene's classification of Aeschylus and Pindar as representative of a later, and more ethical interpretation (*idem* 84).

38   D. Grene "Introduction" *The History: Herodotus passim*; David Grene "Herodotus: The Historian as Dramatist" *The Journal of Philosophy* 58 (1961) 481-487, *et passim*. But, see J. L. Myres *Herodotus: Father of History* 50.

Thus, it is notable that Herodotus shows divine intervention via dreams far more frequently than does Homer. In fact, he does so with about the same frequency as found in the received redaction of Primary History.

Divine intervention in dreams is so common a phenomenon in the ancient world, that its presence in various literatures and theologies may represent more than a prevalent *Weltanschauung*. In particular, the relationship between Homeric epic and such Sumerian, Assyro-Babylonian religious literature as the extant portions of some of the various redactions of Gilgamesh as well as other Mesopotamian literature has been proven by Assyriologists and Classicists alike. Likewise the relationship between Mesopotamian and other ancient Near Eastern literatures has also been amply illustrated. Moreover, the resemblance between Herodotus and Homer in regard to divine intervention in human history has long been accepted.

Thus, by extension, a relationship between Herodotus' theological perspective and that of some ancient Near Eastern writers can be posited. Since Herodotus hailed from Halikarnassus, a city-state that bordered on Caria and had been part of the Persian Empire, it is even possible that Herodotus was directly influenced by ancient Near Eastern religious precepts without Homeric mediation.

For the authors/redactors of much ancient Near Eastern literature, for the Elohist, and even for the two Deuteronomistic Historians (Dtr[1] and Dtr[2]), for the 5th century Greek dramatists whose works are partially extant, and for Herodotus, the godly origin of dreams is generally presented as if it were taken for granted,[39] and as we have seen the dreams themselves are often some form of theophany. I. Mendelsohn's observation that "The OT recognizes one source of dreams: all night visions proceed from God, and his assistance is sought in interpreting them"[40] is particularly important, especially in conjunction with Jensen's note that "Oracular responses by priest or seer might also

---

[39]   See above for a dream theophany as a real manifestation of the divinity.
[40]   I. Mendelsohn "Dream" *IDB (1962) s.v.*

have been given on the basis of dreams...."[41] Clearly, it is not a coincidence that dreams often serve to bring about the realization of fate.

In any case, the gods act directly on the human plane, which as we have seen is fused with the divine, in Herodotus' *History*, Primary History and Aeschylean and Sophoclean Greek drama. Thus, for example, in almost all the Greek tragedies, the gods, be they Olympian or other, are fully functioning *dramatis personae*. In fact, in Aeschylus' *Prometheus Bound*, they are the *dramatis personae*. In Herodotus' work, Apollo personally acts in defense of his treasury (*History* 8.35-39; 9.42)[42] and in Primary History, Elohim in person visits Abraham (*e.g.*, Genesis 17:1-18:15), or Yahweh or Elohim talks with Moses or *vice versa* (Exodus 3:4, 11, 13; 4:1, 10, 13; 5:22, 6:12a; 15:1 ff [[here Moses and the Israelites sing to the divinity]; 17:4; 19:23; 32:11, 31; 33:12, 15, 18; Numbers 10:35, 11:21; 12:13; 16:15, 22, *et passim).*

All the works in question have countless other examples of direct contact between god(s) and men, (and in both the Greek and ancient Near Eastern works, of contact between gods and other gods). This clearly shows that their authors or redactors portrayed the god(s), be they acting alone or amongst themselves or interacting with mankind, as doing so in a form of *History* in which there is no distinction between secular and sacred time and space (above).

Herodotus' use of moira (μοῖρα), ate (ἄτη), hubris (ὕβρις), and other tragic elements such as nemesis (νέμησις) or phthonos (φθόνος) as the basis of the pattern in which both men and nations that rise to great heights are destined to fall shows that this very expectation represents a divine plan. Moreover, Herodotus' inclusion of this divine plan in the architectonics of his *History* is indicative of his attitude toward history.[43] Again, we must iterate and stress that the gods do act in history although their actions are not always direct and they are not always comprehensible to mankind.

---

[41]   Joseph Jensen *God's Word to Israel* (3rd edition Wilmington: Michael Glazier, 1986) 149 note 2.

[42]   J. L. Myres *Herodotus: Father of History* 51.

[43]   But see J. L. Myres (*Herodotus: Father of History* 57 *et passim*) for the belief that there is no divine plan at work in Herodotus' depiction of events.

Thus, Herodotus' distinction between the asserted pretext for an event and the "real 'motive' to which *arche* gives initiative and occasion"[44] must be extended beyond the individual λόγοι into the architectonics of the work. The basis of this is the dogmatic belief that the real motivation for man's actions is ultimately some divine plan, which need not emanate solely from an individual divinity.

The relationship between Herodotus' *History* and Primary History becomes evident when we acknowledge that the coordination of a divine plan with human action in Herodotus' *History* is heightened by Herodotus' almost monotheistic attitude despite his acknowledgment of the multiplicity of divinities.[45] Significantly, the overriding redactor of Primary History, probably Dtr[2], like his predecessor Dtr[1], has not only inherited the Elohistic concept of a divine design, which, as Jenks has stated "is known in advance and understood by men because God reveals himself...'to his servants the prophets' ",[46] but he also assumes the indivisibility of the syncretized deity whose actions in history form the basis of his narrative. In fact, for either Dtr, the actions of the divinity in history are so explicit that they are treated formulaically even when the event differs from the standard presentation. Moreover, for P, the god who took Israel out of Egypt has contractually set certain stipulations; and whenever the nation as a whole or even individual Sons of Israel disregarded these conditions, they were to be accounted as sinning.

The deity in Primary History is not a *deus ex machina*. Rather, he is a *persona* within the more often than not dramatic narrative in which he plays so active a role that the text can be considered a limited, divine biography. Thus, it is not surprising that Primary History has been treated as an account of the Lord God's mighty acts in history as if the deity rather than the Sons of Israel were its hero.

Interestingly enough, even the non-syncretized Israelite and pre-Israelite deities are treated as literary *personae,* whose actions are being represented biographically within the narrative. Hence, by definition

---

44   J. L. Myres *Herodotus: Father of History* 56.
45   For the treatment of the multiple gods as if they were a monolithic entity, see I. M. Linforth "Named and Unnamed Gods in Herodotus" 218.
46   A. W. Jenks *The Elohist and North Israelite Traditions* 32.

Yahweh, Elohim, El, El Shaddai, and all the other godheads of the Is-raelites and their forebears are literary *personae* who act within the narrative context of history. However, for both the 10th century Yah-wist and the 9th century Elohist, it is always man who brings about that which the god both wills and executes.

In this regard, the perspective of Aeschylus, Sophocles, or Herodo-tus does not differ from that of the any of the redactors of Primary His-tory. Likewise, it does not differ from the perspective of the entire work as understood by Ezra. All depict the manifestation of divine will and the intervention of superhuman power as the foundation of the course of history. For them, humans can and do make choices but un-less a hero was allotted more than one prospective fate, the options are limited to those necessary for working out the predetermined end.

Hence, it is not surprising that although the narratives are primarily focused on the relationship between men or between men and gods, they also pay attention to the relationships between the gods them-selves. At times, then, the Greek texts are concerned with the relation-ship between Zeus and Prometheus, as in *Prometheus Bound;* and in Primary History, there is, for example, a concern with the relationship between Yahweh-Elohim and Baal, be the latter's godhead denied or not.

In fact, the thematic denigration or refutation of foreign gods as well as the syncretization of Israelite gods is found throughout Primary History. But this may not go back as far as we think. It may only re-flect a theological overlay emanating from the circle of the Deu-teronomistic Historians or that of the Priestly Redactor. In any case, we iterate that in contrast to earlier beliefs, possibly for the penulti-mate, and certainly for the monotheistic final redactor of Primary His-tory, the godhead is and is presented as if the redactor assumed he had always been singular.

Since we are comparing the final form of the respective texts—even when we pick out individual redactions, we must still presume the corrective and editorial hand of the final redactor,—we may attribute the correspondences between the various works to some form of inter-action between the Greeks and the Jews of the Restoration.

On the other hand, these correspondences may simply reflect some prevailing climate of opinion during the 6th and 5th century BCE. Thus, we may at least assume that their depiction of men and gods was well within the boundaries of accepted religious thought of the 6th or 5th century BCE world.

Not only is there a commonalty of thought and *Weltanschauung*, but of literary technique as well. Clearly, therefore, the striking similarity between the problems in the textual analysis of Herodotus' *History* and those albeit somewhat more complicated in that of Primary History indicates that the use of nothing other than style to differentiate between authors and/or redactors who use identical methodologies is infeasible.[47]

We can only come to an understanding of either text by analyzing each of its facets. Hence we have to supplement our examination of the technique of each author/redactor with a systematic study of other aspects of the works so as to resolve the textual conundrums. In particular, we have to consider such matters as the coincidences in dating; correspondences in the overall format involving literary techniques such as where, under what circumstances, and to what end the author/redactor employs parataxis as opposed to hypotaxis or vice versa; matches in the arrangement of the books; and the use of similar or identical motifs and/or technical terminology.

Thus, it is particularly notable that there is a 5th century dating for Ezra's editing of Primary History and Herodotus' composition of his *History*. Additionally, as we have seen, the two works have parallel motifs, parallel technical usages, and parallel literary techniques. They also have the same number of books. They both depict the same type of back and forth, easterly-westerly and vice versa voyaging of important personages in the first book, which concludes in Egypt in Primary History, and which sets the stage for Egypt in Herodotus' work.

Both focus on Egypt in parts of the second, although in Exodus, the concern is with the escape from that land and in Herodotus' it is with events in it. And Herodotus' *History*, whose Egyptian λόγος is

---

47   In fact, it pertains to all types of literary analyses in which there is more than one author or more than one redactor or both.

found in book 2, devotes more of the book to Egypt than does Primary History, whose Egyptian pericope bridges Genesis and Exodus. Therefore it is interesting that Herodotus continues to discuss Egypt in the first thirty chapters of book 3, albeit interspersed with Egyptian-Persian interaction, and he mentions Egypt elsewhere in this same book. This may well have let his λόγος appear to bridge the two later differentiated books although in fact it does not do so (Chapter One).

Both works depict events in a form of never-never land in their respective forth book, and this also serves as a literary and spatial reflex to Egypt and the Egyptian experience in the second; the same passage from never-never land to the historic land and its appendages (the Eastern city-states on the Asiatic coast or on Islands for Herodotus, and the tribal territories on the Eastern side of the Jordan for the final redaction of Primary History), via a transitional fifth book occurs in both works; and books 6 through 9 treat events in and about the homeland with a sense of impending doom, in both works.

There is some little paratactic variation of λόγοι/pericopes in both Primary History and Herodotus' History.[48] For the most part this is found within the encompassing λόγοι/pericopes of the respective minor series, which themselves are primarily arranged hypotactically.[49] On the other hand, the major series of λόγοι/pericopes is strung together hypotactically until that sequence reaches a principal turning point, a dramatic reversal of action. Then, there is a literary pause in the text after which a new major sequence begins. Occasionally, but not of necessity, this new sequence is in parataxis to the prior one.[50]

---

[48]   See above for the Sinai and Horeb pericopes, for example, as paratactic pericopes in Primary History. For the use of paratactic pericopes in Herodotus, see Henry R. Immerwahr *Form and Thought in Herodotus* (Cleveland: Western Reserve University, 1966) 7.

[49]   We are not referring to the use of parataxis or hypotaxis within sentences or larger grammatical units per se (for which see Erika Lamberts' published dissertation (*Studien zu Parataxe bei Herodot* Wien: Notrig, 1970), but rather the paratactic and hypotactic relationships, wherever they occur between both major and minor λόγοι respectively.

[50]   For the parallelism between the parts, see W. W. How and J. Wells *A Commentary on Herodotus* (2 volumes; New York: Oxford University, 1989) 1.46-47.

In Primary History, the Sinai and the Horeb pericopes parallel one another. There is a caesura and concomitant peripeteia after the description of Covenant conclusion at Sinai. There is a paratactic caesura and concomitant peripeteia in describing Israel at Horeb. Both of these narratives are jointed together again in Deuteronomy 27, which represents the high or at least the breaking point in the narrative that comprises Primary History. This is made to coincide with Israel's understanding of Covenant prior to entrance into the Land. Significantly, an interruption at Deuteronomy 27 gives 76,500 words for the first part of Primary History and 73,500 words for the second, almost dividing the work in half.[51]

In Herodotus' *History*, there is an analogous caesura and concomitant peripeteia that occurs with the commencement of the Ionian Revolt λόγος, which event "marked a new stage in" the escalation of the conflict between Europe and Asia. This intensified gradation had actually begun with the Croesus λόγος and it coincides with a change of focus from the history of the conflict between Europe and Asia, specifically to that between the Greeks and Persia.[52] Most significantly, it leads up to Marathon—a battle only equaled in ideological significance for the Greeks by the fall of Troy.

Herodotus begins his *History* with an introduction (an unnumbered superscription followed by what are now chapters 1.1.1-1.5.3).[53] This is followed by a prehistory of the Greek people, which purports to be a universal history (1.6.1-1.94.6). After this there is a truncated prehistory of 5th century Greece[54] that the implied narrator presents in the guise of describing the Persian conquest of the Asiatic Greeks (1.14.1-1.176.3) and which is properly, therefore, followed by a "Cyrus"

---

[51] By word count, the actual midpoint of the narrative falls in Deuteronomy 22. But contextually this falls in the middle of a pericope and, therefore, is not as significant as the juncture of the two narrative lines that comes at Deuteronomy 27.

[52] See, for example, J. A. S. Evans *Herodotus* (Boston: Twayne, 1982) 79. Herodotus assumes that the conflict really began when Croesus subjugated the coastal Greek cities (Evans *ibid.* 79). For him, therefore, the Ionian revolt represented the point of reversal of action. But modern historians would treat Croesus' *res gestae* as antecedents of the war, whose initiating cause was the Ionian revolt.

[53] The numeration is late and cannot be attributed to Herodotus himself.

[54] This whole entity is often called the Lydian λόγος.

(minor) λόγος (1.177.1-1.216.2). This is followed by an Egyptian (major) λόγος (2.2.2-2.182.1) in which Herodotus explicitly distinguishes between Minos and Polycrates in the midst of his Egyptian λόγος and he concomitantly differentiates between the prehistoric and the historic eras.[55]

The Egyptian λόγος (2.2.2-2.182.1), at whose beginning there is an attempt to ascertain the origins of language (2.2.1-2.3.1), would seem to be out of place; hence, the parallel architectonics in primary history are particularly noteworthy. Moreover, it may be significant, although perhaps merely incidental, that as soon as Herodotus finishes his Egyptian λόγος, he refers to the Palestinian-Syrians (3.5.1) in a brief transitional passage (3.1.3-3.16.5).

An analysis of the structure of Primary History shows that the text begins with an introduction (Genesis 1-11), all or part of which itself served as an introduction to the entire Pentateuch[56] and thematically, to the entire Primary History. By presenting the expulsion from Babylon toward the end of the introduction (Genesis 11:8) and the return to Babylon toward the end of Primary History (2 Kings 24:12-17; 25:6-11), the final redactor of the text stressed that the basic context of the work is the rise and fall of the Israelite nation in the context of a spiritual and physical journey from Babylon back to Babylon. That is, he presented Israel's history as cyclically based. For the Israelites, Babylon is the real place of beginnings and endings.

It is significant that Abram is introduced as part of a genealogical coda-like passage (Genesis 11:29) that concludes the introduction and serves as a transition to the narrative proper, which begins with the account of the three patriarchs, Abraham, Isaac, and Jacob (Genesis 12:1-49:33). It is from these patriarchs that the Israelite nation will arise, not from the nameless people who were scattered over the earth.

Notably, even the patriarchal sagas contained in the narrative depict journeys, both spiritual and physical. The most meaningful of

---

[55] W. W. How and J. Wells "Introduction" *A Commentary on Herodotus* 1.32.

[56] For Genesis 1-11 as the introduction to the entire Pentateuch, see Claus Westermann *Genesis* (2nd edition Neukirchen-Vluyn: Neukirchener, 1976) 2. In fact Genesis 1-11 is also the introduction to the entire Primary History.

these is contained in the tangential and contextually subsequent, but textually overlapping Joseph Novella (Genesis 37:2-50:26) that integrates the Jacob saga into its plot. It is no accident that the account of the descent into, and sojourn in Egypt, which may be an inverse parallel or at least an analog to the expulsion from Babylon, is presented here.

The prologue to Primary History (Genesis 1-11) included a prehistory of the Israelite people that purports to be a universal history. It ends with what has been called an etiological story for the origin of languages[57] although this conclusion has a far more basic function in the narrative than that.

Genesis 1-11 was influenced by and reflects ancient Near Eastern religious precepts. The redactors' of Primary History were only tangentially interested in the beginning of the universe and man, and this topic is peripheral to their main, meta-historical, purpose: to explain and depict the rise of civilization. Herodotus also was far more concerned with the commencement of civilization than with the origins of the universe and man. Thus, he sought to define the first people to be truly human by ascertaining who was the first nation to possess the one uniquely human characteristic, speech.[58]

In any case, the divine figures and human beings do converse in the Primeval History (Genesis 1-11); but there is no mention of the nature of the language prior to the pericope depicting the tower of Babylon. The Yahwist could have had the same aim for including the tower of Babylon and the etiology of multiple languages in his implied narrator's narrative (Genesis 11:1-9) as Herodotus did for including the origin of language (*History* 2.2.1-3.1) in his.

Man becomes civilized when he develops language. But he becomes ethnicized or nationalized by virtue of a distinct language. Con-

---

[57]   For this as an etiological story, see John Van Seters *In Search of History: Historiography in the Ancient World and the Origins of Biblical History* (New Haven: Yale University, 1983) 28.

[58]   We now know that other mammals communicate and some even communicate verbally. (The computer now permits the Great Apes to communicate verbally with man). This obviously was not known to Herodotus, for whom as for all civilized men until recently, speech is defined by words as we conceive them, and represents a peculiarly human characteristic.

sequently, the juncture where "primeval history and sacred history dovetail"[59] is of particular importance. Not only is the basic plot line of an expulsion that is to end in a return introduced here, but this juncture also forms a demarcation point at which the changes from the general to the particular, from a language to languages, from a universal-history to ethno-history become operative.

Thus, as the Primeval History with which the work commenced concerned itself with universal motifs, the remainder of Primary History concerned itself with the Sons of Israel. Other nations are only considered when they have some bearing on the Sons of Israel.

But in particular, whoever placed Genesis 11:1-9 in its present position is, like Herodotus, showing that the primeval state ends and civilization begins only when mankind has language(s). It is the beginning of civilization and not the etiology of language, be it multiple or singular, that is important for Herodotus' implied narrator. And it is of equal importance for the Yahwist's implied narrator—if the Yahwist, who composed this segment, really is responsible for its placement in this portion of the narrative rather than somewhere else.

The genealogy of the sons of Noah's son Shem, from whom the Israelites stem, is the conclusion of the introduction and serves as a coda-like transition into the narrative proper of the Pentateuch[60] and of Primary History in its entirety. The presentation of this genealogy so that it concludes with Terach's journey into Canaan and his death (Genesis 11:31-32), but only after the narrator has introduced Abram into the account, emphasizes the Yahwist's belief that there is a clear break between prehistory and history, and only the history of the Sons of Israel and their post-scattering forefathers really matters. Consequently, even for the Yahwist, temporal history had to have its beginning at Babylon.

This suggests that the Elohist may well have began his narrative with Abraham's call (Genesis 15:1-6)[61] rather than with creation be-

---

59   Gerhard von Rad *Genesis: A Commentary* (revised edition Philadelphia: Westminster, 1972) 153.

60   For this transition, see C. Westermann *Genesis* 746 *ad* 11: 10-26.

61   For E as a substratum of Genesis 15:1-6, see A. W. Jenks *The Elohist and North Israelite Traditions* 34.

cause for him, the "prehistory" did not matter either. Therefore, unlike the Yahwist, who begins his story with creation but was really focused on those who were to be identified as immediate progenitors of the Sons of Israel, the Elohist and Herodotus, who both take creation and prehistory as a given and focus on mankind, were primarily interested in the period when a flourishing mankind was developing a new relationship with the divinity.[62]

The genealogy of the sons of Noah's son Shem after the post-Babylon scattering (Genesis 11:10-32) is fundamentally different from that of the sons of Noah after the flood (Genesis 10:11-32). Shem's sons are part of humanity and are living in an historical time that has coalesced with sacred time. In contrast, Noah's sons are still mythological figures who live in purely sacred time that is portrayed as if it were historical. It is not an accident, therefore, that the narration comprised of the Abraham, Isaac, and Jacob pericopes, which together form a literary unit serving as a truncated Israelite prehistory in which the implied narrator reports the beginning of Israel's rise, follows this minor genealogical pericope (Genesis 10:11-11:32), which itself concludes the major universal prehistory pericope that began with Genesis 1:1.[63]

Significantly, the final redactor of Primary History clearly tied the end of Israel's history to its beginning. The early parts of Genesis (Genesis 1-11), in which the narrator describes the creation of the world and particular events in the lives of the patriarchs depicted in them, takes place in sacred time and sacred space. But in order to set creation and the early patriarchs in real time and, consequently, history, the sense of timelessness basic to the myths, legends and sagas that form the basis of the text is obfuscated.

Once the reader believes that the events and people portrayed in Genesis 1-11 are historical insofar as he thinks that they occur in secular time and space, the narrative in which they are depicted can serve

---

62   The strictly Elohistic redaction of this call has been contested (*e.g.*, G. von Rad *Genesis* 182-183; A. W. Jenks *The Elohist and North Israelite Traditions* 33-34).

63   See J. Van Seters (*In Search of History* 28) for this as a prologue to Abraham's "story".

as an introduction to the account of the "history" proper.[64] Hence, even though the report describes events that occur in sacred time and space, the reader—both implied and real—perceives Genesis 1-11 as forming an *historical* prologue to the epic.[65]

Therefore, despite the prologue's great theological significance, its structural role is simply to set the scene for the body of the epic, whose fundamental theme is the depiction of the coming into being, the life, and the near but not total fall of the Sons of Israel. Thus it is only to be expected that their end at Babylon seems to be the completion of an historical cycle that had its beginning at Babylon.

The (human) predecessors of the Sons of Israel, not yet having established their national identity and, therefore, not yet being named as a nation, go forth from Babylon at the end of the introduction to Primary History. The surviving Sons of Israel, the Judahites, having lost their national identity, and, hence, their name, return to Babylon at the end of Primary History. Significantly, from the perspective of the nations—although not from that of the Judahites, for whom the defeat was inflicted on them by their own god,—the Judahites' god was also defeated. Hence, when the Babylonians brought the Temple pillars and artifacts to Babylon (2 Kings 25:13-17), they would have seen themselves as bringing the god of that temple into exile as well.

Those former Judahites, now in exile, did not share the conqueror's perspective. They could not envision the defeat of their god! Rather, for them, the Babylonian victory that resulted in the overthrow of the Judahite nation was part of the divinity's plan; but the cyclic basis of the narrative of Primary History itself suggests that that victory was not to be the end of the nation. It is for this reason that Yahweh's eventual *Rib* or law case against Judah for covenant violation is perhaps

---

64   Thus, Gary A. Rendsburg (*The Redaction of Genesis* [Winona Lake: Eisenbrauns, 1986] 7, 25, 26, 28) sees Genesis 1:1-11:26 as "an integrated unit" pertaining to universal history, whereas Genesis 12 ff., is only concerned with the Israelites and thus, "particularistic" (*ibid.* 28). See also Hermann Gunkel (*The Legends of Genesis: The Biblical Saga & History* [New York: Schocken, 1964] 13) for the separation at 11:26 between stories having the entire world as their focus and those whose interest is focused on Canaan and the adjoining regions.

65   For this portion as prologue, see D. J. A. Clines *The Theme of the Pentateuch* 61.

even more developed and built up as a leitmotif throughout Primary History than is the earlier law case against Israel. Its intent is to show that Yahweh is responsible for the defeat and loss of identity of his people, but that he himself was not defeated.

Clearly it is the divestiture of nationality, a status predicated on possession, or at least the right to possession of the Land, that itself gives the quondam-Judahites in exile in Babylon the potential for either a rebirth or a new birth from the surviving "shoot," but under a forgiving Yahweh. Those who have not died, cannot be reborn; those who have not been disenfranchised, cannot be re-enfranchised.

In any case, Babylon as a place of exile is a reversal of Babylon as a place of dispersal. And, hence, for the overall redactor of Primary History, all humanity is seen as once again gathered at the place from whence it was once scattered. Just as Israel's prehistory (Genesis 1-11) ends in Babylon, its history also ends there. At the end of 2 Kings, the exiles are back in Babylon. Thus, the final redactor probably conceived of the entire Primary History from Genesis 11 through 2 Kings as a subtending pericope, depicting the rise, hubris, and fall of the Sons of Israel.

But there is yet another basic paradigm in which the leitmotif is that the nation goes from Egypt to Egypt. Despite the overlapping of the Jacob and Joseph accounts, a clearly demarcated pericope begins with Israel's descent into, its stay in, and its escape from Egypt; and this may be defined as an Egyptian pericope.[66] Strikingly, Egypt which was first a place of salvation for Israel and his sons, became a place of suffering and virtual exile for them. Likewise, at the end of Primary History, Egypt is depicted as a place of salvation. Perhaps, we may infer that it will become a place of suffering and virtual exile once again.

R. E. Friedman sets forth what he calls "a compelling case for seeing the literary history of the Deuteronomistic History as comprising two editions, the first Josianic (Dtr[1]), the second Exilic (Dtr[2])."[67] But

---

[66]   Notably, the second book and second major λόγος in Herodotus is his Egyptian λόγος.

[67]   Richard Elliott Friedman "From Egypt to Egypt: Dtr[1] and Dtr[2]" *Traditions in Transformation: Turning Points in Biblical Faith* (Baruch Halpern and Jon D. Levenson, ed. Winona Lake: Eisenbrauns, 1981) 185.

his argument presents an interesting conundrum in that, on the one hand, we may assume a distinction between Dtr² and a different, final redactor, who is responsible for integrating the various components of Primary History into one meaningful unit; and, on the other hand, we may also assume that they could be the same person.

Notably, the leitmotif of a journey from Babylon to Babylon in relationship to another leitmotif, that of Israel's history as a journey from Egypt to Egypt,[68] may possibly be a means of distinguishing the final redaction of Primary History from DtrH as revised and redacted by Dtr². It also suggests, but is not a sufficient or definitive proof that Dtr² was the penultimate rather than the final redactor of Primary History as found in the Essential or Fundamental Bible, and that the final redaction must then be attributed to another, unknown person or group.

Since, if there were two redactors of DtrH, Dtr¹ is Josianic, he could not be responsible for the leitmotif "from Babylon to Babylon." And since Dtr² is exilic he knew that the Judahites, at least those who counted from a theological perspective, had returned to Babylon. Either he is different from the redactor who used the "from Babylon to Babylon" leitmotif, or he really is the final redactor of the narrative and he had his own reasons for presenting the leitmotifs "from Egypt to Egypt" and "from Babylon to Babylon" in tandem with one another.

The latter hypothesis is made quite viable by R. E. Friedman's observation:

> The final sentence of the story of the people states: 'And all the people, young and old, and the officers of the soldiers arose and came to Egypt, for they feared the Babylonians' (2 Kings. 25:26).[69]

There may well be not one, but two subtending pericopes in Primary History, then.

Analogously, the whole of Herodotus' narrative may be conceived of as having two subtending λόγοι: the first depicting the rise, hubris,

---

68   For the view that the journey was from Egypt to Egypt, see R. E. Friedman "From Egypt to Egypt: Dtr¹ and Dtr²" 167-192.
69   R. E. Friedman "From Egypt to Egypt: Dtr¹ and Dtr²" 189.

and fall of Persia, and the second, the rise, hubris, and, by implication, the projected fall of Greece.

Once he concludes the introduction, Herodotus begins his narrative with early Greek history. Not only are there analogies between the *Weltanschauungen*, at least of the implied narrators, but there are literary correspondences in the two works as well.

Herodotus' *History* and Primary History are definitely both didactic and national chronicles (in the non-technical sense), and, as we have seen, they were also prose epics[70] in despite of their prologues.[71] Notably, however, they differ from both *Iliad* and *Odyssey* in two very important and salient ways. The Homeric works are not national epics; and each of them is about half the length of either Herodotus' *History* or Primary History. The Hellenistic (Alexandrian) Grammarians may have paid particular attention to Primary History and Herodotus' *History* in tandem with one another precisely because they were both didactic, and thus representative of a genre that was particularly popular during the Hellenistic era, and because they were clearly national epics albeit in prose.

Primary History is presented as a tragic, primarily prose combined Roman à Clef and Documentary Novel in epic format. Even if the respective works were not divided in parallel formats, then, they would have to be considered somewhat analogous to one another. Herodotus' *History* is also presented as a tragic, primarily prose Roman à Clef and Documentary Novel in epic format, depicting the coming into being, the life, and giving signs of the potential fall of the Greek "nation" or its specific component parts, with its potential for rebirth.

---

70   Although all the examples usually classified as epic are in verse, particularly in dactylic hexameter, we do not know whether verse was a *sine qua non* for a lengthy work to be defined as epic even during the period of the early Homeridae. In fact, since our knowledge is predicated on the traditions found in *extant* literature and on statements in Aristotle's *Poetics* that represent his *opinion* and may not have been commonly accepted even in his own time, there is no real basis for our presumption that all epics were in verse. What we have may not be representative of the whole of the genre.

71   In the case of Herodotus, the architectonic prologue comprised of the events depicted in the books prior to the Ionian Revolt is meant here. This is not the same as the literary prologue.

And like Dtr[2], who sees sin and punishment as basic to his narrative, Herodotus sees crime and punishment as basic to the cycle depicted in his account. Although Herodotus renders this rise and fall as one in a chain of the events upon which the history of the world is built, he does so in such a way that the rise and fall of other nations prior to the Ionian revolt is also an historical prologue to the main theme of his narrative, which the Hellenistic Grammarians may well have treated as a national epic.

Because the accounts of Homer and the Homeridae are not national epics despite their use as such both in antiquity and ever after, the Hellenistic Grammarians would not have compared either Primary History or Herodotus' *History*, each of which tells the story of either one or more folk or nations, with the Homeric writings save under the generalized rubric of ἔπος,[72] which includes more than epic proper.

Albright suggested that there were "recensional differences between the Hebrew and the Greek texts" of the books that comprise Primary History, emanating from *different pre-Hellenistic* Hebrew recensions.[73] This lends credence to the hypothesis that the Grammarians may have been aware of the major structural units of Primary History, maybe in other text types or recensions than that of the Septuagint, and perhaps even of a Vorlage of MT. So the Hellenistic Grammarians in Pergamum or Alexandria, having access to the Hebrew Scriptures in Greek and to Targums in Aramaic, and those in Alexandria having ac-

---

[72]   *Iliad,* for example, tells of the wrath of Achilles just as *Odyssey* tells of the wanderings and homecoming of Odysseus, and the Alexandrian *Argonautica* tells of Jason and the Argonauts. On the other hand, Virgil's *Aeneid* is somewhat different. Although it presents the story of Aeneas' wanderings and his founding of a new nation in Italy, it is an intentional blending of a personal epic with national history, whose intent is to support Augustan ideology.

What little we understand of the early Homeridae suggests the same type of story telling as in Homer, but possibly with less skill. And the Hellenistic epic writers, the so called "Alexandrian Homeridae" (including Apollonius of Rhodes), were relating the same sort of tale as Homer though perhaps with less passion.

[73]   William Foxwell Albright *Yahweh and the Gods of Canaan: A Historical Analysis of Two Contrasting Faiths* (Winona Lake: Eisenbrauns, undated reprint of 1968 School of Oriental and African Studies edition) 28-29.

cess to Hebrew texts as well,[74] would have recognized the epic and national type category parallels. And, consequently, they would have perceived both works as being built on the same paradigm.

But most significantly, it is precisely the late dating of Primary History and the outlook about the divine we have already discussed that is so important for our supposition that there is a relationship between Herodotus' *History* and Primary History or between Herodotus himself and the redaction of Primary History received and re-divided by Ezra during the 5th century BCE. Since, for all practical purposes, Ezra's era coincides with that in which Herodotus was writing his work, we can assume either that Herodotus was influenced by Primary History, both as Ezra had received it and as he re-divided it, or that the data Herodotus received had been influenced by Primary History even before the time of Ezra. The evidence afforded by the near parallels in variant book divisions in both works, however, suggests the former. The later hypothesis is unlikely precisely because it presupposes that Herodotus himself divided his books in the received format.

We have discussed the presence of correlative leitmotifs and the mutual conformance of the ordering of λόγοι/pericopes. Additionally, however, the congruity in book ordering is extremely significant to our belief that there is more than an accidental relationship between the two works. In fact, the division of both Herodotus' *History* and Primary History into *nine* books is of paramount relevance to the argument that there is some degree of contiguity between Herodotus' *History* and Primary History.

---

[74]   We assume the latter on the basis of the traditions regarding the translation of LXX from an Hebrew Text, albeit of a different tradition than that of MT, having taken place in Alexandria. We do not really know who did the translating although the tradition relates that they were Jews who were conversant in both languages.

But the tradition is ideologically oriented. If, in reality, the translations had been done by or under the supervision of the Grammarians, then there is a question of their fluency in Hebrew and/or their first hand knowledge of the texts. Although the Grammarians may have only had access to those who understood Hebrew and not to the texts in Hebrew, this is not likely—particularly for those known for their scholarship and their love of collecting "books."

It is unlikely that the Hellenistic Grammarians, who not only collected but edited books and who had been exposed to number mysticism of many types, were not cognizant of the number symbolism inherent in their division of Herodotus' *History* and in the division of
Primary History as they may have inherited it. In any case, if the same
Grammarians studied both Herodotus' work and Primary History, they
would have been aware of the literary and historical parallels between
the two texts. But if Gunkel's hypothesis regarding the nine part apportionment of the introduction (Genesis 1-11) is valid,[75] the number nine
may have had some particular meaning for the final redactor of Primary History centuries before the Hellenistic scholars edited, arranged,
or simply analyzed and wrote scholia to the various texts that came
into their hands.

Although we do not know how Herodotus divide his book, we do
appreciate that Herodotus' *History* was divided into its present nine
books by or during the Hellenistic-early Roman era just as Primary
History was divided into its present nine books.[76] The Hellenistic-early
Roman divisions for Herodotus may have been traditional, but it is
equally possible that they had no relationship to earlier divisions. On
the other hand, we can state with conviction that the Pentateuch was
separated off from the other Biblical books in the time of or, as we believe, by Ezra. Moreover, as we have already noted, there is a demarcation in Primary History between the Pentateuchal narrative and the
Deuteronomistic History; between the artificially truncated
Tetrateuchal narrative (if it existed as such), Deuteronomy with its
Deuteronomistic framework, and the Deuteronomistic History; between that same Tetrateuchal narrative and the Deuteronomistic History including the framework of Deuteronomy, as Noth suggests;[77] and

---

75   Gerhard von Rad "The Form-Critical Problem of the Hexateuch" *The
Problem of the Hexateuch and Other Essays* (London: SCM, 1984) 62.

76   But see James A. Sanders (*Canon as Paradigm: From Sacred Story to Sacred Text* [Philadelphia: Fortress, 1987] 127-128) for the suggestion that the text
was "fluid" even through the greater part of the Herodian era.

77   B. W. Anderson "Introduction" to Martin Noth *A History of Pentateuchal
Traditions* (Chico: Scholars, 1981) xiv. Not everybody, however, accepts the existence of a framework (see A. Graeme Auld *Joshua, Moses and the Land:*

between the Hexateuchal narrative, which really did not include the work of the Deuteronomist whereas it did include Joshua, and the remainder of the Deuteronomistic History depicting Israel in the Land.[78] But in both works, these divisions are later than and subordinated to that between λόγοι/pericopes.

Conceivably, the Alexandrian editors responsible for the arrangement of Herodotus' *History* divided it so as to make it correspond with Primary History. But then we would have expected some juggling with the Egyptian λόγος/pericope so as to make the two works coincide more exactly. This makes the more likely the possibility that they may have tailored one or the other to fit some mystic or maybe even some popular paradigm. Unfortunately we can do no more than hypothesize.

If the divisions were Hellenistic, then, having been set in place by the Grammarians, they still do not suffice to permit us to draw conclusions regarding Ezra's influence on Herodotus in this particular matter. We suggest, however, that the Hellenistic Grammarians used the format of Primary History to configure Herodotus' work, perhaps under the realization that Herodotus' narrative had been influenced by Primary History or possibly because they saw congeners that they may have thought inexplicable unless the works were related to one another.

Although temporal contiguity is not in and of itself excessively significant, Ezra separated the Pentateuch from Primary History because of or so as to bring about a meaningful shift in the:

Tetrateuch-Pentateuch-Hexateuch in a Generation Since 1938 [Edinburgh: T. & T. Clark, 1980] 111-112).

[78] A. G. Auld (*Joshua, Moses and the Land* 15) points out that both Noth and von Rad view the theme of settlement in the Land "as the goal of the Pentateuch/Hexateuch." The theme really demands the inclusion of Joshua since the basic story cannot end with either Numbers of Deuteronomy. Hence, we favor the academic tradition that prevailed toward the end of the 19th century, in which it was believed that some source strata—including and particularly P—found in the earlier books extended into Joshua and even "continued through the book and indeed only found their fulfillment there" (Robert G. Boling *Joshua : A New Translation with Notes and Commentary* [Garden City: Doubleday, 1982, *The Anchor Bible*] G. Ernest Wright "Introduction" 55). This brings about a literary closure since the apportionment of the Land among the tribes can be seen as a fulfillment of the promises made in Genesis as recorded by P and included in his presentation.

focus and target of biblical religion from an essentially historical mode (that is, divine acts in human history) to the mode of law (that is, divine words or commands to regulate the behavior of the human community).[79]

Like Primary History, Herodotus' *History* is concerned with "the mode of law". As we have stressed Herodotus repeatedly depicts the rise to power, the hubris and consequent or, by extension, expected fall of each king or nation upon which his narrative focuses. Although man commits hubris by a free act of the will, that very act is regulated by divine precognition represented by the hallowed words of the Delphic oracle.

It can hardly be accidental that Herodotus and Ezra, *both contemporaries of one another*, each base their historical formulation in tragic format on the same mode of law. If one of them had access to the other's work, it would have been Herodotus who had access to Primary History as both re-divided and received by Ezra, although it is doubtful that Herodotus, whom we realize knew Imperial Aramaic, the *lingua Franca* of western the Persian Empire including the satrapy of "Beyond the River," but for whom there is no suggestion that he knew Hebrew, would have had it in Hebrew. Hence, he could have become acquainted with either a translation or targumic form of Primary History in that tongue. The reverse is not likely since Ezra, who had to have known Imperial Aramaic, is not known to have had a command of Greek or even to have had interaction with the Greek world.

Meaningfully, therefore, Herodotus' implied narrator visits Elephantine (*History* 2.29-30 *et alii*), a place where he may also have heard stories about the Sons of Israel in either Greek or Aramaic or both. These may have been different than that in our version of Primary History, but that is not significant. Herodotus, moreover, attributes knowledge of Syria-Palestine to his implied narrator (*History* 3.5.1) in a brief transitional passage (*History* 3.1.3-3.16.5). But the

---

[79] Editorial introduction to David Noel Freedman's "The Formation of the Canon of the Old Testament: The Selection and Identification of the Torah as the Supreme Authority of the Post-exilic Community" *Religion and Law: Biblical-Judaic and Islamic Perspectives* (Edwin B. Firmage, Bernard G. Weiss, John W. Welch, ed. Winona Lake: Eisenbrauns: 1990) 315.

lack of textual detail prohibits us from knowing if the author really had any knowledge of it.

Unfortunately, there is no data to support the hypothesis that Ezra and Herodotus were personally acquainted with one another. But if Herodotus really did visit Syria-Palestine as his fictive implied narrator did, the possibility that they met does exist.

Although we must be very hesitant to assume that the real author himself went to the places of which his implied narrator either has knowledge or is depicted as having visited, we must remember that he is the real creator of the implied narrator and of the narrative as a whole, and, ipso facto, he had to be familiar with the details he attributes to his implied narrator whether or not they represent valid data.

What we do not know is how he received that data. Even when the data are invalid, he may have obtained them from another source or he may have made them up himself. But even when his evidence is valid, he may also have obtained it from a secondary source or he may have had first hand knowledge of it, be it by a visitation to a foreign land or by an acquaintance with a primary source either in its original or in a translated form.

Consequently, the real author, Herodotus, may have been acquainted with Primary History, but in an Aramaic translation or targum. This, however, is not provable; and we can only say that the parallels suggest that Herodotus may have known at first hand or he simply may have heard about the work of the editor, most likely Ezra, who we think separated the Pentateuch from Primary History.[80] The numerous correspondences suggest that if Herodotus did not know anything about Primary History, then the respective works reflect the same climate of opinion to an astonishing and almost unbelievable extent.

On the other hand, since the period in which the various text traditions were flourishing and that in which *Vorlage* of the Masoretic text was "stabilized" *coincides exactly* with that of the Alexandrian Grammarians who are traditionally dated from the 3rd century BCE through

---

[80]   For this separation, see D. N. Freedman "The Formation of the Canon of the Old Testament: The Selection and Identification of the Torah as the Supreme Authority of the Post-exilic Community" 323.

the 1st century CE,[81] it is both possible and likely that coincidences in the two works reflect the hand of the same Hellenistic redactor or group of redactors. This is more than suggested by the notable concurrence of at least four different but mutually corresponding architectonic bases in Herodotus' *History* and Primary History(as received in MT) respectively.[82]

Since the probability that both works could accidentally be divided respectively into sections of four, one, and four; four and five; five and four; six and three, is rather small, it is likely that the totality of these divisions is the work of the Grammarians. This does not exclude an earlier set of divisions, based more on the coincidence of major λόγοι/pericopes than on book divisions as such that may have been put in place by Herodotus and the final redactor of Primary History respectively.

---

[81]   See Brevard S. Childs (*Introduction to the Old Testament as Scripture* 6 [Philadelphia: Fortress, 1979] 102) for "the period of textual fluidity" in OT. See also James A. Sanders *Canon as Paradigm: From Sacred Story to Sacred Text* 127-128.

[82]   The paradigms for the Septuagint differ from those of the Masoretic text, because the former includes a tenth book, Ruth. There is a late theological warrant for the inclusion of Ruth in its position in the Septuagint. Its normative validity would seem to depend on the foundations upon which rests the messianic expectation of the Alexandrian Jewish community in the 3rd-2nd century BCE. Descriptively, it may well lack the strength of argument accorded it in the subsequent Christian tradition for which it has become normative if in fact Ruth is postexilic as many think.

Chapter Four: Conclusion

One of the distinctive attributes of Primary History and Herodotus' *History* is that the λόγοι/pericopes often extend beyond the divisions of a book. And in Herodotus' work, there is even an individual sentence that begins at the end of book 8 and ends at the beginning of book 9—and this within a λόγος. Moreover, there are Herodotean manuscript traditions in which this type of bridging occurs more frequently than is generally assumed.[1]

Because manuscript scrolls could be lengthened at will, the presence of trans-book λόγοι raises some doubts about our own logical inference that the book divisions in both works were merely mechanical.

These doubts can be assuaged regarding the Herodotean work, however, by acknowledging that the need for a reasonably sized scroll could account for the placement of all separations of the books where they occur save for that of 8 and 9.[2] They can also be alleviated regarding Primary History since the same need for a reasonably sized scroll could account for the placement of all the separations of the books where they occur save that of 8, Samuel, and 9, Kings. Notable, however, is that here too we have a very significant parallel between the works.

There is a difference that is slight from a literary perspective. In Herodotus' *History* a single sentence is divided so as to extend from book 8 into book 9, whereas in Primary History, a major pericope, is divided so as to extend from book 8 into book 9 by placing its final minor pericope in book 9 (1 Kings 1-2:12).

That the death of David forms a minor pericope that seems to be self contained in Kings gives the illusion that it is to be treated as a separate entity from the major pericope, found in the preceding book,

---

1   R. A. McNeal "On Editing Herodotus" *L'Antiquité Classique* 52 (1983) 127.

2   This is strange indeed precisely because the lengthening of either book to accommodate that single sentence would not have made a significant difference in book length. Hence, in this case alone, we must rule out a mechanical separation since other manuscript traditions had been altered to preempt exactly this type of bridging elsewhere in Herodotus. For this, see R. A. McNeal "On Editing Herodotus" 127.

Samuel, of which this minor pericope is a part and to which it is the conclusion. This however, forces the reader envision a continuum bridging Samuel and Kings, when in fact there should be a break between them, just as the Herodotean sentence bridging books 8 and 9 force the reader of that narrative to do likewise. And this suggests that even here, the separation into books is merely perfunctory since logically we would expect the break to come at the end of a λόγος\pericope.

Inasmuch as an ordering of the λόγοι elicits similar although not the same results as a division into books, we cannot draw any information about the responsibility for the latter from the former. Although we do not know who divided Herodotus' *History* into the books we have, we may assume that some divisions were in place by the time the Hellenistic Grammarians edited the work, but they need not be the same as what we have received. In the latter case, the Grammarians may have made the received divisions.

Assuming, but not taking the latter as proven, we think that it is likely that precisely because the narrative breaks are not always concomitant with the book divisions,[3] the Alexandrian book divisions had no real correspondence to Herodotus' possibly mechanically imposed separation of different scrolls. And, moreover, the breaks have no real conformity with his narrative separations, which themselves are indicated by the partitions between λόγοι. And we have no way of knowing whether Herodotus made his book divisions conform to the parameters of his λόγοι.

Since we cannot determine whether the earliest book divisions of either Herodotus' *History* or Primary History coincide with those we now have,—and in the case of Herodotus, the modern divisions are at best Hellenistic,—it is particularly important that those who divided them into the respective books as we have them did so according to some plan or specific format. But we can only give an analysis of either Herodotus' *History* or Primary History on the basis of its own received text since we cannot consider analytically what we do not

---

[3]   John L. Myres *Herodotus: Father of History* (Oxford: Oxford University/Clarendon, 1953) 65.

have. Our understanding of the real author's, Herodotus', intent or that of any of the non-final redactors of Primary History is limited then precisely because we are working with a final version of the text.

If the book divisions are merely mechanical and the λόγοι/pericopes are ordered as the work Herodotus finally "published" and as the final redactor of Primary History, that is the redactor responsible for the Essential Bible, finally handed on his, then these respective arrangements are probably characteristic of the *Vorlagen* of the received text. Granting this, we could assume that when we study the λόγοι/pericopes, the redaction we are analyzing is Herodotus' and the final redactor's of the Essential Bible respectively and not that of Alexandrians or even later scholars. Consequently the object of analysis of either text must be the unity of the subtending λόγος/pericope if we are to ascertain the intent of either Herodotus or the final redactor of Primary History.

On the other hand, a study of the unity, patterning, order, and divisions of the books will lead to an understanding of the Hellenistic Grammarians' alterations, however slight, of both Herodotus' *History*'s and Primary History's textual format. Since naming is a different parameter from dividing. we may state, in the case of Herodotus' work, that the book division by the Grammarians was probably more mechanical than literary. But as in the case of Herodotus' own divisions, there were literary aspects to it, and it was not solely done to accommodate text to a particular scroll length.

There is no suggestion that the Hellenistic Grammarians who studied Primary History changed any of the divisions in the (proto) Masoretic text although, presuming the same Hellenistic Grammarians worked on both, they (or someone) did change the book ordering in the Septuagint. It is possible that in Primary History scroll length is the basis of the book division. But this was not predetermined and the redactor could have added papyrus to fit the varying length of each of the nine books .

It would seem logical to have book divisions correspond to the parameters of the major λόγοι/pericopes. But the overlapping λόγοι/pericopes in both Primary History and Herodotus' *History* as well as the overlapping sentence in the latter militate against this. Although the protrusion of the final sentence of book 8 into book 9 of Herodotus has been contested and the various translations disguise its extension between two books, we have no right to assume with Fornara and others that "the separation between Books VIII and IX is not Herodotus".[4] If the precept of *difficilior lectio* is applicable, the opposite supposition is the more likely. Hence, if the Alexandrian redactors did not emend the text so as to separate the two books, it was because they could not do so.[5]

The real basis for either Herodotus' or the Grammarians' division of the text of his *History*, is not clear. We believe that the overlapping of λόγοι may have represented some Herodotean architectonic design as Benardete has suggested.[6] But there may be some entirely different justification for it. In either case, it is apparent that there are three or four or even more formats rather than only one that must be analyzed if we are to understand the nature of the *History*.

Likewise we cannot ascertain the real basis for either the final redactor's division of Primary History in the form that was the precursor of the Masoretic Text or the Alexandrians' ordering of it in the form that was the precursor of the Septuagint. The theological justifications for the division are after the fact, and others would apply equally as well to hypothetically different separations into books.

As in Herodotus' *History*, the overlapping of λόγοι/pericopes indicates totally different demarcations from those delineated by book divisions. Consequently in Primary History also not one, but a number of formats must be analyzed if we are to understand the nature of the text. And in particular there are two textual structures, each of which may well be independent of the other, subtending the narrative in Herodotus' *History* and Primary History respectively.

---

4   Charles W. Fornara *Herodotus: An Interpretative Essay* (Oxford: Oxford University/Clarendon, 1971) 83.

5   There are various reasons why they could not do so: for example, it could have been well enough known to have been used as a school text exemplar.

6   For the book divisions and λόγοι, see Seth Benardete *Herodotean Inquiries* (The Hague: Martinus Nijhoff, 1969) 4, 153-155. We follow Benardete regarding the division and even its nature but not regarding the justification for the division.

We suggest that the relative order of λόγοι/pericopes rather than of books forms the basic structure of both Herodotus' *History* and the final redaction of Primary History. And we also think that both Herodotus and the final redactor conceived of his respective work in terms of λόγοι/pericopes rather than books.

The book divisions were superimposed on Herodotus' chain of λόγοι in a manner similar to that in which they had been superimposed on the chain of pericopes in Primary *History* (above, Chapters One - Three). Nevertheless it is the relative order of books, whether or not their divisions were mechanically imposed, that the Grammarians took as the basic structure of each work. And in the case of Primary History, moreover, this is reflected in the subsequently canonized form of the text.

But unlike Primary History, where we have been able to date with relative certainty various redactions, neither the final form of the Herodotean λόγοι nor that of the book divisions gives any evidence about the date that any particular book or λόγος was composed. The current accepted opinion is that the λόγοι that comprise books 7 through 9 were written before those which constitute books 1 through 6, but this is not justified.

These two major units may have been composed as λόγοι, as we believe. Some, however, do hold that they were been composed as books. If so, they could not have been concomitant with the books in the received text. These divisions, then, would have no literary significance in and of themselves since *ipso facto* the extension of λόγοι beyond book divisions affirms a lack of closure, which despite the beliefs of some modern theorists, is necessary for a work to be considered whole and complete.

It is notable that there are literary justifications for both the book and the λόγοι groupings although not for their division into their current books. Hence, we conclude that as in Primary History where the ordering of pericopes precedes that of books, so in Herodotus' *History*, the ordering of λόγοι also precedes that of books. Consequently, it is not at all likely that Herodotus composed the work book by book, hence presuming composition by individual books,[7] particularly since he changed the book sequence after the sections of the *History* had all been finished.[8]

In any case, the basic narrative pattern of both works is that of λόγοι/pericopes within or tangential to λόγοι/pericopes even within or tangential to other λόγοι/pericopes.[9] These λόγοι/pericopes are more meaningful than the book divisions.[10] The λόγοι/pericopes are divided into segments that are complete in and of themselves and yet they are joined to one another in what is both a logical and a tangential progression so as to form the work as a whole.[11]

Each of the sections, however, encompasses smaller components, each of which is also complete within itself. Consequently each work can be described as a series of major λόγοι/pericopes that are themselves composed of a series of minor λόγοι/pericopes, each of which may contain other minor λόγοι/pericopes.

---

[7]   For the danger in correlating Herodotus' "publication" with the methodology of book publishing in the modern world, see W. W. How and J. Wells *A Commentary on Herodotus* (2 volumes; New York: Oxford University, 1989) 1.13.

[8]   Thus, for example W. W. How and J. Wells (*A Commentary on Herodotus* 1. 12-13) indicate that A. Bauer (*Die Entstehung des Herodotischen Geschichtswerkes* [Vienna, 1878] 171—this book is unavailable to us) believes that books 7 through 9 were composed circa 445. Although these were early, they need not be the earliest. Moreover, Bauer (*ibid.* 173) thinks that Herodotus changed the order of the λόγοι he had written, and then "published" what is now book 2. See also R. W. Macan *Herodotus VII-IX* (London: MacMillan and Company, 1908) xlv-lxvii. For further discussion of 19th century beliefs regarding the priority of books 7 through 9, see J. L. Myres *Herodotus: Father of History passim.*

[9]   There is an enormous body of literature depicting the division into pericopes of the Hebrew Scriptures/Old Testament. For λόγοι as framing devices, see Henry R. Immerwahr *Form and Thought in Herodotus* (Cleveland: Western Reserve University, 1966) 15.

[10]   Thus, significantly, M. Noth believes that the joining together of the units of tradition (the major pericopes) is secondary to the individual saga (major pericopes, or perhaps even individual pericopes) in the Pentateuch. See B. W. Anderson "Introduction" to Martin Noth *A History of Pentateuchal Traditions* (Chico: Scholars, 1981) xxv. This is true of the entire Primary History, however.

[11]   J. L. Myres (*Herodotus: Father of History* 81-88) envisions a pedimental, that is a scenic division, related to the basic architectonics of Greek temples as basic to the architectonics of Herodotus' history. See also Stewart Flory "The Personality of Herodotus" *Arion* 8 (1969) 101.

Other than the fact that λόγοι/pericopes are basic to both Herodotus' own, and Primary History 's final redactor's architectonics, we do not know how either actually arranged the segments of the work as a whole. It is more than likely that the author Herodotus' and the final redactor's last ordering of the λόγοι/pericopes in their respective works is in accord with their ordering within or throughout the books as we have them. But the placement of these λόγοι/pericopes in books alters the reader's perception of the delineating function of the λόγοι/pericopes.

Again we must iterate that it is more than coincidental that the basic architectonic feature of both works is their respective division into two parts consisting of four followed by five books, five followed by four books, or six followed by three books; and their alternative division into two parts consisting of four books, an axial fifth book that partakes of both, and then four more books. It is also notable that in both works, the division of four followed by five books, may well be the most significant arrangement.

Both Herodotus' *History* and Primary History are introduced by an anthropological prehistory in which the background of events is predicated. Both have an Egyptian λόγος/pericope. And both are concerned with great and wondrous deeds, both human and divine, as part of human history. Moreover, in both, the first four books form a background to the historical data focusing on the Land, be it mainland Greece or Palestine, in the last four books, to which they are connected by a transitional book 5. But the differ precisely in regard to that fifth book. In book 5, Herodotus implied narrator depicts events in secular time and space whereas Primary History's depicts events in sacred time and space.

With the conclusion of Book 4, Herodotus seems to be finishing up the narrative of his peregrinations. He is ready to develop what is ostensibly his major theme, the war between the Greeks and the Persians. Now his focus really turns to the immediate antecedents of that war and thence to Greece. He is also ready to develop what is actually his major theme, the rise and fall of Greece which is based on his major leitmotif whereby the protagonist rises, commits hubris, and falls.

Only by unifying can the Greeks beat back the Persians. However, as the implied narrator shows, particularly after Marathon, victory leads to and intensifies disunification as the same time as it accords the Athenians incredible power that in and of itself induces hubristic behavior, and an impending destruction even when it is not expected.

The narrative of Primary History does not reach the point where it is about to conclude the Sons' of Israel foreign peregrinations at the end of book 4, but rather at Numbers 11:33. The narrative from Numbers 11:34 through Joshua 21:45 (with the exception of Deuteronomy, which from a literary perspective is properly misplaced) focuses on the new and one of the major themes of Primary History, the antecedents of, and entry into the Land. But here too there is disunity. The complaints of Aaron and Miriam (Numbers 12), the misleading reports of the scouts (Numbers 13:25-33), the possibility of revolt (Numbers 14:1-10), and the rebellion of Korah (Numbers 16:1-11), and Dathan and Abiram (Numbers 16:12-24) all indicate this lack of oneness. Hence, here too, unification is necessary; and only when this occurs do the Israelites begin to experience the victory (Numbers 21 ff) that will lead up to the Conquest.

But the tragic paradigm holds good in both works, and even before the Sons of Israel enter the Land or the Athenians and, most suggestively, the Pelasgans, whom Herodotus knew to be the most ancient inhabitants of Greece (*History* 1.56), are victorious at Marathon, the seeds of future destruction are sown. In Primary History, a second census is taken and the Yahweh gives Moses instruction about the land allotment (Numbers 26). This is recapitulated in Numbers 33:50-54. In Herodotus' *History,* the Spartans arrive too late to take part in the battle of Marathon (*History* 6.120).

Herodotus implied narrator depicts the Persian War as if it were an "all Greek" enterprise despite the Medization of some (*History* 9. 16-18 *et* passim). But the Greeks even at the acme of their prowess never really unify, as is epitomized by the late arrival of the Spartans at Marathon. And they must be treated as separate national entities despite the Herodotean illusion of oneness that is suggested by the presence of the Pelasgians at that same battle.

From a literary perspective, the high point of the narrative in Primary History is the "Conquest" (Joshua 1-12) and this is analogous to the successful Greek defense against Persia, particularly at and as exemplified by Marathon. The Conquest is also depicted as an "all Israel" enterprise at whose successful conclusion, the Israelites, who are at the apparent acme of their prowess, divide the Land (Joshua 13-21) and symbolically separate into their component tribes. In fact, there are numerous examples, epitomized, however, by the return of the trans-Jordanian tribes to their territory (Joshua 22),[12] that show that this unity is a literary illusion. However, this merely foreshadows the more theologically meaningful oneness of the United Monarchy that Dtr also depicts as an illusion, and a short lived one at that. The division of Solomon's kingdom cannot be repaired by purely human means.

Both Herodotus' *History* and Primary History are narrated in such a way as to make the sense of oneness extremely prominent so as to justify the tragic paradigm. The tribes go to their separate territories; the United Monarchy falls, and the Sons of Israel fall just as the Greek city-states shall all fall. It does not matter that historic reality represented by the *Realpolitik* that is the basis of the events as they may actually have occurred, which is often ignored or else so subsumed into the narrative that its full impact is obliterated in accordance with literary demands, most likely differed from those in the literary, and, hence, fictionally defined world portrayed in Herodotus' *History* or Primary History.

---

[12] This emblematic division is actuated for the trans-Jordanian tribes when they build the altar at the Jordan and return to what is henceforth to be their home (Joshua 22).

Bibliography of Works Cited in the Text

Aalders H. Wzn, G. J. D.
1969   "*De vader der geschiedenis*" *Hermeneus* 40:105-114

Ackroyd, Peter R.
1975   "The Old Testament in the Making" *The Cambridge History of the Bible vol. 1From the Beginnings to Jerome* (New York/New Rochelle: Cambridge University, Ackroyd, P. R. & Evans, C. F. ed.) 67-113

Aichele, Jr., George
1985   *The Limits of Story* Philadelphia/Chico: Fortress/Scholars

Ahlström, G. W.
1966   "Oral and Written Transmission: Some Considerations" *HTR* 59: 69-81

Albright, William Foxwell
Undated reprint of 1968 editio   *Yahweh and the Gods of Canaan: A Historical Analysis of Two Contrasting Faiths* Winona Lake: Eisenbrauns,School of Oriental and African Studies edition

Alter, Robert
1981   *The Art of Biblical Narrative* New York: Basic Books

——and Kermode, Frank eds.
1987   *The Literary Guide to the Bible* Cambridge: Harvard University

Anderson, Bernhard W.
1981   "Introduction" to Martin Noth's *A History of Pentateuchal Traditions* Chico: Scholars.

Auld, A. Graeme
1980   *Joshua, Moses and the Land: Tetrateuch-Pentateuch-Hexateuch in a Generation Since 1938* Edinburgh: T. & T. Clark

Baker, D. W.
1983   "Diversity and Unity in the Literary Structure of Genesis" *Essays on the Patriarchal Narratives* (Winona Lake: Eisenbrauns, A. R. Millard & D. J. Wiseman, ed.) 197-215

Barbour, Amy, ed.
Undated reprint of 1929 editio *Selections From Herodotus* Norman: University of Oklahoma, reprint of D. C. Heath, edition

Barr, James
1983 *Holy Scripture: Canon, Authority, Criticism* Philadelphia: Westminster

Barth, Hannelore
1968 "*Zur Bewertung und Auswahl des Stoffes durch Herodot (Die Begriffe* θῶμα, θωμάζω, θωμάσιος *und* θωμαστός") *Klio* 50: 93-110

Barton, John
1984 *Reading the Old Testament: Method in Biblical Study* Philadelphia: Westminster

Belsey, Catherine
1988 *Critical Practice* London: Routledge, reprint of the 1980 Methuen edition

Benardete, Seth
1969 *Herodotean Inquiries* The Hague: Martinus Nijhoff

K. Elliger and W. Rudolph, al. ed.
1967/77 *Biblia Hebraica Stuttgartensia* Stuttgart: Deutsche Bibelstiftung

Boling, Robert G.
1982 *Joshua: A New Translation with Notes and Commentary* Garden City: Doubleday

Booth, Wayne
1961 *The Rhetoric of Fiction* Chicago: University of Chicago

Bornitz, Hans-Friedrich
1968 *Herodot-Studien: Beiträge zum Verstandnis der Einheit des Geschichtswerks* Berlin: Walter de Gruyter

Brooks, Cleanth
1971 *A Shaping Joy: Studies In The Writer's Craft* New York: Harcourt Brace Jovanovich

Brown, T. S.
1962 "The Greek Sense of Time in History as Suggested by their accounts of Egypt" *Historia* 11: 257-270

Burkert, Walter
1985   *Greek Religion* Cambridge: Harvard University

Burrows, Millar
1983   "Ancient Israel" *The Idea of History in the An-
                             cient Near East* (New Haven: AOS, Robert C.
                             Dentan, ed.) 99-131

Bury, J. B.
1958   *The Ancient Greek Historians* New York:
                             Dover.

Childs, Brevard S.
1979   *Introduction to the Old Testament as Scripture*
                             Philadelphia: Fortress

Cicero
1928   *de Legibus* London: William Heinemann, *Loeb*

Clines, David J. A.
1982   *The Theme of the Pentateuch* Sheffield; *JSOT*

Cobet, J.
1986   "Herodotus and Thucydides on war (sic)" *Past
                             Perspectives in Greek and Roman Historical
                             Writing* (Cambridge: Cambridge University, I.
                             S. Moxon, J. D. Smart, A. J. Woodman, ed.) 1-
                             18

Crahay, Roland
1956   *La littérature oraculaire chez Hérodote* Paris:
                             Société d'Édition <<Les Belles Lettres>>

Cross, Frank Moore
1980   *The Ancient Library of Qûmran & Modern
                             Biblical Studies* rev. ed.; Grand Rapids, Baker
                             Book House, reprint of 1961 Doubleday edi-
                             tion
1973   *Canaanite Myth and Hebrew Epic: Essays in
                             the History of the Religion of Israel* Cambridge:
                             Harvard University

Cuddon, J. A.
1979   *A Dictionary of Literary Terms* London: Pen-
                             guin

de Selincourt, Aubrey
1982   *The World of Herodotus* San Francisco: North
                             Point

Di Girolamo, Costanzo
1981   *A Critical Theory of Literature* Madison: Uni-
                             versity of Wisconsin

Dombrowsky, Alexander
1962/63   "Herodotus and Hippocrates on the Anthropol-
                             ogy of the Scythians" *Annals of the Ukrainian
                             Academy of Arts and Sciences* 10:85-91

Donnelly S. J., Malachi J.
1934   "The "Epic' of Herodotus" *Classical Bulletin*
                             11: 4-5

Eissfeldt, Otto
1976   *The Old Testament an Introduction: The His-
                             tory of the Formation of the Old Testament*
                             New York *et al.*: Harper & Row

Engnell, Ivan
1969   *A Rigid Scrutiny: Critical Essays on the Old
                             Testament* Nashville, Vanderbilt University,
                             John T. Willis and Helmer Ringgren ed.

Evans, J. A. S.
1982   *Herodotus* Boston: Twayne

Flory, Stewart
1980   "Who Read Herodotus' Histories?" *AJPh* 101:
                             12-28

1969   "The Personality of Herodotus" *Arion* 8: 99-
                             109

Focke, Friedrich
1927   *Herodot als Historiker* Stuttgart: W. Kohlham-
                             mer

Fornara, Charles W.
1971   *Herodotus: An Interpretative Essay* Oxford:
                             Oxford University/Clarendon

Forrest, W. G.
1957   "Colonization and the Rise of Delphi" *Historia*
                             6:160-175

Freedman, David Noel
1991   *The Unity of the Hebrew Bible* Ann Arbor:
                              University of Michigan
1990   "The Formation of the Canon of the Old Testa-
                              ment: The Selection and Identification of the
                              Torah as the Supreme Authority of the Post-ex-
                              ilic Community" *Religion and Law: Biblical-
                              Judaic and Islamic Perspectives* (Winona Lake:
                              Eisenbrauns, Edwin B. Firmage, Bernard G.
                              Weiss, John W. Welch, ed.) 315-331
1987   "The Earliest Bible" *Backgrounds for the Bible*
                              (Winona Lake: Eisenbrauns, Michael Patrick
                              O'Connor and David Noel Freedman, eds.) 29-
                              37
1980   *Pottery, Poetry, and Prophecy: Studies in Early
                              Hebrew Poetry* Winona Lake: Eisenbrauns
1979   "Early Israelite Poetry and Historical Recon-
                              structions" *Symposia Celebrating the Seventy
                              Fifth Anniversary of the founding of the
                              American Schools of Oriental Research (1900-
                              1975)* (Cambridge: American Schools of Orien-
                              tal Research, Frank Moore Cross, ed.) 85-96
1962   "The Deuteronomic History" *IDB Supp.* 226-
                              228
1962   "Pentateuch" *IDB* 3: 711-727

French, Valerie
1980   "Herodotus: Revisionist Historian" *Panhelleni-
                              ca: Essays in Ancient History and Historiogra-
                              phy in Honor of Truesdell S. Brown* (Lawrence:
                              Coronado, Stanley M. Burstein and Louis A.
                              Okin, ed.) 31-42

Friedman, Richard Elliott
1989   *Who Wrote the Bible?* New York *et al.*: Harper
                              & Row
1981   "From Egypt to Egypt: Dtr[1] and Dtr[2]" *Tradi-
                              tions in Transformation: Turning Points in Bib-
                              lical Faith* (Winona Lake: Eisenbrauns, Baruch
                              Halpern and Jon D. Levenson, eds.) 167-192

Frye, Northrop
1990   *Words with Power: Being a Second Study of
                              The Bible and Literature* San Diego/New York:
                              Harcourt Brace Jovanovich
1971   *Anatomy of Criticism: Four Essays* Princeton:
                              Princeton University

Gabel, John B. and Wheeler, Charles B.
1990
The Bible as Literature: An Introduction New York: Oxford University, 2nd edition

Gayre of Gayre, R.
1973-1974
"Herodotus" *Mankind Quarterly* 14: 156-181

Geertz, Clifford
1979
"Religion as a Cultural System" *Reader in Comparative Religion: An Anthropological Approach* (New York/Philadelphia, San Francisco: Harper & Row,William A. Lessa & Evon Z. Vogt, ed. 4th edition) 78-89

Gentili, Bruno
1988
Poetry and its Public in Ancient Greece: From Homer to the Fifth Century Baltimore: Johns Hopkins.

Glover, Terrot Reaveley
1969
Herodotus Freeport: Books for Libraries, reprint of 1924 edition

Gomme, A. W.
1954
The Greek Attitude to Poetry and History Berkeley and Los Angeles: University of California

Gottwald, Norman K.
1985
The Hebrew Bible—A Socio-Literary Introduction Philadelphia: Fortress

Gould, John
1989
Herodotus New York: St. Martin's

Greene, William Chase
1963
Moira: Gate, Good, and Evil in Greek Thought New York: Harper & Row

Grell, Chantal
1985
"*Hérodote et la Bible. Tradition chrétienne et histoire ancienne dans la France moderne (XVI-XVIIIe siècles)*" *Histoire de l'historiographie* 7:) 60-91

Grene, David
1987
The History: Herodotus Chicago: University of Chicago
1961
"Herodotus: The Historian as Dramatist" *The Journal of Philosophy* 58: 477-488

Gunkel, Hermann
1964   *The Legends of Genesis: The Biblical Saga &*
                             History New York: Schocken

Gunn, David M.
1976   "On Oral Tradition: A Response to John Van
                             Seters" *Semeia* 5: 155-163

Hall, F. W. and Geldart, W.
ed.
1906   Aristophanes *Comoediae* Oxford: Oxford Uni-
                             versity/Clarendon, 2nd edition, vol. 1

Hardy, J. ed.
1932   Aristotle *Poétique* Paris: Société d'Édition
                             <<Les Belles Lettres>>

Harriott, Rosemary M.
1986   *Aristophanes: Poet and Dramatist* Baltimore:
                             Johns Hopkins University

Hartog, François
1988   *The Mirror of Herodotus: The Representation of*
                             the Other in the Writing of History Berkeley:
                             University of California

Hayes, John H. and Hollada
Carl R.
1987   *Biblical Exegesis: A Beginner's Handbook* At-
                             lanta: John Knox, revised ed.

Hellmann, Fritz
1934   *Herodotos' Kroisos-Logos* Berlin: Weidmann-
                             sche

Henige, David
1982   *Oral Historiography* New York: Longman

Hertzberg, Hans Wilhelm
1964   *I & II Samuel: A Commentary* Philadelphia:
                             Westminster

Holman, C. Hugh and Harmo
William
1986   *A Handbook to Literature* New York: Macmil-
                             lan

How, W. W. and Wells, J.
1989   *A Commentary on Herodotus* 2 vols.; New
                             York: Oxford University, reprint of corrected
                             1928 edition

Huber, Ludwig
1965   *Religiöse und politische Beweggründe des Han-
                       delns in der Geschichtsschreibung der Herod.*
                       PhD Diss.; Tübingen: Eberhard-Karls-Univer-
                       sität

Carolus Hude ed.
1927   Herodotus *Historiae*; Oxford: Oxford Univer-
                       sity/Clarendon, 3rd edition, 2 vols.

Humphreys, W. Lee
1985   *The Tragic Vision and the Hebrew Tradition*
                       Philadelphia: Fortress

Hunter, Virginia
1982   *Past and Process in Herodotus and Thucydides*
                       Princeton: Princeton University

Immerwahr, Henry R.
1985   "Herodotus" *The Cambridge History of Classi-
                       cal Literature I Greek Literature* P. E. Easterling
                       and B. M. W. Knox, ed.; (Cambridge: Cam-
                       bridge University) 426-441.
1966   *Form and Thought in Herodotus* Cleveland:
                       Western Reserve University
1957   "The Samian Stories of Herodotus" *Classical
                       Journal* 52: 312-322
1954   "Historical Action in Herodotus" *TAPA* 85: 14-
                       65

Iser, Wolfgang
1978   *The Act of Reading: A Theory of Aesthetic Re-
                       sponse* Baltimore: Johns Hopkins University

Jacoby, F.
1913   "Herodotos" *PW* 8 Supp. 2: *col.* 205-520

Jaeger, Werner
1965   *Paideia: The Ideals of Greek Culture Volume I:
                       Archaic Greece; The Mind of Athens* New
                       York: Oxford University, 2nd. ed.

Jenks, Alan W.
1977   *The Elohist and North Israelite Traditions* Mis-
                       soula: Scholars

Jensen, Joseph
1986   *God's Word to Israel* 3rd ed.; Wilmington: Mi-
                       chael Glazier

Jones, Henricus Stuart, ed.
1942   Thucydides *Historiae* Oxford: Oxford University/Clarendon, reprint with emended and augmented critical apparatus, 2 vol. ed.; *Tomos Prior*

Kelber, Werner H.
1988   "Narrative and Disclosure: Mechanisms of Concealing, Revealing, and Reveiling (sic)" *Semeia* 43: 1-20

Knierim, Rolf
1985   "Criticism of Literary Features, Form, Tradition, and Redaction" *The Hebrew Bible and its Modern Interpreters* Douglas A. Knight and Gene M. Tucker, ed.; (Fortress/Scholars: Philadelphia/Chico) 123-165

Kuhrt, Amélie
1988   "The Persian Empire, pt. 3a" *CAH* 4 (Cambridge: Cambridge University, 2nd edition) 112-138

Lamberts, Erika
1970   *Studien zu Parataxe bei Herodot* Wien: Notrig

Lang, Mabel L.
1984   "Oral History with a Difference" *PAPhS* 128: 93-103

Latte, Kurt
1956   "*Die Anfänge der griechischen Geschichtschreibunt*" *Histoire et Historiens dans L'Antiquite* (Genève: Vandoeuvres) 1-37

Lattimore, Richmond
1958   "The Composition of the History of Herodotus" *Classical Philology* 53: 9-21

Legrand, Ph. -E.
1955   "Introduction" *Hérodote* Paris: Société d' Edition <<Les Belles Lettres>>

Lincoln, Bruce
1986   *Myth, Cosmos, and Society: Indo-European Themes of Creation and Destruction* Cambridge: Harvard University

Linforth, Ivan M.
1926-1929a   "Greek Gods and Foreign Gods in Herodotus"
                    University of California Publications in Classi-
                    cal Philology 9: 1-25
1926-1929b   "Named and Unnamed Gods in Herodotus"
                    University of California Publications in Classi-
                    cal Philology 9: 201-243

Macan, R. W.
1908   *Herodotus VII-IX* London: MacMillan and
                    Company

MacKendrick , P.
1954   "Herodotus: The Making of a World Historian"
                    The Classical Weekly 47: 145-152

Malkin, Irad
1987   *Religion and Colonization in Ancient Greece*
                    Leiden: Brill

Mandell, Sara
1990   "The Language, Eastern Sources, and Literary
                    Posture of Herodotus" *Ancient World* 21: 103-
                    108
1969 (= Sindel, Sara)   *A Literary Analysis of books Thirty One*
                    through Forty Five of Livy's Ab Urbe Condita
                    PhD Diss., New York University

Marrett, R. R. ed.
1980   "Herodotus and Anthropology" *Anthropology*
                    and the Classics (Oxford: Oxford University)
                    121-168

Martin, Luther H.
1987   *Hellenistic Religions: An Introduction* New
                    York: Oxford University

McEvenue, Sean E.
1975   "A Comparison of Narrative Styles in the Hagar
                    Stories" *Classical Hebrew Narrative* Semeia 3:
                    64-80

McNeal, R. A., ed.
1986   *Herodotus Book I* Lanham: University Press of
                    America
1983   "On Editing Herodotus" *L'Antiquité Classique*
                    52: 110-129.

Mendelsohn, I.
1962   "Dream" *IDB* 1:868-869

Mikalson, Jon D
1991   *Honor Thy Gods: Popular Religion in Greek
                                  Tragedy* Chapel Hill and London: The Univer-
                                  sity of North Carolina Press

Millard, A. R.
1983   "Methods of Studying the Patriarchal Narra-
                                  tives as Ancient Texts" *Essays on the Patriar-
                                  chal Narratives*(Winona Lake: Eisenbrauns, A.
                                  R. Millard & D. J Wiseman, ed.) 35-51

Miller, J. Maxwell
1985   "Israelite History" *The Hebrew Bible and Its
                                  Modern Interpreters* (Philadelphia: For-
                                  tress/Chico:Scholars, , Knight, Douglas A. and
                                  Tucker, Gene M. eds.) 1-30

Miscall, Peter D.
1983   *The Workings of Old Testament Narrative* For-
                                  tress/Scholars: Philadelphia/Chico

Momigliano, Arnaldo
1957   "*Erodoto e la Storiografia Moderna: Alcuni
                                  Problemi Presentati ad un Convegno di Uman-
                                  isti*" *Aevum* 31: 74-84

Murray, Oswyn
1986   "Greek Historians" *The Oxford History of the
                                  Classical World* (Oxford: Oxford University,
                                  John Boardman, Jasper Griffin, and Oswyn
                                  Murray, ed.) 186-203

Myres, John L.
1953   *Herodotus: Father of History* Oxford: Oxford
                                  University/Clarendon

Nelson, Richard D.
1981   *The Double Redaction of the Deuteronomistic History* Sheffield: JSOT

Noth, Martin
1981   *A History of Pentateuchal Traditions* Chico: Scholars
1943   *Überlieferungsgeschichtliche Studien I: die sammelnden und bearbeitenden Geschichtswerke im Alten Testament* Halle: Max Niemeyer

Parke, H. W. and Wor-mell,
E. W.
1956   *The Delphic Oracle* Oxford: Oxford University

Fridericus Spiro, ed.
1959   Pausanias *Graeciae Descriptio*; (Stuttgart: B..G..Teubner, 3 vol edition) vol. 3

Pfeiffer, R. H.
1962   "Ezra" *IDB* 2:214-215

Phillips, Anthony
1973   *Deuteronomy The Cambridge Bible Commentary on the New English Bible* Cambridge: Cambridge University

Polzin, Robert
1981   "Reporting Speech in the Book of Deuteronomy: Toward a Compositional Analysis of the Deuteronomic History" *Traditions in Transformation: Turning Points in Biblical Faith* (Winona Lake: Eisenbrauns, Baruch Halpern and Jon D. Levenson, eds.) 193-211
1980   *MOSES and the DEUTERONOMIST: A Literary Study of the Deuteronomic History* Part One New York: Sea-bury
1975   "'The Ancestress of Israel in Danger' in Danger" *Semeia* 3: 81-98

Powell, Mark Allan
1990   *What is Narrative Criticism?* Minneapolis: Fortress

Rendsburg, Gary A.
1986   *The Redaction of Genesis* Winona Lake: Eisenbrauns

Rendtorff , Rolf
1986   *The Old Testament: An Introduction* Philadel-
                             phia: Fortress

Rosenmeyer, T. G.
1982   "History or Poetry?" The Example of Herodo-
                             tus" *Clio* 11: 239-259

Rowley, H. H.
1962   "Canon of the OT" 1:49*IDB* 8-520

Rutherford, R. B., ed.
1992   Homer: Odyssey Books XIX and XX Cam-
                             bridge: Cambridge University

Rylaarsdom, J. Coert
1971   "Introduction" to G. M. Tucker's *Form Criti-
                             cism of the Old Testament* Philadelphia: For-
                             tress

Sanders, James A.
1987   *Canon as Paradigm: From Sacred Story to Sa-
                             cred Text* Philadelphia: Fortress
1962   "Hermeneutics" *IDB* Supp. 402-407.

Schmid, Wilhelm and Stähle
Otto
1946   *Geschichte der Griechischen Literatur, HAW*
                             7.1.4 Mün-chen: C. H. Beck

Segal, Charles
1986   "Greek Tragedy and Society: A Structuralist
                             Perspective" *Greek Tragedy and political The-
                             ory* (Berkeley: University of California,J. Peter
                             Euben, ed.) 43-75

Sellin, Ernst
1968   *Introduction to the Old Testament* Revised &
                             Rewritten by Georg Fohrer; Nashville: Abing-
                             don

Snell, Bruno
1960   *The Discovery of the Mind: The Greek Origins
                             of European Thought* New York/Evanston:
                             Harper & Row

Sternberg, Meir
1985   *The Poetics of Biblical Narrative: Ideological
                             Literature and the Drama of Reading* Blooming-
                             ton: Indiana University

Thompson, J. A. K.
1935   *The Art of the Logos* London: George Allen &
                           Unwin

Toldorov, Tzvetan
1990   *Genres in Discourse* Cambridge: Cambridge
                           University
1979   "Language and Literature," *The Structuralist
                           Controversy* Richard Macksey and Eugenio Do-
                           nato, eds.; Baltimore: Johns Hopkins University

Tucker, Gene M.
1971   *Form Criticism of the Old Testament* Philadel-
                           phia: Fortress

Van Seters, John
1983   *In Search of History: Historiography in the An-
                           cient World and the Origins of Biblical History*
                           New Haven: Yale University
1976   "Oral Patterns or Literary Conventions in Bib-
                           lical Narrative" *Semeia* 5 : 139-154

Vernant, Jean-Pierre
1981a   "Imitations of the Will in Greek Tragedy" *Trag-
                           edy and Myth in Ancient Greece* (Atlantic
                           Highlands: Humanities, Jean-Pierre Vernant
                           and Pierre Vidal-Naquet, ed.) 28-62
1981b   "Tensions and Ambiguities in Greek Tragedy"
                           Tragedy and Myth in Ancient Greece
                           (Humanities: Atlantic Highlands, Jean-Pierre
                           Vernant and Pierre Vidal-Naquet, ed.) 6-27

von Rad, Gerhard
1984   *The Problem of the Hexateuch and Other Es-
                           says* London: SCM
1972   *Genesis: A Commentary* revised ed.; Philadel-
                           phia: Westminster

Waters, K. H.
1985   *Herodotos the Historian: His Problems, Meth-
                           ods and Originality* Norman: University of
                           Oklahoma

Weingreen, J.
1982   *Introduction to the Critical Study of the Text of
                           the Hebrew Bible* New York: Oxford Univer-
                           sity/Clarendon

Wellek, René   and   Warre
Austin
1975   *Theory of Literature* New York: Harcourt Brace
                                        Jovanovich, 3rd edition

Wellhausen, Julius
1973   *Prolegomena to the History of Israel* Glouces-
                                        ter: Peter Smith

Wells, Joseph
1970   *Studies in Herodotus* Freeport: Books for Li-
                                        braries, reprint of 1923.edition
1926   "Herodotus as a Traveller" *Proceedings of the
                                        Hellenic Travellers' Club* 20-31

Weerdenburg, Heleen Sancisi
and Kuhrt, Amélie, ed.
1987   "Herodotus and Oral History" *Achaemenid His-
                                        tory II. The Greek Sources* (Nederlands Insti-
                                        tuut voor het Nabije Oosten: Leiden) 93-115

Westermann, Claus
1976   *Genesis* 2nd ed.; Neukirchen-Vluyn: Neukirch-
                                        ener

White, Hayden
1984   "The Question of Narrative in Contemporary
                                        Historical Theory" *History and Theory* 23: 1-33

White, M. E.
1969   "Herodotus' Starting-Point" *Phoenix* 23 : 39-48

Wiseman, D. J.
1975   "Books in the Ancient Near East and in the Old
                                        Testament" *The Cambridge History of the Bible
                                        vol. 1 From the Beginnings to Jerome* P. R.
                                        Ackroyd & C. F. Evans, ed.; (New York/New
                                        Rochelle: Cambridge University) 30-48

Wright, G. Ernest
1982   "Introduction" to Robert G. Boling's *Joshua: A
                                        New Translation with Notes and Commentary*
                                        Garden City: Doubleday

Würthwein, Ernst
1979   *The Text of the Old Testament: An Introduction
                                        to the Biblia Hebraica* Grand Rapids: Eerdmans

Yamauchi, Edwin M.
1990   *Persia and the Bible* Grand Rapids: Baker
                                        House

Young, T. Cuyler
1988   "The Persian Empire, pt. 1-3" *CAH* 4
                        (Cambridge: Cambridge University, 2nd edi-
                        tion) 1-111

South Florida Studies in the History of Judaism

DATE DUE

SEP 12 '90			